Dragon Ball Culture

Volume 1

ORIGIN

Derek Padula

thedaoofdragonball.com

Legal Disclaimer

Copyright © 2014, by Derek Padula.

Written and published by Derek Padula in The United States of America, all rights reserved.

Cataloging In-Publication Data

Padula, Derek.

Dragon Ball Culture Volume 1: Origin / Derek Padula

Includes bibliographical references and index.

ISBN: 978-0-9831205-8-2

1. Martial arts – Comic books, strips, etc. 2. Heroes. 3. Good and evil. 4. Imaginary wars and battles. 5. Ethics, ancient. 6. Spiritual life – Buddhism. 7. Fantasy comic books, strips, etc. – Japan – 20th century – History and Criticism.

PN6790.J33 – P2 2012

741.5952 – 23

LCCN: 2014922138

Contents

Acknowledgements

THANK YOU FOR reading *Dragon Ball Culture*.

I am grateful to Akira Toriyama, the creator of the world's greatest *anime* and *manga*. Thank you for working so hard!

This book required 12 years of effort to write. Thank you to my parents, family, and friends for supporting me.

Thank you to my professors at Western Michigan University for providing the education in Chinese and Japanese culture, history, and language that made this book possible. They include Dr. Timothy Light, Dr. Stephen Covell, Dr. Wáng Xiǎojūn, Dr. Jeffrey Angles, Dr. Gregory Veeck, and all the faculty at WMU in the Department of Comparative Religion and Department of World Languages and Literatures.

Thank you to my martial arts and meditation instructors, including Sifu Sam Chan at Chan's Kung Fu in Grand Rapids, Michigan, Shīfu Shì Yángāo in Běijīng, China, and Shīfu Lǐ Hóngzhì of Fǎlún Dàfǎ. The insights you'll find in this book are the result of my experiences under their tutelage.

Special thanks to the staff and forum of *kanzenshuu.com* for their dedication to *Dragon Ball*. Almost all of the translated quotes of Akira Toriyama's interviews, the introduction comments in the *Dragon Ball manga*, and the guidebooks that I refer to come from their website. This book would be a lesser product without their efforts. Particular thanks to Julian "SaiyaJedi" Grybowski for answering my questions and helping with the hard to find info on Toriyama's past.

Thank you to Sunny Mann for assisting my writing and taking this book to the next level.

Finally, thank you to my fans who have cheered me on!

To *Dragon Ball* fans across the world:
DRAGON BALL FOREVER!!

Introduction

SEE DRAGON BALL with new eyes. This book is your cultural tour guide to *Dragon Ball*, the world's most recognized *anime* and *manga* series.[1]

Dragon Ball is about a young martial artist named Son Gokū who travels on a quest to increase his power. Written and illustrated by Akira Toriyama from 1984 to 1995, *Dragon Ball* is a comic meant to entertain and inspire you by telling Son Gokū's journey through life. It is one of the best-selling series of all time, having sold over 230 million volumes of *manga* in Japan and been localized into over 40 countries.[2] It has countless fans, including myself.

This book goes deep into the core of what makes *Dragon Ball* so special, and shows you why you love it—or will learn to love it. You will gain a better understanding of the ancient cultural artifacts and storytelling techniques Toriyama uses during the creation of *Dragon Ball*. He simplifies these ideas to the point where anyone can accept them, but he never explains them. Only now are they explained as we explore Toriyama's mind.

If you are experiencing *Dragon Ball* for the first time, then welcome to one of the most charming, influential, and grand stories ever told.

---

1   *Dragon Ball* is the world's most recognized *anime* and *manga* series according to a global report published by Orikon Kabushiki-gai-sha (オリコン株式会社, Oricon Co., Ltd., founded 1999) on August 7, 2012. *http://www.oricon.co.jp/special/145/#rk*

2   *Dragon Ball* has sold over 230 million volumes of *manga* in Japan: *http://db30th.com/into/into01.html*. If sales outside of Japan are included, the total exceeds 300 million volumes: *http://comipress.com/article/2008/12/31/3733*

If you are a *Dragon Ball* veteran who has read every chapter of the *manga*, watched every episode of the *anime*, seen all the movies, played all the games, and are wearing a *Dragon Ball* T-shirt as you read this, then you may think you have *Dragon Ball* figured out; but that's not the case.

Forget everything you think you know. I will get you to reassess your established notions, shatter the misinformation you've been given by less informed fans or localized versions, and show you the true *Dragon Ball Culture*.

Dragon Ball and Culture

Dragon Ball is the world's most culturally rich *anime* and *manga*, and by the time you finish this book you will see the proof on every page. There is so much culture embedded in *Dragon Ball* that you can delve into it for years and still find something fresh. I know because I spent 12 years writing this book and still have more to say.

Dragon Ball is a modern testament to traditional culture and a traditional testament to modern culture. It's a series that combines East Asian martial arts and extrasensory powers with Western technology and science fiction, such as time machines, robots, and flying cars. This mix of East and West creates an ecosystem allowing for gods and aliens to intermingle while we travel across a Chinese landscape filled with immortal martial arts masters and cyborgs. It's a supernormal place where dinosaurs walk among humans, and a mundane place where people shop in malls, work in office buildings, and earn their driver's license. The *Dragon Ball* world represents a fantastic version of the globalized world of today mixed with classic storytelling elements, making it relatable while mystical. It is a fusion *manga* of interwoven cultures that has global appeal.

Yet as a fan of *Dragon Ball* you may not fully understand

the culture the series is derived from. That's because Toriyama strives to tell a story that is "easy to understand," but in so doing he creates a story that is difficult to explain.

Here I will reveal something old in something new. I'll give you the context to see what you think you know in a new light, which will by happenstance be an old light. The esoteric ideologies in *Dragon Ball* will be made public for the first time.

Culture through Action

Akira Toriyama is a master storyteller because he lets his action do the talking. He has Son Gokū or the villains take action that leads to more action, with minimal dialogue to hold it together. The lack of description is why it appears simple and is easy to read or watch, but the contextual glue behind these actions goes back thousands of years.

The traditional beliefs and values in *Dragon Ball* are founded upon a Buddhist and Dàoist framework inspired by *Journey to the West*, a 16th century Chinese novel. This adventure story popularizes the ancient folktales and religious concepts within China. Then, the novel and its belief systems travel from China to Japan. Finally, in the 1980s, Toriyama incorporates its traditional culture into a modern work of *manga* and introduces these elements to the masses through action-oriented combat and humor. By writing his work for 12-year-old boys and focusing on the action, Toriyama lowers the barrier to entry and makes the culture accessible to everyone on a more simplified level, promoted through mass media and distribution channels.

He illustrates this culture in a way that is less religious and more martial. For example, instead of using an existing character from the story verbatim, he alters their appearance, turns them into a martial artist, and has them carry a symbol or take an action that reflects on their original role. What remains is only visible on the surface or through their deeds, but it points back to an ancient origin.

By using action instead of doctrine he creates a series that is acceptable to all and offensive to none. In being so accepted, it plants cultural seeds in the minds of millions of impressionable youth who see the leaves on the tree but don't examine the roots from which it sprung. How many *Dragon Ball* fans understand the symbolism within their actions when they 'power up' and fire imaginary energy beams at one another? To them it's simply fun, mystical, and uplifting. But there's more to the story. *Dragon Ball* isn't just about punching and screaming. It's about heart, character development, and what this means to you.

Symbols and the Eyes to See

Dragon Ball speaks to our humanity through symbols. Symbols are letters, graphics, marks, and cues that contain meaning. *Dragon Ball* is filled with symbols, from the Japanese characters on Gokū's martial arts uniform to his magical cloud and the dragon balls themselves.

Just as those without the eyes to see beauty will miss it, those without the knowledge to decipher symbols will miss their message. Once you've learned how to perceive these symbols, then you can see the beauty in *Dragon Ball* and carry it within you. You'll recognize the multi-layered depth of the story and further appreciate its humor.

The majority of symbols in *Dragon Ball* come from East Asian culture. To better understand these symbols, I've spent over 16 years walking the path that *Dragon Ball* inspired me to walk. This includes training with the Shàolín monks and *tàijí* sword masters of China, practicing Fǎlún Dàfǎ meditation, becoming a scholar of 5,000 years of East

Asian history, studying Chinese and Japanese language, art, and beliefs, plus popular culture from the West.

Dragon Ball is a fusion of these elements, so to fully understand *Dragon Ball* I felt I had to learn everything there is to know. And let me tell you, that's difficult to do. You're fortunate in that you don't have to do it from scratch. Just read this book and you will become an expert in *Dragon Ball's* symbols, with the eyes to see their deeper meaning.

Meaning and Art

Toriyama may have created *Dragon Ball* as a gag *manga* (漫画, "comic") that was then adapted into an *anime* (アニメ, "animation"), but it grew into a meaningful work of art.

It is correct to associate comic book and TV culture with meaningful art if it stirs the soul of its perceiver. *Dragon Ball* has a power that can be found in the greatest paintings and sculptures. It tells a timeless tale through a medium of old and new, traditional and modern, while appearing simple yet being deep. It is a vibrant record of an era.

As the series and the characters within it mature, so do you. It becomes a part of your life because it's filled with culture that you accept over decades of youth and young adulthood. Each time you return to this series it becomes further tied to your identity and shapes your worldview. It takes root inside you and alters your perceptions as you inherit its spirit. You might not have realized it, but you'll come to understand what I mean as our story unfolds.

Dragon Ball is art, but it's art that Toriyama leaves for you to interpret. Some fans feel that *Dragon Ball* is no more than an action-adventure comic with fighting, screaming, big muscles, and explosions. Others feel that it's a heartfelt epic that inspires them to overcome hardships, endure, and believe in their hidden potential. Perception is everything.

In order to change your perception you have to become familiar with the meaning of Toriyama's work. Only then will you realize why the series is so popular.

This book represents my effort to interpret and explain *Dragon Ball's* meaning. It is not a trivia book. It is a volume of culture and truth. Even though there may be fans of *Dragon Ball* who have a notion of the series as a certain, unchangeable thing, I seek to show you how to enjoy it on a deeper level. Your perception of the series will grow richer. In turn you will have a better understanding of the culture that led to its creation, and of yourself.

Dragon Ball Brings Joy

Each generation that experiences *Dragon Ball* feels its inner joy. Toriyama stopped writing *Dragon Ball manga* in 1995, but to this day fans cry out for more. They don't want it to end because it would mean the end of the connection to their childhood; to their cultural roots as experienced each day with Son Gokū and friends. They want to feel that sensation of open-hearted excitement, adventure, and intensity that *Dragon Ball* emanates from within its dragon soul.

Thus there are always fans who complete the series and ask, "What's next?"

The true journey has just begun. You're about to see *Dragon Ball* with new eyes.

***

Step with me through the doorway of *Dragon Ball Culture*.

Approach

DRAGON BALL IS a massive series. It consists of 519 chapters of *manga*, 508 episodes of *anime*, plus the films, video games, and additional content that continue to be produced.

How do you approach such a vast topic?

Structure

Dragon Ball Culture is 7 volumes long. It explores Chapters 1 to 194 of the *Dragon Ball manga* plus select content from Episodes 1 to 153 of the *anime*. This includes *anime* filler episodes between certain chapters of the *manga*, after its conclusion, and all 4 *Dragon Ball* movies.

It does not explore the *"Dragon Ball Z"* portion of the series, from Chapters 195 to 519, but I will mention those chapters on occasion. Why did I put that title in quotes? Because Akira Toriyama's *manga* is just called *Dragon Ball* from start to finish. It's the *anime* staff in Japan who change the name of their adaptation after Chapter 194 of the *manga* to *"Dragon Ball Z"* for marketing purposes. There is no such division in Toriyama's original work.

"Dragon Ball Z" is the more popular portion of the series, so why not write about this first? *Dragon Ball* is a martial arts adventure that follows the principle of mastering the basics and establishing a solid foundation. This is because Akira Toriyama follows the basics in his craft, as a product of a traditional Japanese worldview. The concepts that are established in the first 194 chapters of the *Dragon Ball manga* create a foundation upon which the rest of the franchise is built. It all starts here. If you want to understand

"*Dragon Ball Z*" and the movies, video games, and other official works, you must begin with the basics of *Dragon Ball*.

Dragon Ball Culture Volume 1 reveals the origin of *Dragon Ball*. Here you'll learn about Akira Toriyama's life and discover how and why he creates a series that changes the world. This is the first biography about Akira Toriyama to be published in English. No *Dragon Ball* fan has ever encountered this, and it's the missing piece to your understanding of the series. I feel that Toriyama's story is just as interesting as Gokū's. After all, without Toriyama, Gokū doesn't exist.

Dragon Ball Culture Volumes 2 through 7 explore Gokū's story. This is organized into 3 parts that mirror its original structure in the first 16 of 42 *tankōbon* (単行本, "standalone volumes") of the *manga*.

A *tankōbon* is a sequential collection of the serialized *manga*. Each *tankōbon* volume contains about 12 chapters, starting at Chapter 1 and proceeding forward.

This means Volumes 2 and 3 of *Dragon Ball Culture* will explore Part 1 of Gokū's story (*tankōbon* 1 through 4). Volume 4 will explore Part 2 (*tankōbon* 5 through 9). Volumes 5 and 6 will explore Part 3 (*tankōbon* 9 through 16). And Volume 7 will explore the *anime*.

I'll walk you through Gokū's journey from the first page to the last.

Process

I recommend reading a portion of the *manga* or watching the *anime*, proceeding through a chapter of *Dragon Ball Culture*, and then continuing this process one chapter at a time until you finish both *Dragon Ball* and the book.

Source

What is the genuine *Dragon Ball*? Is it only the Japanese *manga*, or does it include the *anime*, movies, games, toys, spin-offs, localized versions, and other merchandise? Since Toriyama wrote the *manga*, but not the *anime*, there are endless debates among fans about which parts of the series are canonical, and what the true "canon" is.

Canonical is a term that refers to the authoritative version of something. For example, canonical texts of a religion are those transcribed in their original language during or near the time the teachings are spoken. Every version that follows is an abstraction from this original source, with different interpretations or translations adding further layers of abstraction. So if you want to receive the original teachings, you have to return to the source.

Dragon Ball is a long-running series that has been added onto by other writers and adapted into various forms. As the series continues to expand in scope and spin-offs are added into the mix we end up with a problem: There is no authority to define what is and is not canonical.

As a result, canonicity is a sensitive topic. Some fans include the *anime* adaptations, while others include the movies, games, merchandise, and fan-created works. In particular, their localized version of the *anime* is often their only experience with the series, so it becomes their standard. Adding mud to the waters is that Toriyama did contribute character designs in movies and spin-offs, but his degree of influence either varies or is unclear.

Canonicity is a complicated issue, but for sure the *manga* is the ultimate standard since it comes from the creator. That's why I use the original Japanese *manga* as my reference. I return to the source so that I can bring you the true *Dragon Ball*.

That said, I'm not here to argue about what is canonical

and what isn't. My goal is to focus on what's important to you, which is the content that makes the series more entertaining and rich. That's why I also include the Japanese *anime* when necessary to fill in the blanks or add insight. I do this because if there is content meaningful enough to the story to discuss, has cultural value, or is a popular topic, then I should explain it.

No matter how you prefer to enjoy *Dragon Ball*, seeing the original content will enhance your experience.

Identity

Some *Dragon Ball* fans don't know that the series comes from Japan. They watch the *anime* in their localized language and never give its origin a second thought.

This is often the case with fans in the United States who grow up watching the censored English dub by FUNimation alongside Western cartoons, with its script changes, added-in references to American culture (such as cowboys or surfers), and jokes that were never in the original.

Yet another case of mistaken identity is to think *Dragon Ball* is Chinese because it has so much Chinese culture.

Nonetheless, the fact remains that *Dragon Ball* is a product of a young Japanese man living in a post-World War II Japan; himself a product of a multicultural environment.

Language

If you want to understand a culture, you must first speak its language. That's why I use Japanese terms for every aspect of the series, from characters to techniques and beyond.

I understand this might feel weird at first because it's

foreign. That's how everyone feels when they're learning something new for the first time. But it's beneficial because you'll learn about a foreign language and culture through a vehicle you already accept. This makes it easy and fun.

When I wrote and published my first book, *Dragon Ball Z "It's Over 9,000!" When Worldviews Collide* (2012), I intended it to be read by an American audience. That's why I used the FUNimation English dub names for the characters, such as Krillin and Vegeta. I never imagined that it would become an international success with readers in Brazil, Japan, New Zealand, Germany, Russia, Spain, the UK, and South Africa. Now that I know I'm writing for an international audience, I have to make adjustments that appeal to a wider demographic. The way I do that is by going back to the original source language, rather than catering to a specific localization and alienating everyone else. As the saying goes: One man's Yamcha is another man's Jamsza.

Another reason for using Japanese is because the localized dubs alter the original Japanese script, including the names of characters, places, and martial arts techniques. Or worse, they outright censor the content.

I dislike censorship and feel that it is disrespectful to the artist's original intent. This book remains true to Toriyama's intent, and that means you may see things you never knew were there. The fact that cultural content is stripped out or made shallow in the localized dubs is one of the reasons why this book needed to be written. If you're a dub fan it may make you curious enough to watch the subtitled *anime* in Japanese and see what you've been missing.

You may even be inspired to learn Japanese so that you can enjoy the series as Toriyama intended. This is a worthwhile effort because if you compare the Japanese version to your own localized version you'll see that there are changes on every level, and sometimes only the most basic content is kept in order to maintain the flow of the story. Subtle word choices, accents, and personality differences between characters are lost in translation. It's like you've only heard the mid-range of the audio signal instead of the highs, mids, and lows, together. If you want the full spectrum, you have to go back to the source.

Of course, I grew up watching the American dub and this book wouldn't exist without it. So I'm not here to tell you which version of *Dragon Ball* is the best, and I'm not going to comment on the countless alterations in certain localizations as they come up. There are too many, and to do it in every chapter would appear derogatory. Instead I'll let the translated examples of the Japanese speak for themselves. *Dragon Ball* is an incredible series no matter which language you prefer.

Translation

Translating *Dragon Ball* is difficult. I experienced the same challenges during the writing process that localizers have, so I'll tell you up front how I addressed them.

The main issue is that the vocabulary of *Dragon Ball* is composed of three different languages: Japanese, English, and Chinese. It would be simple if there were no overlap among them, but that's not the case. We have Japanese terms, fabricated Japanese terms, English terms, English terms approximated in Japanese, terms that are a combination of English and Japanese, Chinese terms, Chinese terms translated into Japanese millennia ago, and Chinese terms translated into modern Japanese. Furthermore, many of the Japanese or Chinese terms stem from East Indian Sanskrit.

These terms are essential to understanding the cultural content of the *Dragon Ball* series and will be defined and explained each time they are introduced. By the end of the book you'll be fluent in canonical *Dragon Ball* terminology.

There's a full Glossary in the back of each volume for

your reference. If you want a reminder of what a word means, then jump to the Glossary, read it, and jump back.

To understand the words they have to be written in a language you speak. So the Japanese terms in this book will be in *rōmaji* (ローマ字, "Romanized Japanese"), not in a localized equivalent. For example, the United States' localized English name for Krillin will be written as Kuririn (クリリン, pronounced 'Ku-ri-rin') because that is the Romanized pronunciation of how Akira Toriyama writes it in Japanese. The Chinese terms will likewise be written in the equivalent *pīnyīn* (拼音, "spelled sound"). So each time I introduce a new term I'll show you the Roman alphabet version followed by the original language. This makes it easy for you to learn as you go.

Whenever I use a non-English term I put the Romanized equivalent first, followed by the original and its translation. For example, Papaiya-*shima* (パパイヤ島, "Papaya Island"). The scholarly way is to write パパイヤ島 (Papaiya-*shima*, "Papaya Island"), but I think that's dumb. If you don't speak that language, why put it first?

You might be hearing the characters' original names for the first time. Toriyama gives meaningful names to his characters, so to change their names is to change their identity. If I localized their names, then it would be a disservice to you because you'd be deprived of a full immersion into the culture from which Toriyama's work emerged.

However, this creates a problem. Should an exception be made for the Japanese 'L' and 'R' issue, since there is no letter 'L' in the Japanese alphabet? I decided it was all or nothing, because if I make an exception for one character, such as saying Bulma instead of the original Buruma (ブルマ), than why not for another? Toriyama does sometimes write his characters names in the Latin alphabet on their clothing, but it's a fraction of the time compared to when other characters say their name in Japanese. If I made those exceptions, then it would become confusing.

The same logic applies to the English terms that Toriyama approximates into Japanese. I don't use the English terms because that's not how Toriyama writes them, and things will get lost in translation if I localize the terms. Dozens of exceptions could be made, but what right do I have to make them? And why make an exception for one term and not another? To solve this problem I go 100% Japanese.

You may have trouble pronouncing the foreign terms, so there's a Pronunciation Guide at the front of the book, and whenever a difficult to pronounce term appears for the first time I'll put the proper pronunciation next to it. Try to pronounce each word the best you can, but you can call the words whatever you want; what matters is that you have fun with the adventure and learn as you go.

Summary

Because there is culture on every page of Dragon Ball it means I have to summarize the storytelling content in-between the cultural content. I don't like doing this because I respect the series too much to be seen as a plagiarist. Yet an alternative solution escapes me, so I try to summarize as little as possible in order to reach the next cultural curiosity. I do this with full respect of Toriyama's work and all of the copyright owners and license holders. The intent is to add value to the original work.

This book does not replace the *manga* or *anime*. I believe the usage of the content falls within fair use and scholarly guidelines for the purpose of education and literary criticism. If anything, it will make you want to buy the official works. Please support the official release.

Images

Dragon Ball Culture does not have licensed images. I'd love to have them, but I don't own the rights to Toriyama's work and the licenses are expensive and complicated. Should this book sell well, then that may allow me to add them in. Fortunately, *Dragon Ball* is an illustrative work, so you can always refer to it.

Progression

Dragon Ball is a testament to the chronological progression of Akira Toriyama's life. As Toriyama wrote each chapter he offered a comment at the front that shed light into his mindset at the time of publication. He was also interviewed over the course of the series. I combine his comments with his interviews in a linear fashion to help you feel what it's like to follow Toriyama's progression through the series as it is being published. You'll put on Toriyama's shoes and walk the path that he walked.

These comments are a gift because they give me the ability to track down the source of inspiration that he uses for each chapter. I relived his experiences by watching the same movies, TV shows, and other life events that he refers to. For example, there are instances where we see a character who looks like an actor from a movie that comes out the same week that Toriyama writes the chapter he appears in, or where Gokū does a martial arts technique that is used in a *gōngfu* (功夫, "kung fu") film from earlier that year. Same for costume designs, environments, and scenarios. There are hundreds of these examples, and it required a great effort to put the different pieces back together in a chronological way over the course of the series.

Evolution

There's a lot about *Dragon Ball* that hasn't been explained, but I still do my best to explain it. I researched every aspect of *Dragon Ball*, its creator, and its culture to try and solve the mysteries that fans have wondered about; but it's an ever-evolving project.

This means taking educated guesses and forming theories for which little information is available. I have to be brave, step out into the spotlight and make presumptions. When I do this I'll use phrases such as "I believe," or "I suspect," and then provide the rationale for why. Yes, I might be wrong and everyone will see it, but the incorrect theories will be sifted out while the correct theories will carry on. That's what it means to be bold and do something new.

It also means this book may never be perfect. Perfect information is impossible because knowledge is infinite yet our time is finite. I've done my best to make it as perfect as I can within the time I have.

There's never been a book like this that enriches the collective understanding of *Dragon Ball* fans across the world. As one body, let our dragon soul rise higher!

Pronunciation Guide

Akira Toriyama is a master wordsmith who plays with the pronunciation of words, names, and places. This is part of the charm of *Dragon Ball* and a reason why I present the content to you in its original form.

However, there are foreign terms that you may not know how to pronounce because Toriyama borrows from Chinese, Sanskrit, and English, and fuses them into his native Japanese. This pronunciation guide will give you the basic linguistic knowledge needed to enhance your appreciation of *Dragon Ball*.

Chinese Language

The Chinese believe their culture is divinely bestowed, and therefore semi-divine. Chinese folktales say that the Chinese language is handed down by the gods, and that's why the Chinese use *hànzì* (漢字, pronounced 'hahn-zuh,' "Hàn characters") in their language.[1] *Hànzì* are ideograms: a series of strokes that illustrate an image or carry meaning. Each combination of strokes has a different meaning, and there are thousands of combinations.

For example, the word *dà* (大, "big") depicts a man with his arms and legs spread out to the side. Some of the *hànzì* have changed over their thousands of years of use, so they

---

1   The Chinese refer to their written text as *hànzì* (漢字, "Hàn characters") and to themselves as the *hànrén* (漢人, "Hàn people"). These both refer to the Hàn Dynasty (漢朝, Hàn-*cháo*, "Dry Riverbed Dynasty," 206 B.C. – 220 A.D.), a golden age of Chinese civilization.

don't always look like their intended meaning, while others look closer. For example, *gǒu* (狗, "dog") doesn't look like a dog to me, but in *mǎ* (馬, "horse") I can see the mane and four legs of a horse. Thus the meaning of Chinese characters is left open to interpretation.

Westerners often have a difficult time memorizing the sounds of so many images compared to a Western alphabet. That's why there is a phonetic teaching aid called *pīnyīn* (拼音, "written sound") that writes the sound of each character in Romanized letters. I start each new Chinese term with the *pīnyīn* equivalent of the Mandarin pronunciation. Mandarin (Chinese: *pǔtōnghuà*, 普通話, "common speech") is one of many dialects spoken in China, but is the standard and national dialect of modern China, so it will be the most accessible to international readers.[2]

There are two types of *hànzì* written in the world today. The first type are the *zhèngtǐ-zì* (正體字, "traditional characters"). These characters have been in use for thousands of years, and are still used in Táiwān, Hong Kong, Macau, and overseas Chinese communities. But many of them were replaced, modified, or forbidden from use by the Chinese Communist Party after they took control of China in 1949. The *hànzì* were altered because the atheist doctrines of Chinese Communism were opposed to their cultural, historical, or religious content. Therefore the second type of *hànzì*

---

2   The word Mandarin comes from the Chinese *Mǎndàrén* (满大人, "*Mǎn* Great Man," or "*Mǎn* Master"). *Mǎn* (满) refers to the *Mǎnzhōurén* (满洲人, "Manchurian," or "Full Continent People"), the foreign rulers of China during the Qīng Dynasty (清朝, Qīng-*cháo*, "Clarity Dynasty," 1644 – 1912 A.D.). *Mǎndàrén* was used by the Chinese people to refer to their foreign rulers, and in turn, their language. The term spread across the world during the 19th century and is now synoymous with the language, but in modern China they call this dialect *pǔtōnghuà* (普通話, "common speech") because it is the standard dialect of Northeast and central China.

are the *jiǎnhuà-zì* (簡化字, "simplified characters") used in mainland China.

I use the traditional characters because they contain the original culture that is lost when using the simplified characters. Toriyama often uses these symbols to connect his characters to ancient China and its spiritual concepts. I'll give explanations of the deeper meaning behind certain *hànzì* when relevant to *Dragon Ball.*

Chinese Pronunciations

The key letters to focus on are 'c,' 'j,' 'q,' 'x,' and 'r.'

C: Like 'ts,' as in 'bits.' So 'cao' is pronounced 'tsao.'

J: Like 'zh,' as in 'jeep.' So 'ji' is pronounced 'zhee.' The 'i' sound is like this as well, but can sometimes have a falling sound. For example, the 'zì' in '*hànzì*' is pronounced 'zuh.'

Q: Like 'ch,' as in 'cheap.' So 'qun' is pronounced 'choon.'

X: Like 'sh,' as in 'show.' So 'xia' is pronounced 'shiah.'

R: An 'r' most often sounds like the English 'r.' For example, 'rou' is pronounced 'row.' But with a Mandarin accent it can be slurred as 'rr,' like in 'rouge,' or 'er,' like in 'urban.'

Then there are the two-letter combinations of 'ao,' 'ch,' 'qu,' 'sh,' 'wu,' 'xi,' 'yi,' and 'zh.'

AO: Like the 'ow' in 'cow.' So 'pao' is pronounced 'pow.'

CH: Like the 'ch' in 'chair.' So 'chao' is pronounced 'chow.'

QU: Like the 'choo' in 'chew.' So 'quan' is pronounced 'chew-ahn.'

SH: Like the 'sh' in 'share.' So 'shao' is pronounced, 'show,' like in 'shower.'

WU: Like the 'oo' in 'room.' The 'w' is partially spoken.

XI: Like the 'sh' in 'sheep.' So 'xi' is pronounced 'shee.'

YI: Like the 'ee' in 'bee.' So 'yi' is pronounced 'ee.'

ZH: Like the 'j' in 'jam.' So 'zhao' is pronounced 'jow.'

There's more to Chinese—like tones—but this will suffice.

Japanese Language

Chinese culture has a major influence on the development of Japanese culture and language. The biggest exportation of Chinese culture is during the Táng Dynasty (唐朝, Táng-cháo, "Boastful Pestle Dynasty," 618 – 907 A.D.). It's here when the Chinese *hànzì*, Buddhist, Dàoist, and native folk cultures of China are adopted by the Japanese literati. This leads to the Japanese using the *hànzì* (漢字) and calling them *kanji* (漢字, pronounced 'kahn-jee').

When the Japanese first hear Chinese they try to approximate the sounds in their native Japanese phonetics. This leads to what's called the *on'yomi* (音読み, "sound reading") pronunciation. For example, the *hànzì* of *jiǎo* (餃, "dumpling") in *on'yomi* Japanese is pronounced *chao*.

After hundreds of years, the Japanese make the *kanji* their own and give them localized pronunciations that differ from the Chinese. This is called the *kun'yomi* (訓読み, "translated reading") pronunciation, and is more modern. So in *kun'yomi* Japanese, *jiǎo* (餃) is pronounced *gyō*.

This means that every *kanji* has two (or more) pronunciations. And there are thousands of *kanji*.

One way to tell which pronunciation to use is by whether the *kanji* is by itself or positioned next to another. For example, the *hànzì* of *shén* (神, "god," or "spirit") by itself in Japanese is pronounced with *kun'yomi* as *kami*. But if you position it next to another *kanji* then it is pronounced with *on'yomi* as *shin*, such as in *shinrei* (神雷, "soul"). *Kun'yomi* tend to be multisyllabic in their pronunciation, while *on'yomi* are monosyllabic like their Chinese counterparts.

From this, the Japanese develop a writing system of their own, culturally synchronous with the islands. They do this because *kanji* convey information in an image, but don't have a phonetic value of a syllable.

So in addition to *on'yomi* and *kun'yomi* the Japanese have their own alphabet symbols comprised of phonetic sounds, such as *ka* (か), *ki* (き), *ku* (く), *ke* (け), *ko* (こ), and *na* (な), *ni* (に), *nu* (ぬ), *ne* (ね), *no* (の), written with different characters. You combine the different syllables together to make words. The outlier is the *n* (ん) consonant, which can be said by itself or joined with others, acting like a regular syllable. For example, *konbanwa* (こんばんは, "good evening") combines the syllables of 'ko-n-ba-n-wa' together.

There are two alphabets used in Japanese, each comprised of *kana* (仮名, "scripts").

The first is *hiragana* (平仮名, "ordinary scripts"). This consists of 46 round letters and shapes, and is used to write native words and grammatical particles for which there are no *kanji*, or as the written pronunciation of *kanji*. For example, the suffix of *san* (さん, "Mr.," "Mrs.," or "Miss") has two hiragana of *sa* (さ) and *n* (ん) combined. As in, Toriyama-*san* (鳥山さん, "Mr. Toriyama").

The second is *katakana* (片仮名, "fragmentary scripts"). This consists of 48 sharp letters and shapes, and is used to write foreign, technical, and scientific terms. For example, America is written as *Amerika* (アメリカ, pronounced 'A-me-ri-ka') in *katakana*. They do the same for certain Chinese words, such as the game of *májiàng* (麻將, "mahjong"), written as *mājan* (マージャン, pronounced 'maa-jahn').

Katakana plays an important role in *manga* because it is used for sound effects and onomatopoeia: the words created to sound like real-life sounds. For example, the sound of 'bang' in Japanese is *don* (ドン). There is a full set of cultural sounds that differ from what you're used to. For instance, in the West a dog makes a sound like 'woof, woof,' but in Japanese it's *wan-wan* (ワンワン). And unlike in Western comics where a word is written in bold italics to add emphasis, in *manga* it's done with *katakana*.

In the same vein, *hiragana* and *katakana* are used to express emotion. For example, if Gokū is excited about something, he'll say the sound of *waku-waku* (わくわく) in *hiragana*, rather than the equivalent of "I'm excited." And if a character becomes angry, they will say *pun-pun* (プンプン) in *katakana*. These actions, sounds, and emotions are a language all their own.

You'll notice in the *manga* that Toriyama uses a combination of English and Japanese sound effects, such as writing "BOOOM!!" in big English letters in one panel, and then "*DON!!*" in *katakana* in the next. This is part of his style, and it's noteworthy because he does this for his Japanese audience of the 1980s who may not speak the language. This is because English is considered cool in Japan.

The Japanese start to incorporate English *gairaigo* (外来語, "loanwords") into their language in the late 19th century during a process of modernization; especially after World War I (1914 – 1918) with the introduction of radio. English and foreign philosophies are perceived as attractive, but due to the syllabic nature of the Japanese language, many words are difficult to speak. So the words undergo rephonalization, meaning that the sounds are converted to the syllabic writing systems—mostly in *katakana*. For example, 'orange juice' becomes *orenji jūsu* (オレンジジュース). Because of the longstanding 'coolness' of using these words that persists to today, Japanese citizens often do not realize these words were originally foreign. In 2003 my Japanese roommate in Běijīng didn't know that 'orange' and 'juice' were foreign words, and just knew that you call the drink *orenji jūsu*.

Toriyama loves to use loanwords. Not only because they sound foreign and cool, but because of his comedic wit. He'll name characters after foreign foods, create futuristic devices with scientific names, and have Chinese or Japanese characters speak English in rephonalized Japanese in order to connect them to Western culture.

In *Dragon Ball* you're going to see *kanji*, *hiragana*, and *katakana*. I'll refer to the ancient *on'yomi* and modern *kun'yomi* as examples present themselves to show how

Toriyama plays with ancient and modern pronunciations.

There is also a reading aid to help you pronounce *kanji*, called *furigana* (振り仮名, "pronunciation scripts"). It consists of writing *hiragana* or *katakana* letters above or to the side of *kanji*. I mention it whenever Toriyama does something silly with his word jokes intended for a Japanese audience. He'll write a word a certain way and then include *furigana* text next to it that drives home a pun. If you don't know Japanese, the joke gets lost in translation, so I'll point them out.

Similar to the Chinese terms, I'll start each new Japanese term with the *rōmaji* (ローマ字, "Roman letters") equivalent of the Japanese pronunciation.

Japanese Pronunciations

I believe that most of your attempts to pronounce the Japanese words will be close to how they sound. And if you're a *Dragon Ball* fan, you've probably heard most of them before. So I won't give detailed examples of Japanese like in the Chinese above.

The only thing to pay attention to are the vowels of 'ā,' 'ī,' 'ū,' 'ē,' and 'ō.' When you see one of these macrons above a vowel it means you elongate the sound.

For example, the 'kū' sound in Gokū has a macron on it in the original Japanese. So his name is pronounced 'Gokuu.' The same goes for the 'ō' sound in words like 'Daima-ō,' pronounced 'dye-ma-oh.' And the 'ī' in words like *bīru* (ビール, "beer"), pronounced 'bee-ru.'

Sanskrit

Sanskrit is an ancient language of India that shaped the cultures of our world, similar to Latin and Greek. It provides the roots for countless words in multiple languages.

Many Buddhist words originate in India, are approximated in Chinese, and are then approximated again in Japanese. So I often mention a word in Sanskrit followed by its Chinese and Japanese counterpart. For example, the Buddhist term *citta-santāna* (Sanskrit: चित्तसंतान, Chinese: *xīn-xiāngxù*, 心相續, Japanese: *shin-sōzoku*, "continual heart") refers to the continual series of moments in our existence that we call our consciousness.

In these multi-language cases I don't include the Japanese *kanji* when it's the same as the Chinese *hànzì*, or vice versa.

Toriyama does not use Sanskrit; he uses a Japanese or Chinese approximation. But to understand their meaning we have to reference the original terms from India.

Sometimes a Sanskrit word doesn't exist in Japanese and Chinese, or is unique to that culture. Or there are times when it reduces the readability to include it. In those cases you can find the variants in the Glossary.

I'm not going to give a pronunciation guide on Sanskrit. It's there for your enhanced appreciation of the Chinese and Japanese, and for the linguists who enjoy seeing how words change over time and influence our world.

Have Fun

It's okay if you have trouble pronouncing these words. Gokū would have a hard time with them as well. But that wouldn't slow him down, would it? He'd give it his best shot and keep moving forward. So have fun on your adventure!

Origin

TO DISCOVER *DRAGON Ball's* origin we will enter the mind of Akira Toriyama.

We'll trace his story from childhood to young adulthood and figure out how he ticks.

Along the way you'll find out what makes him a star, where his inspiration for *Dragon Ball* comes from, and why it is the most beloved *anime* and *manga* in the world.

Akira Toriyama

"TORIYAMA THE MAGNIFICENT" springs from his mother's womb with pen in hand. Doves fly from his mouth as he says, "Give me paper, and ink, and I will bring joy to the hearts of men." Then the earth quakes and the people rejoice!

Toriyama is Born

Of course, in reality there is no miraculous birth. Toriyama is born on April 5, 1955, in Nagoya-*shi*, Aichi-*ken*, Japan.[1–2] He's the first child of Karazu and Tombi Toriyama, followed two years later by his sister, Uzura.[3]

Akira Toriyama (鳥山 明, "Bright Bird Mountain") is written in three *kanji*: *tori* (鳥, "bird"), *yama* (山, "mountain"), and *akira* (明, "bright," "light," or "brilliant").

Nagoya is the "central capital" of Japan because of its location on the main island. It's a metropolitan area, but Toriyama grows up in the countryside, in Kiyosu-*shi* (清須市, "Clear-headed City"). He still prefers to live in Kiyosu because it's a quiet area far from the crowds.

---

1   Nagoya-*shi* (名古屋市, "Ancient Name Dwelling City"). Aichi-*ken* (愛知県, "Loving Wisdom Prefecture").

2   Japan has 47 *ken* (県, "prefectures"), which are regions of the country. Each has its own local customs.

3   Toriyama's family is a typical *ie* (家, "family home") consisting of a father, mother, son, and daughter. An *ie* is a family structure emphasized by the Japanese government during the 1930s to '50s (especially during World War II) for the purposes of propaganda and nationalism. It is similar to the ideal American family of the same era.

Springtime of Youth

'Tag! You're it!' Toriyama runs through the countryside of Kiyosu as he plays with his friends, breathes in fresh air, and watches the birds. It's Toriyama's springtime of youth.

Toriyama recalls his childhood: "The kids were full of life ... and we played passionately on the streets until the sun set, yet we're all excellent people now as adults."[4-5]

When he's not playing games with other kids he's enjoying the work of history's most famous *manga-ka* (漫画家, "comic author"), Tezuka Osamu (手塚 治虫, November 1928 – February, 9, 1989). In particular, Tezuka's seminal work, *Tetsuwan Atomu* (鉄腕アトム, "*Mighty Atom*," or "*Astro Boy*," 1952). Toriyama says in the *Dragon Ball: Bōken Special* guidebook that his favorite *manga* is, "*Tetsuwan Atomu*. There used to be this magazine called *Shōnen*, and I liked practically every *manga* that ran in it."[6]

After World War II (1939 – 1945), Japan's *manga* industry explodes in popularity in the 1950s and 60s. So *manga* is something he grows up with in the same way that American boys grow up with comic books. While *manga-ka* can express themselves through different genres targeted at adults, women, young girls, or specific genres such as sports or political issues, Toriyama reads *shōnen manga*

---

4   "The kids were full of life" comes from the three volume collection of his *manga* short stories called *Toriyama Akira ○ Saku gekijō* (鳥山明○作劇場, "*Akira Toriyama's Manga Theater*," 1983, 1988, and 1997).

5   Almost all of the translations of Toriyama's interviews or comments in official publications that I use in this book come from *http://kanzenshuu.com/translations/* and are available for you to read online. Thank you to the *Kanzenshuu* staff for their dedication to the series.

6   *Dragon Ball: Bōken Special* (ドラゴンボール 冒険SPECIAL, "*Dragon Ball: Adventure Special*," 1987) is the first official *Dragon Ball* guidebook and includes rare information and interviews.

(少年漫画, "young boys' comics"). These are *manga* that usually star a young boy that the reader can relate to as they go on adventures or experience funny situations.

So he enjoys reading *manga* as a child and gets inspired by the beautiful artwork and entertaining stories to draw his own. In *Saku gekijō* (1983) he continues, "As a child I was very naughty, but I loved to draw. I always drew animals and vehicles because it's what I liked." And in the *American Shonen Jump*, Volume 1, #1 (January 2003), he says, "I started copy-drawing other people's *manga* characters when I was about 5 years old."

He says that when he was in kindergarten he saw the Disney film *101 Dalmatians* (1961) and, "I almost fell backwards, thinking, 'How I would like to draw like that!'" After this experience he never stops drawing. Toriyama says in *Daizenshū 6: Movies & TV Specials* (1995),[7] "When I was a child there were drawing schools called Zugaya-*san* (図画屋さん, "Mr. Drawing Shop"). Local children would gather together and draw pictures and be noisy. I remember one day, I drew a picture from *101 Dalmatians*, won a prize, became ecstatic, and here I am now." This art school is likely a small local business chain in his home town where friends gather to have fun. Art is just a pastime until he enters this drawing contest and wins. Afterward, it becomes a passion.

Toriyama says his family was poor and unable to afford toys and other fun things for him to play with. He recalls in the *Menzu non-no* (メンズノンノ, "Men's Non-No") magazine interview (2014) that he drew, "Things that I wanted. At the time, I wanted a horse the most, so I drew it, thinking, 'It'd probably be fun to ride down the neighborhood streets, clip-clopping as I go.'" He draws a horse again and again,

---

7   The *Daizenshū* (大全集, *"Great Complete Collections"*) are ten official guidebooks to the *Dragon Ball* series published shortly after the completion of the *manga*, from 1995 to 1996. They are filled with information, artwork, and interviews.

imagining that he is bringing it to life and riding in the streets. Finally in *Daizenshū 6* he says, "My first memory of a satisfactory drawing was that of a horse. I still remember it. I knew I got the joints right." He continues, "I've always liked to draw. When I was little, we didn't have many forms of entertainment like we do today, so we were all drawing pictures. In elementary school, we were all drawing *manga* or *anime* characters and showing them to each other."

At this age Toriyama doesn't know his life will be dedicated to drawing art or the global impact his drawings will have. Nor does he think that his talents are exceptional. "Perhaps I just kept on drawing. We all start out with around the same drawing skills don't we? I started to do portraits of friends and whatnot and started to think drawing was fun."

He discovers he has the artist's eye. "I have had this habit since I was a kid of always looking around at my surroundings. Even when I go shopping, more-so than the shopping itself, it's fun to just observe the town. When you're drawing a work, it comes in handy for things like street scenes, small objects, clothes, and such." He takes a mental snapshot whenever an external scene or object inspires his imagination. Then he translates the internal image onto paper, doodling away until he renders it or loses interest. "I burn them into my memory." But sometimes his memory fails him and he has to be creative to fill in the gaps. "But I do remember the rough image." So the end result isn't photorealistic, but is close enough for you to admire. This ability to capture an image in his mind's eye and then transfer it to paper is a gift that provides versatility. He says, "I think there's probably nothing I can't draw."

After school gets out he spends his afternoons in the street, "doing mischief until it got dark. And then at home, I spent all my time drawing." He grows up in an era before the *gakushū juku* (学習塾, "tutoring classes") are common, where students do additional studying after their regular school hours are complete. If he didn't have that creative freedom to just be a kid and play games with his friends, then he wouldn't grow up to be the man he is.

Despite not studying all the time, he still does well in school. In the 1981 *Ribon* (りぼん, *"Ribbon"*) magazine interview he says that in elementary school he "got all 5's on his report cards" (the highest marks), and that his favorite subjects are "arts and crafts! Poor at math."[8] So even at a young age he leans toward the creative arts and away from mathematics. And he admits in the *Tetsuko no Heya* (徹子の部屋, *"Tetsuko's Room,"* 1983) interview, "My textbooks were relatively full of doodles."

Then one day he goes to a neighbor's house and sees TV for the first time. It's love at first sight. "I was perplexed ... As a child I was seeing more and more interesting things." His curiosity compels him to continue watching for what will appear next. The whole world sits inside that box.

From this moment onward TV becomes a constant companion in Toriyama's life. In his own words he is, "raised on TV."

Raised on TV

Television shapes Toriyama's worldview, and the work he produces as an adult reflects his childhood entertainment.

Since he is born in 1955 he grows up watching TV shows in the 1960s, '70s, and '80s. This is called the Shōwa-*jidai* (昭和時代, *"Era of Enlightened Peace"*) period of television. The Japanese define their calendar years and history based on the Emperor's reign. So the Shōwa-*jidai* encompasses the

---

8   An archive of the *Ribon* (りぼん, *"Ribbon"*) magazine interview with Toriyama from October, 1981, in Japanese: *http://www.geocities. jp/kongzimi/duihua-toriyama.html*

reign of the Shōwa-*tennō* Hirohito (昭和天皇裕仁, "Enlightened Peace Emperor Hirohito," April 21, 1909 – January 7, 1989), lasting from December 25, 1926 through January 7, 1989. After this it becomes the Heisei-*jidai* (平成時代, "Era of Accomplished Balance") period when Hirohito's son, Akihito (明仁, "Second Born Brightness," born December 23, 1933), succeeds the throne on November 12, 1990. That's the period we are currently in.

The *Shōwa* era of television has a lighthearted and simple tone. It's typified by costumed superheroes fighting against giant "monsters of the week," while comedy shows and *anime* entertain people with tales of fantasy and romance, whether with robots in outer space or mischievous boys on Earth. It's a time when the Japanese entertainment industry exercises its creative muscle and many classic series are born. This is the cultural response to the World War II era.

As a result of growing up during this time, Toriyama is instilled with the idea of creating products of a lighthearted and simple nature. He prefers to leave you with a feeling of being entertained and refreshed, rather than make things violent, dark, or serious. To make a comparison for a Western audience, it's similar to American cartoons produced in the 1970s, such as *Super Friends* (1973) and *The Tom and Jerry Show* (1975), and the 1980s, such as *Transformers* (1984) and *G.I. Joe: A Real American Hero* (1985). These shows contain simple fun and occasional moral messages, and even though they are filled with action, nobody experiences violent deaths or sexual scenarios.

Toriyama still carries this attitude with him today. When commenting on his 2013 film, *Dragon Ball Z: Kami to Kami* in the *Akira Toriyama x Shōko Nakagawa Interview* (2013) he says, "Recent *anime* have gotten to have pretty complex character relationships, but in that area I developed things simply while leaving in a whiff of *Shōwa*, so I'll be happiest if I can get them to understand the fun of the characters. Something this simple and pure isn't depicted all that much, so I'd like for them to enjoy simply seeing something that's easy to understand!!" Even though he is 24 years into the *Heisei* era and his compatriots are creating darker stories, Toriyama still prefers to keep his stories lighthearted and entertaining. That's part of why his work maintains a fresh spirit, and becomes classic.[9]

So what shows did he watch? In *Daizenshū 3* he says, "I watched shows like *Tetsuwan Atomu* and *Tetsujin Nijūhachi-gō* up until about the fourth grade. In the second half of primary school, I liked live-action shows and giant-monster movies, and then in junior high, I got into regular movies. ... Apart from that, I also watched *Osomatsu-kun*; everybody was imitating Iyami's "*shē!*" pose. I also liked *Eitoman*."

Tetsuwan Atomu (1963) is the first *anime* series ever made. It's based on Tezuka's *manga*, and according to Toriyama is "the one that stays deepest in my memory." *Tetsujin Nijūhachi-gō* (鉄人28号, "*Iron Man No. 28*," 1963) is the first "giant robot" type of *anime*, where a boy controls a robot with a remote control. It's likewise based on a *manga* created by Yokoyama Mitsuteru (横山 光輝, June 18, 1934 – April 15, 2004). *Osomatsu-kun* (おそ松くん, 1966) is a comedy *anime* about the antics of sextuplets with buckteeth. Once again it's based on a *manga*, this time by Akatsuka Fujio (赤塚 不二夫, September 14, 1935 – August 2, 2008), considered "the gag *manga* king." The *shē* (シェー) pose is one of the main character Iyami's (イヤミ) signature physical comedy jokes, where he turns up one foot while standing on the other leg, and then puts one hand above his head in a funny position. It became a popular trend across Japan. And *Eitoman* (8マン, "*8 Man*," 1963) is an *anime* about a human turned android who uses martial arts to defeat villains and maintain world peace. The series is, as you now expect to hear, based on a

---

9   *Dragon Ball Z: Kami to Kami* (ドラゴンボールZ 神と神, *Doragon Bōru Zetto: Kami to Kami*, "*Dragon Ball Z: God and God*," or "*Battle of Gods*," 2013) is the 18th animated *Dragon Ball* feature film.

manga, by Hirai Kazumasa (平井 和正, born May 13, 1938) and Jirō Kuwata (桑田 二郎, born April 17, 1935). It predates the Hollywood *Robocop* (1987) and others like it by over two decades.

Toriyama just cited the 4 shows that influenced him the most as a child, and they are all based on *manga.* If there's a lesson to be learned here, it's that if you want your stories to be turned into *anime,* then you should become a *manga-ka.* Toriyama learns this lesson well.

In addition to *anime* he becomes a big fan of live-action *tokusatsu* (特撮, "special [effects] filming") shows. These are costumed superhero series where a character does *henshin* (変身, "transformation") to change their body into an ultra-powerful warrior who uses martial arts and supernormal techniques to defeat the weekly monster. The monster is often portrayed by a man in a suit, and they battle one another in their giant forms and crush the city.

Two iconic series spark the genre and influence Toriyama's work. *Urutoraman* (ウルトラマン, "*Ultraman,*" 1966) is about a special police force operative who is accidentally killed by a falling alien's spacecraft. The alien feels bad that he killed him, so he enters his body and takes his place as the transforming red and silver Urutoraman that fights against the alien monsters that attack Earth. Toriyama loves this show, including its first sequel, *Urutorasebun* (ウルトラセブン, "*Ultra Seven*"), and repeatedly references or parodies it. This series and its many sequels create the *kyodai hīrō* (巨大ヒーロー, "giant hero") genre, where a regular-sized man grows to towering proportions.

Kamen Raidā (仮面ライダー, "*Kamen Rider,*" 1971) is about a young man who undergoes a cybernetic transformation to become a *kaizō ningen* (改造人間, "remodeled human," or "cyborg") with the traits of a grasshopper. He fights against the mysterious terrorist organization known as *Shokkā* (ショッカー, "Shocker"), who kidnaps people, brainwashes them, and uses the same *kaizō ningen* process to turn them into animal-based villains. Many of the villains in Toriyama's works are inspired by this series, including scientists who perform similar operations. *Kamen Raidā* goes on to have over a dozen sequels and theatrical films.

In addition to these programs, he watches decades of other television and entertainment, such as variety shows. But the biggest influence are the movies.

Cinema Lover

In *Daizenshū 1* Toriyama is asked what he uses for reference materials and he says, "Stuff like movies that I watched a long time ago stay in my head, so maybe I used those. Of course, I think that movies are the most useful. I've been ridiculously fond of movies since way back when." And in the *American Shonen Jump* #1 interview he says, "I always play the stories out as movie scenes in my head and imagine how they would unfold." Toriyama relies on his childhood memory of watching movies as the basis of reference for his works; from the vehicles and weapons to the actors.

One of his favorite genres is *kaijū* (怪獣, "strange beast"). The iconic example of a *kaijū* is *Gojira* (ゴジラ, *"Godzilla,"* 1954), a film about a giant radioactive lizard monster that attacks Tōkyō (東京, "Eastern Capital"). But the film is much more than a simple monster movie, it's a poetic portrayal of Japan's experience of being bombed by atomic weapons and the social fallout of science gone wrong. It's because of nuclear weapons that Gojira is born, so Gojira's existence and the devastation he wreaks upon Tōkyō is a reminder of what occurred in 1945 as a result of Japan's extreme *bushidō* (武士道, "the way of the warrior") militarism.

The film is produced by Tōhō Kabushiki-gaisha (東宝株式会社, "Tōhō Studios," founded 1932), Japan's largest film studio.[10] The movie launches the *kaijū* genre and *tokusatsu* special effects cinema that leads to the televised series mentioned above, such as *Urutoraman*. Without *Gojira* in the movies there would be no such TV shows. The director of special effects and supervisor of *Gojira* is the famous Tsuburaya Eiji (円谷 英二, July 10, 1901 – January 25, 1970). He creates *Urutoraman* and works with Tōhō to establish this genre throughout the 1960s during Toriyama's formative years. The young boy absorbs Eiji's special effects wizardry on both the silver screen and small screen.

Toriyama watches *Gojira's* sequels and spin-offs, such as Mosura (モスラ, "*Mothra*," 1961), and *Kingu Kongu tai Gojira* (キングコング対ゴジラ, "*King Kong versus Godzilla*," 1962). Likewise the radioactive turtle, *Gamera* (ガメラ, 1965), produced by rival studio Daiei Eiga Kabushiki-gaisha (大映映画株式會社, "Daiei Motion Picture Company," founded 1942), becomes his personal favorite.

Gojira starts the genre off on a somber note, but they become more childish, and to be blunt, ridiculous, as the years go on. Toriyama prefers the latter. He enjoys the child-like stories of the sequels made in the late-1960s and into the '70s. They aren't award-winning films, but they are fun to watch, and he frequents the theaters to watch them.

Calling upon his childhood memories of these monsters, Toriyama has Gojira, Gamera, and the other *kaijū* appear in his *manga* at random times just for the sake of a laugh. Likewise, his depictions of massive blasts of energy that explode in huge mushroom clouds like an atomic bomb are no doubt inspired by the concepts depicted in these movies. As are the aliens who visit from outer space and the scientists who want to study the strange beasts or create high tech inventions to destroy them. These movies teach Toriyama how to focus his work on entertainment.

---

10   A *kabushiki-gaisha* (株式会社, "stock company") is a type of corporation defined under Japanese law as having stock.

Tōhō also produces *samurai* (侍, "noble warriors") and martial arts drama classics called *jidai-geki* (時代劇, "period drama") that influence Toriyama's work, such as Akira Kurosawa's (黒澤 明, March 23, 1910 – September 6, 1998) masterpiece, *Yōjinbō* (用心棒, "Yojimbo," 1961).

The other film company in Toriyama's life is Tōei Kabu-shiki-gaisha (東映株式会社, "Tōei," founded 1950). They are responsible for many classic *tokusatsu* films and series as well as adventure films such as *Dai Tōzoku* (大盗賊, "The Great Bandit," 1963), known internationally as *Samurai Pirate* and in America as *The Lost World of Sinbad*. It's a classic film full of fantasy, swashbuckling, witches, kings, hermits, and a magical staff that can grow on command. Toriyama uses it for inspiration in *Dragon Ball*. Tōei is the company that goes on to create *anime* versions of his *manga*, so they hold a special place in his heart—and bank account.

Throughout *Dragon Ball Culture* you'll see examples of how Toriyama takes the faces of famous actors that he grew up watching, and then adds them into *Dragon Ball*. He turns them into a *gōngfu* ("kung fu") fighter, wrestler, witch, deity, or some other character for the purposes of his story. He copies them outright for the sake of humor, and then moves on without telling a soul.

So Toriyama loves the movies, but as an adult he doesn't go to the theaters much. Instead he prefers to watch them on his old friend called TV. "It doesn't matter what channel. I generally leave the television on while I'm working. Because of this, I can't watch anything with subtitles, since then I couldn't work. (laughs) I'm basically working, but I'll watch when I can tell by the music that an interesting scene is on. I focus on those movies that I want to see no matter what, but all the rest just flow by."

Western Cinema

Western cinema also has an influence on Toriyama's mind, and he loves watching foreign films. For example, *Jaws* (1975), *Star Wars* (1977), *Alien* (1979), *Blade Runner* (1982), and *The Terminator* (1984) each leave an impression. The *James Bond* films (starting in 1962 with *Dr. No*) also play a large role. In the *American Shonen Jump* #1 interview he says, "I love sci-fi movies. Especially the first *Alien* movie— that's my favorite. I incorporated science fiction into *Dragon Ball* to expand its scope."

Toriyama adds subtle references and blatant mimicry into the series, most often for comical effect. These include monsters from outer space, artificial humans, robots programmed to assassinate the hero, futuristic cities next to quaint villages, time travel, and special effects wizardry.

Disney's *101 Dalmatians* (1961) serves to inspire his artwork as a child, as does *Cinderella* (1950) and other classics. He says in the *V-Jump* December 2013 interview, "I admired Disney films and *Tom and Jerry* from a young age because they were really well-done. Even as a kid, I got a real shock at seeing the difference with Japan in terms of things like drawing skill."

Western superhero films such as the iconic *Superman* (1978) often appear as parodies or as inspirations for storylines in his *manga*. For example, Suppaman (スッパマン, "Sourman"), with the alternate identity of Kuraaku Kenta (暗悪健太, i.e. "Clark Kent"), whom Gokū will meet in Part 2 of *Dragon Ball*.

Toriyama loves World War II period films in particular. He's fascinated by the details of the guns, vehicles (tanks, airplanes, and motorcycles), soldier's uniforms, and paraphernalia. It doesn't matter if it's the American and Allied Forces, the Nazi's, or the Japanese, he loves it all.

Toriyama includes a lot of these war related phenomenon in *Dragon Ball*. He draws these real-world items in his Chinese fantasy driven world, but since he draws them in his signature style, nothing looks out of place.

Toriyama's interest in Western cinema is what causes him to incorporate Hollywood pop culture into his *manga* as jokes or plot devices. Then to make his series more entertaining he mixes these with Asian legends and Chinese belief systems.

Gōngfu Cinema

His love of movies continues with Hong Kong *gōngfu* films. He starts watching these in the 1970s when Hong Kong filmmakers decide to export their films to neighboring countries to increase revenue.

Toriyama recalls his experience with *Enter the Dragon* (1973) in the *TV Anime Guide: Dragon Ball Z Son Gokū Densetsu* (2003): "I saw *Enter the Dragon* starring Bruce Lee, back when I was a student; I remember I got so hopped up on it that I went to the movie theater for about 10 days straight. I saw it about three times a day, and even now, I watch it on video. As a film I first saw during the emotional turmoil of adolescence, it influenced me greatly."

Bruce Lee (Chinese: Lee Jun-fan, 李振藩, November 27, 1940 – July 20, 1973)[11] is arguably the world's most famous martial artist. Despite only filming 4 movies before his unfortunate passing at the age of 32, he is almost single handedly responsible for bringing *gōngfu* movies to the American mainstream. He was a pioneer in several regards, such as his willingness to teach Westerners the martial arts. His trademark "style of no style" influences Toriyama's own

---

11   Lee Jun-fan (李振藩) is Bruce Lee's name in Cantonese. In Mandarin it is pronounced Lǐ Zhènfān.

fighting choreography in his battle sequences, and Bruce's films inspire scenarios and environments throughout his work. *Enter the Dragon* (1973) changes Toriyama's life.

He continues, "There was a boom in *gōngfu* movies... and around that time I saw Jackie Chan in *Drunken Master* and got hooked. Altogether I must have watched that over 200 times as well." In the *American Shonen Jump* interview he goes on to say, "If I hadn't seen this movie, I would never have come up with *Dragon Ball*."

Jackie Chan (Chinese: Chan Kong-sang, 陳港生, born April 7, 1954),[12] brings *gōngfu* cinema to the mainstream in the 1970s and '80s with his action-packed fight scenes and humorous stories. Jackie's *Zuì-quán* (醉拳, "*Drunken Master*," 1978) is a classic film that Toriyama repeatedly mines for inspiration. Another one is *Zájiā xiǎozi* (Chinese: 雜家小子, "*Knockabout*," 1979). This film stars Sammo Hung (Chinese: Hung Gam-bou, 洪金寶, born January 7, 1952)[13] and Yuen Biao (Chinese: Jyun Biu, 元彪, born July 26, 1957).[14] These two counterparts of Jackie are talented and humorous martial artists and actors. Their comedic fight sequences inspire Toriyama's battles to be exciting and funny.

The similarity in their films should come as no surprise, since they all studied together at the same Peking Opera School and China Drama Academy (founded 1952) in Hong Kong. There they learned how to perform tumbling, stunts, and cinematic martial arts under a grueling training regimen of up to 18 hours a day for 10 years straight. The training was painful to endure, but these young disciples would go on to become superstars in the films produced

12   Chan Kong-sang (陳港生) is Jackie Chan's name in Cantonese. In Mandarin it is pronounced Chén Gǎngshēng.

13   Hung Gam-bou (陳港生) is Sammo Hung's name in Cantonese. In Mandarin it is pronounced Hóng Jīnbǎo.

14   Jyun Biu (元彪) is Yuen Biao's name in Cantonese. In Mandarin it is pronounced Yuán Biāo.

by the "Shaw Brothers" (Chinese: Shào shì xiōngdì, 邵氏兄弟, 1958 – 2011), who made over 1,000 movies, and by the "Golden Harvest Entertainment Group" (Chinese: Jiāhé yúlè jítuán yǒuxiàn gōngsī, 嘉禾娛樂集團有限公司, founded 1970), that produced and distributed Bruce Lee and Jackie Chan's movies.

Toriyama adores these actors, and his obsession with watching the movies from these two studios burns their images and storytelling methods into his brain. They later influence his martial arts tournaments and fighting styles.

It's also where he receives a large dose of his understanding of traditional Chinese culture. He's not a scholar, after all. It's through these movies that he absorbs the culture and makes it his own.

Cinematic Influences

Akira Toriyama is the result of his cinematic influences. His art is the art of transforming someone else's art into new art, as a cultural synthesis of different concepts into a new life form. Therefore his original works are unoriginal, yet unprecedented.

Toriyama is a student of cinema, the science of humor, and the art of action. As the years of his youth go by he fills his notebooks full of sketches, but he stops reading *manga* and instead spends his time watching TV and going to movies. Then years later when he decides to pick up the pen and write an actual *manga* with a story, he draws upon his memories to do so. What do his memories consist of, but movies and TV?

Toriyama's love of television and cinema means he's more influenced by movies than he is by *manga*. It's not his fellow *manga-ka* who produce *manga* in the 1960s and '70s that influence his stories. It's the *anime* versions of their *manga*, along with everything else that's on TV. Seems a bit odd since he makes *manga* for a living, doesn't it?

How strange then that he never strives to become a director of live-action films or of *anime*. Instead he strives to become a *manga-ka*. That's because he loves to draw and it's through his *manga* that he tells his cinematic stories. He gets to be the director, artist, special effects wizard, and actor in his own movies. He gets to control every aspect of the film. At least in theory, if it weren't for his pesky editors.

The end result is that *Dragon Ball* is a *manga* that feels cinematic. It's such a cinematic series that it comes ready-made for a good Hollywood adaptation. All the producers have to do is stay true to Toriyama's source material and they'll be golden.

Model Hobbyist

Since Toriyama grows up spending a lot of time by himself, he needs hobbies. And one of them is assembling models and painting miniatures. In the *American Shonen Jump #1* interview he says, "I have a lot of hobbies, but I've kept up with model-building the longest. In particular, I love military models."

This is a perfect activity to do while watching TV. I can confirm this since I did the same thing as a child. I'd spend hours watching *Dragon Ball Z* on TV while I assembled and painted model airplanes and Warhammer miniatures.[15]

For Toriyama it's a hobby that continues to this day. In *Daizenshū 5* he says, "I'm always going to the toy store; I

---

15   Warhammer is a tabletop wargame created by the British gaming and miniature company Games Workshop (founded 1975). As a young man I played this game and its science-fiction themed version, Warhammer: 40,000, as the High Elves and Eldar, respectively.

even have a room full of plastic models. With plastic models, if you don't buy them right then, they might go out of production soon. So I'd buy them, thinking, 'If I decide I want to build it later, I'll be out of luck,' and before I knew it, it ended up like this." In his home he has so many models that the boxes of unbuilt kits are piled on top of one another. It's the same case for his art studio. Just imagine what his bedroom looked like as a teenager.

He also says in *Daizenshū 1* that his hobby helps him do his job. He sees a vehicle in a movie and then, "I use reference materials afterwards, when I'm drawing things like cars or airplanes. Plastic models are useful for this, because you can look at them from a variety of angles." This helps train his eye to pay attention to details.

With his increasing interest in television, movies, and models, Toriyama no longer has time to read *manga*. It stays like this for the rest of his life because he remains continually busy with work. So he's the type of guy that would rather watch the movie than read the book.

How ironic that a *manga-ka* doesn't read *manga*.

Auto Enthusiast

In line with being a fan of model vehicles and tanks, Toriyama is an auto enthusiast and loves to draw foreign cars.

He says in *Dr. Slump* Volume 10, "I think my love for cars and motorbikes and all things mechanical comes from my old man. Back in the day, my dad did super cool things like race motorbikes, and after he broke a bone and quit, he went into auto repair. I still remember seeing that "Toriyama Motors" sign when I was a kid. (It went out of business pretty quick, unfortunately.) In any case, my dad's a big fan of cars and motorcyles too." So this is where Toriyama's fascination begins. He adds, "My favorite cars are small things with great curves. I'm all about the style, and if it goes fast, too, I've got no complaints." Then in Volume 15 he expresses his adoration for motorcycles, "I love off-road bikes, and modded bikes, and American bikes... I love them all!"

You'll see a wide range of automobiles in *Dragon Ball*, from large American cars from the 1950s with fins on the back, to French racers and tiny Italian imports. They don't look photorealistic, but they're close enough to count.

In *Daizenshū 1* Toriyama comments on how his cars look deformed yet still realistic, saying, "Yeah, I do that because if you try and draw the car's design exactly correct, it takes a ridiculous amount of time. If you don't draw it accurately, it'll end up looking completely off somewhere. But if you draw it deformed, it's alright for a few things to be off. ... The characters are all deformed humans anyway, so it'd be odd if everything else wasn't deformed as well."[16]

Meka Enthusiast

He's also a big fan of *meka* (メカ, "mecha"), the Japanese shorthand for the English "mechanical." This is a catch-all term for science fiction stories that feature mechanical

---

16   It takes a lot of research to figure out which cars Toriyama references, but the accuracy of his drawings makes it possible to find their make and model. Of course, to become familiar with the wide world of automobiles requires more work. Fortunately my father and mother grew up in the Motor City of Detroit, so I asked for their help in identifying certain models. The same research is needed for Toriyama's boats, motorcycles, and planes. These often required several days of continual research to find, involving a lot of cross-references, examination of subtle differences across years, and paying close attention to the vehicles in films that he watched.

or robotic vehicles that can be piloted by a human, or to human beings who undergo a scientific enhancement.

Japan is the birthplace of *meka*, with their giant robots and mobile suits, such as those featured in the *Gandamu* (ガンダム, "*Gundam*," 1979) space opera series of *anime* and *manga*. There's a multi-billion dollar industry of model toys centered on *Gandamu* called *Ganpura* (ガンプラ, "Gunpla"), a portmanteau of "*Gandamu* Plastic Model."

Toriyama grows up building models and playing with *meka* into his adulthood. As a result we see a lot of *meka* in his *manga*.

He says in *Daizenshū 1*, "It's the most fun to think up original *meka*. (laughs) I draw them thinking about how you get into them and where the engine is located and whatnot. Sure enough, when you draw cars and things that exist in the real word, you have to check reference materials every time you draw them. But with things that I thought up on my own, I don't have this problem, since you can't say anything. Since I thought of it, I can just say that it's okay like this. (laughs)."

Introvert

Toriyama spends a lot of time alone because he is an introvert. An introvert is someone who benefits more from being alone then they do by being around others. They feel energized and comfortable by themselves, yet drained around people. As a result they spend time in their own mind, exploring their thoughts and feelings or crafting artwork, philosophy, poetry, or similar types of expression as they become absorbed by their work.

Toriyama discusses his introverted personality when he writes an autobiographical *manga* for *Daizenshū 1*. Along with the illustrations he says, "When I look at it, I don't really like people, and socializing is really awful. Outside of my family, friends, and those connected to my job, I don't think I actively want to meet anyone." That's a strong statement. He's saying that except for those people he already knows or works with, he doesn't want to meet anyone else.

He often experiences this conflict in his career because to do his job he has to stay in society and travel to the city. He continues by saying, "Even a hick like me ended up having to come to Tōkyō three times this month. Uhhhh... pardon me... I hate how the city has so many people."

Like a hermit he views people as bothersome and prefers to live as far away from them as possible. "I've always lived in the country, after all. Nevertheless, somehow or another people kept dropping in, so I had to move to even farther out in the sticks to live comfortably."

I can relate, as I'm fine being by myself and not communicating with others for days at a time. Particularly during my high school and college years I often thought about going away to a temple and cutting myself off from society. It's because of the emotional and social conflicts, and I'm a sensitive guy, so the unpleasant encounters would weigh on my mind for days. I thought, "People, they're the worst!" However, I grew out of my shell, learned how to be patient and compassionate, and now enjoy the company of others and benefit from conversation. Yet in general I still prefer to be alone. It's that balance of spending a long period of time alone in deep concentration on my work combined with interacting with others that enriches the quality of both my life and the work. If I weren't like this, then there's no way I could have written this book because of the thousands of hours of deep concentration required to write it. Nevertheless, I function in society just fine and can manage others and have a direct communication style. So being introverted doesn't by default mean that you're shy or incapable of speaking with others. However, Toriyama struggles with these types of things because his introversion goes beyond normal.

When he starts in the industry he is more outgoing, allowing his face to be photographed and being open about his personal preferences. But as he becomes more famous he avoids interviews as much as possible, doesn't want to be on TV or radio, and avoids anything that involves other people. That's not to say he doesn't do more interviews, because in total he does over 200 of them, but they're usually quick, silly, and light.

This is why he's a difficult man to write about. To make it worse, there's never been a biography written about the man's life in Japanese or English. What you're reading right now is the closest thing to one. So in order to understand Toriyama you have to read everything he's ever said and put the pieces back together to paint a picture.

You might be wondering if Toriyama suffers from a psychological disorder such as agoraphobia (fear of crowds and open spaces) or sociophobia (fear of society or people in general). It's never been stated, but he does exhibit these traits. We see this when he travels to New York City in late 2002 for the premiere of the *American Shonen Jump* magazine. Christopher Sabat (born April 22, 1973) is the Voice Director at FUNimation,[17] the American license holder and English dubbing company for the *Dragon Ball* series. He attends the premiere as well, and then in a July, 2014 interview recorded to promote a *Dragon Ball Z* film, recalls that Toriyama was nervous and sweating at the event, and he left as quickly as he could after answering questions. There were people who wanted Toriyama's picture, but he preferred to not be photographed. From this you can see that he's not incapable of being around others, but he does feel uncomfortable in crowds and prefers to be alone.

His internal self is the opposite of his external self. On the

---

17   Because of their success with *Dragon Ball*, FUNimation is the largest *anime* dubbing studio in North America.

outside he lives within his comfort zone and avoids people. But in his artwork he pushes himself past his comfort zone and takes his characters on wild adventures filled with hundreds of zany people. This is his introverted mind at work. He does things in his story that are the opposite of his own preferences, just so he can take the characters in new directions and surprise the reader. So there's a dynamic interplay of internal and external going on, where in his outside life he avoids people and spends his time engrossed in his hobbies and artistic pursuits, while inside his mind there is a rich world filled with fantasy, science fiction, huge robots, and supernormal powers.

Toriyama is famous for his artwork, not for his personality, but I believe that it's because of his introverted personality that his artwork is so rich. His art is an expression of himself and the ideal world he'd like to live in.

It's a world that others like to visit.

Product of His Environment

The work of an artist is a reflection of the artist's mind, and Toriyama's *manga* is a synthesis of different cultural elements because Toriyama is a synthesis of different cultural influences. Many of the abovementioned influences on Toriyama are a result of American influences on Japan in the 20th century, and how this foreign culture mixed with traditional Japanese culture to create a fusion society.

Consider the following. The American military ends the Pacific War by dropping the fission bombs of Fat Man (August 6, 1945) on Hiroshima-*shi* (広島市, "Vast Island City") and Little Boy (August 9, 1945) on Nagasaki-*shi* (長崎市, "Long and Rugged Mountains City"). The following devastation leads to the surrender of Japan on September 2, 1945. The bombs affect the psyche of Japan and generate a strong anti-nuclear weapon sentiment alongside a fascination with science and technology. This is followed by the 6-year occupation and reconstruction period of the Japanese homeland by the American forces, resulting in an influx of American mentalities and pop culture.

Toriyama is born 10 years afterward, in the middle of the 20th century during a time of profound transformation. Japan strives to re-establish itself, build up its economy, adopt democracy, break away from its Imperial roots, and examine its extreme *bushidō* militarism. They look to America as the model to emulate. During the 1950s America is all about the established prototypical family and societal expectations, in the 1960s it's all about counter-culture and rebelling against the establishment. Toriyama is born in the '50s but is a child of the '60s, so there is a fair amount of this counter-culture in his mind.

The ensuing American military's forced top-down revolution in Japan toward free market capitalism ushers in a new wave of popular culture through television and film. Disney, *King Kong*, classic automobiles, and other Western imports spark the creation of the homegrown Japanese *anime*, *kaijū*, superheroes, and *meka*, over the course of his youth. These industries create works that turn Toriyama into a free thinker who loves Western and Japanese culture.

While this Western worldview is influencing Japan, he's also growing up in an environment with a rich set of cultural traditions and over 3,000 years of history, rooted in its religions. Toriyama never mentions his religious beliefs, but most Japanese have faith in several belief systems without considering themselves religious. It's just part of the social consciousness. These belief systems are primarily Buddhism and Shintō, with a bit of Confucianism.

Shintō (神道, "The Way of the Gods") is the native belief system of Japan; a development of shamanistic beliefs that mixes with Chinese Dàoism, Buddhism, and Confucianism across millennia. The three of them fuse together into one collective belief system called *shinbutsu shūgō* (神仏習合, "the amalgamation of *kami* and Buddhā").[18] The faiths do not compete with each other. A family can have a Buddhist altar, a Shintō shrine, and a place to venerate their ancestors in the same home. If you grow up in Japan during the mid-20th century like Toriyama does, this seems normal.

Toriyama doesn't say much in his interviews about his experiences with Japanese culture as a child, but it's clear from his work that he understands it well. He no doubt attends *matsuri* (祭, "festival," or "holiday") ceremonies, such as the *bon* (盆, "ancestor veneration day") and *sakura* (桜, "cherry blossom") festivals. Other forms of traditional culture include the *kabuki* (歌舞伎, "song, dance, and skill") play, *nō* (能, "skillful") dance, the *kyōgen* (狂言, "mad words") comedy dance, and *bunraku* (文楽, "puppetry") performances. Hundreds of *matsuri* are held every year in honor of Shintō, Buddhist, or Confucian beliefs. I suspect this is the reason why he is able to depict so many of these cultural elements in his work.

Japan's military tradition and heroism inherent in *bushidō* influences popular culture. The government-led efforts to turn the martial arts away from World War II militarism and toward sport leads to the idea that martial arts are cool and something young men can get into. This results in a lot of martial arts related *anime*, movies, and television programs displaying the idea of a man who uses his mind and body to defeat monsters, whether through traditional means or scientific. Toriyama absorbs these works in his childhood, and we then see them later in *Dragon Ball*.

Not all Japanese people are as creative as Toriyama, but he would not be able to become the man he is without the environment in which he is raised. The influences of his childhood are the result of a unique period of time where

---

18   *Kami* (神, Chinese: *shén*, "god," or "spirit") are the spiritual beings or essences of deities in Shintō.

he experiences a synthesized multiculturalism in-progress. In turn, Toriyama channels these cultural influences into his work and creates synthesized multicultural *manga* that appeals to everyone.

Budding Art Career

Now that we've established the influences on Toriyama during his youth, let's turn to his teenage years.

It's 1971 and Toriyama is 15 years old. He loves to draw, so he makes a bold decision to enroll in the art-focused "Aichi Prefectural Okoshi Technical High School" (Aichi-ken-ritsu okoshi kōgyō kōtō gakkō, 愛知県立起工業高等学校) in the *dezain-ka* (デザイン科, "Design Course"). In Japan there are technical schools where students specialize in a certain field, such as engineering or design. Why specialize in design? Toriyama's father, mother, and little sister don't draw, and his friends just like to draw *manga* for a bit of fun, so they don't influence him enough to want to become a *manga-ka*. It's graphic design that strikes his fancy, so he passes the entrance exam and walks through the door.

However, he doesn't fancy the discipline of a standard education. "I still liked to draw, but I liked having fun even more. When I finished school I would go to eat noodles, go to a toy store, department store, go bowling, play pool, etc. Never once did I go straight home." He says in his *Sutārogu* (スターログ, "*Starlog*") magazine interview (1980), "When I was in high school, I was in the *manga* club. I was the president too, for what it's worth." But he doesn't do what he's there for: "The truth is that I almost never read *manga*, and rarely drew them," and, "I didn't complete a single one. (laughs) So I can't actually say that I made any *manga*." Even so, it's here where he learns the fundamentals of art that he will use for the rest of his life.

Three more years go by, and Toriyama graduates from high school with a specialty in publicity.

But he has a dilemma. "I had to face the decision of which path to take, whether to go to college or to get a job."

Toriyama is young, optimistic, naïve, and confident in his abilities. "My parents didn't agree, but I did not hesitate for a moment to decide I wanted to work and had no desire to study more." He thinks, "My drawings are so good that I will succeed soon! Hehe, I was very young."

Two years go by before he gets his first job, working for an advertising and design firm in Kyōto (京都, "Capital City"). Almost all of his work consists of fliers, where he has to illustrate objects or animals onto the flier. "Among those, there were clients who didn't have the money to take photos, and they'd make a request where they wanted me to depict chickens in illustrations. Then when I drew a chicken and showed it to them, they'd say, "This is a rooster, so it's no good. We only sell hens." (laughs)."

Toriyama often works overtime and doesn't get home until 2 or 3 a.m., so as a result, he's tired and wants to sleep in. He says, "I was very cunning, so I did well. But I have trouble waking up in the morning and am always late." Showing up late is not something you're supposed to do at any job, but especially on your first job, and it's even worse at a Japanese company because you are expected to conform to conventions. "It was only about 10 or 15 minutes, but if you were late three times it was treated the same as missing an entire day. ... Moreover, as it was a rather large company they were picky about the dress code. I like to dress any way I feel like it, so I was scolded often. In a word, I did not fit in well with society."

Toriyama doesn't want to conform to the rigid conduct of Japanese society. He's an artist, someone who stays up late, is disorderly, and believes he is innately talented. That's the opposite of a typical Japanese *sararīman* (サラリーマン, "salary man") who wears a suit and tie, stays quiet, and follows his boss's orders so he can bring home a paycheck. Toriyama's a free thinker and is not into meeting people's expectations. In fact, he strives to defy your expectations at every turn. That conformist stuff ain't gonna' fly.

It's also not a job that pushes his creative abilities, as he recalls drawing underwear, lingerie, baby rompers, and other real-world items in department store brochures. In *Daizenshū 6* he says, "I was complaining all the while, "Whaaat? Why do I have to draw a hundred pairs of socks?!" His job is to draw socks so attractive to the reader that they'll feel a soul-stirring drive to buy them. Exciting, right?

His poor behavior at work means that he never receives a promotion, and he is late so often that they reduce his bonus. "When I compared my bonus with a girl in the administrative section who had just joined the company, mine was a lot less, even though I was in my third year. I thought this wouldn't do, so I decided to quit my job."

But looking back on his time at the firm he says, "Now I recognize that it's something that helped me because it allowed me to see the system from within. Students that are also *manga-ka* can never learn these things by working on their own." So he believes that entering the workforce provides an education you cannot receive in college.

However, Toriyama is now out of work and he still doesn't want to earn a degree. What's he going to do?

Taking a Chance

Our young artist needs money so he can keep having fun, but all he knows how to do is draw. His parents want him to go job-hunting, but for whatever reason he can't get a full time job, so in the meantime he does part-time design and illustration work, such as for advertising fliers.

Nagoya is a countryside town filled with café's, and he

idles away most of his time here, unsure of what else to do. His parents give him 500 *yen* (¥, ~$5 USD) as a daily allowance, which he blows on snacks and cigarettes, but this can't last forever. He's floating through life.

Then, "One day while I was reading a volume of *manga* in a café I saw an article about a contest that asked for submissions." The *manga* is *Shūkan Shōnen Magajin* (週刊少年マガジン, "*Juvenile Magazine Weekly*"), and the reward for the winning artist is a 500,000 *yen* (¥) (~$5,000 USD) prize and publication in the *manga*.

Toriyama draws and draws, but when he returns to the café and looks at the fine print in the ad, he sees that he missed the submission deadline!

The next contest is a ways out, "So I thought, 'How about *Shōnen Jump*?' And when I looked, they were also doing the same sort of contest." The reward for this one is a lesser 100,000 *yen* (~$1,000 USD) prize and publication in the *manga*. "I thought it was a bit low, but in terms of timing, I decided to send my entry in to them."

This monthly contest for *Shōnen Jump* is held by Kabushiki-gaisha Shūeisha (株式会社集英社, "Shūeisha Publishing Co., Ltd.," founded 1925), the largest *manga* publisher in Japan, located in Tōkyō. The contest is called the *Monthly Young Jump Award* and is used as a promotion to find new talent for the *manga* anthology called *Weekly Shōnen Jump* (週刊少年ジャンプ, *Shūkan Shōnen Janpu*, first issue July 2, 1968). This is one of several combination paperback books where one chapter of a *manga* is presented next to a series of others, around 10 to 15 serialized *manga* per book, and about 200 to 400 pages total. Millions of these paperbacks are printed each week, so it's the goal of many *manga-ka* to have their creations serialized in this format in order to gain recognition. Not all *manga* do well, but such distribution is similar to having a television program air during the primetime slots on a major network.

According to Toriyama, on his 23rd birthday he decides

that entering this contest sounds better than finding another job. He says, "I wanted to win that prize! So this was the first time I drew a real *manga*." This cash prize is the reason why Toriyama becomes a *manga-ka*.[19]

In 1977 he submits his entry to *Weekly Shōnen Jump*, titled *Awawa wārudo* (あわわワールド, "*Awawa World*"). It's a comical story about two *samurai* in feudal Japan who meet a Superman-like character. This is the first example of what I call Toriyama's fusion style of *manga*, where he blends traditional Japanese culture and modern Western pop culture to create original and funny stories.

Awawa wārudo does not win any awards. "When I sent it in I was so confident in myself, but it was not even selected for a prize. I was strongly disappointed, but above all I was just angry." Toriyama's youthful confidence clashes with the judges' inability to recognize his talent, but he remains undeterred and tries again next year. "I was confident in my art, so the fact that I lost out was really frustrating. Almost entirely out of stubbornness, I set my heart on not giving up until I got the prize money. I immediately drew my next work and sent it in."

He competes in 1978 with *Nazo no rein jakku* (謎のレインジャック, "*Mysterious Rain Jack*"). This is a *Star Wars* parody featuring aliens, storm troopers, R2-D2, C-3PO, Japanese police guards, talking animals, a Japanese thunder ogre who reports the weather on TV, and a main character that

---

19   There are two categories that Toriyama considers entering in the *Shūkan Shōnen Magajin manga* contest: *Sutōrī manga* (ストーリー漫画, "story comic") and *gyagu manga* (ギャグ漫画, "gag comic"). As a golden rule, *sutōrī manga* are 31 pages long while *gyagu manga* are 15 pages long; but the prize amount is the same for both, so Toriyama decides to become a *gyagu manga-ka*. That way he can get the same pay for half the work. Even though it's half the work, he still misses the deadline for the submission, and that is why he then sends his entry to Shūeisha. If this hadn't happened, he would not have been discovered.

looks like Clint Eastwood (born May 31, 1930) in the film *Dirty Harry* (1971).

This doesn't win any awards either because it's disqualified for being a parody of a licensed work. What is it with these judges? Don't they know genius when they see it?

Toriyama is upset. It's been 4 ½ years since he graduated from high school, and so far all he's accomplished is working at a company where he draws socks, and submitting two failed entries in a *manga* contest.

He's down on his luck and is tired of it. Maybe he should go to school? Maybe he should get a real job where he is forced to wear a suit? The man is unsure of himself. However, all of that is about to change.

"I received a call from an angel."

Torishima Kazuhiko

The voice on the phone tells him, "You might have promise. Draw some more pages and send them directly to me."

It's Torishima Kazuhiko (鳥嶋 和彦, "Bird Island Peaceful Prince," born October 19, 1952), an editor for *Weekly Shōnen Jump* at Shūeisha, in Tōkyō. He's been at Shūeisha since he graduated from the prestigious Keiō Gijuku Daigaku (慶應義塾大学, "Keiō University") in 1976.

What kind of man is he? Torishima-*san* recalls how he became an editor in his 2007 interview with *Tokyopop* magazine's German branch at the Leipzig Book Fair. "It's a funny story because I can't say, 'Yes, of course. It's always been my dream.' After my studies I thought about what I wanted to do in general and then created a list of things I do better than others. ... In the end I was only sure of having read more books than other people my age. Therefore I could become an author or editor." He says that 'author' wasn't an option because, "those kinds of people have to learn about and remember all kinds of unpleasant things, whereas I forget everything after three days."

He applies for a job as an editor and writes a humorous story during the writing test that was built on the word-play between "jeans," "genes," and the name of a famous ancient Japanese queen. "It was apparently so funny that other testers asked me to recite it to them as well. Out of 5,000 applicants, only 14 were ultimately taken on. Luckily, I was one of them. ... Then I was assigned to *Weekly Shōnen Jump*. I actually wanted to publish art books or *Playboy*." He grins and says that's because *Playboy* had the best editors and the Japanese edition included a serialized novel. Really, Torishima-*san*, that was the *only* reason?

Torishima-*san* is much like Toriyama, in that he falls into the job. Neither of them have the lifelong dream of working as professional *manga* creators, but here they are none-theless. So at this point he has been an editor for 2 years and is only 3 years older than Toriyama, but as Toriyama's senior and the one who decides whose work is published and whose isn't, his words carry great weight.

Opening the Door

Toriyama's *manga* was rejected, so why is he receiving this call? Torishima-*san* recalls in his Kazé (2014) interview, "I was 25 years old, and every month the *Jump* magazine received works from young *manga-ka*. Which is still how it works. Every month, one of us had to choose a young author and take him under our wing to make him evolve. Toriyama applied during the month it was my turn to choose. We received between 100 and 150 candidates every month. I was the youngest employee at that time. I read all the works we got that month, and his was the one that caught my attention."[20]

Why? He says in *Daizenshū 1*, "The first manuscript that Toriyama-*kun* sent me was a *Star Wars* parody. Parodies can't win any prize money. They're not original and it's difficult to publish them. Only, his lettering left an unusual impression on me. *Kakimoji* (描き文字, "sound-effects") are usually drawn as *katakana*, but he had drawn them as *rōmaji* letters of the alphabet. I thought this was extraordinarily refreshing, groundbreaking, and kind of cool. So I contacted him."

It isn't Toriyama's illustrations or jokes that matter most. It's his use of English lettering instead of the usual Japanese *katakana* that catches the editor's eye. Toriyama's use of *rōmaji* is likely a result of his continual absorption of Western movies and culture through television. His style is different enough from other entries to make his work stand out, and this minor part of his *manga* is what gets his foot in the door. Without this simple thing there would be no Akira Toriyama the world-famous *manga-ka*, and there would be no *Dragon Ball*.

Toriyama feels hope.

Like one of his martial arts characters in *Dragon Ball*, he works with high intensity to improve his skills. "I started drawing and sending in sleeves of pages." However, "I had no idea how to draw a *manga*, so every single one of them was rejected. So it was like, as I drew, I gradually learned how to do it."

Toriyama is living with his parents, has no money, and spends all his time drawing *manga* so he can impress this editor at Shūeisha. He recalls in *Tetsuko no Heya* (1983), "I was pretty much unemployed, so [I'd say] things like,

---

20   Kazé is a French licensor of *Dragon Ball*. In 2014 they published a 7-part interview with Torishima-*san* on their Bluray release of *Dragon Ball Kai* (2009). Here is Part 1 of 7, from which I quote his recollection of discovering Toriyama: *https://youtu.be/ju2WjBTCllc*

"Mom, I'm gonna' buy some cigarettes. Can I have 150 *yen*?" or "I wanna' go out to a café, so I need 200 *yen*."[21]

Toriyama recalls in his 1986 interview with *Terebaru* magazine that, "About 500 pages of drafts had been rejected by publishers before I debuted. ... When these drafts were rejected I was really depressed. But I call it even when I take advantage of them later."[22] And in *Tetsuko no Heya*, "I think during that time, my skills were really improving by leaps and bounds."

But Torishima-*san* isn't the kind of master who encourages his new disciple with praise. On the contrary, Toriyama remembers him saying things like, "This is no good; it's not interesting at all. Why don't you draw something more interesting?" He acts like a strict *gōngfu* master, who rather than hold their disciples' hand and teach them how to improve, forces them to undergo painful lessons until

---

21   Torishima-*san* elaborates in his Kazé interview on how impressed he was by Toriyama's entries. "My *senpai* (先輩, "senior employees") chose authors they believed in more. But I stayed with my choice. The reason I chose him was because of how clean his work looked. The young authors often excessively correct their sheets with a white pen. However, Toriyama's sheets didn't show any trace of having been corrected. They were clean! Secondly, his sheets were unique. What I mean by that is, the *kakimoji* ("sound-effects"). Or as they're also known, onomatopoeia. They're normally written in Japanese, but with Toriyama, all of the *kakimoji* were in the Roman alphabet, and not in *kana*. At the time, that was innovative. It was beautiful. That's what struck me. So I told the editorial staff about my choice of being in charge of him." He then says, "That's how I became his editor. First I sent a telegram to Nagoya, reading: "You have talent. Call me fast. Signed: Torishima." That's how my relationship with him began." So according to Torishima-*san*, he first sent a telegram, and this lead to their phone call.

22   Toriyama's interview with *Terebaru* (1986): *http://www.furinkan. com/takahashi/takahashi4.html*

they self-enlighten and meet the masters' high standard. Toriyama says, "I'm the kind of person who really doesn't like to lose, so I'd repeat this cycle of him telling me it wasn't interesting, me getting ticked off and drawing again, and sending it in."

He continues this exhausting effort for three months. "And after some time I made my debut."

Toriyama's Debut

Toriyama premieres in *Weekly Shōnen Jump* #52 in November, 1978 with his first published *manga* titled *Wandā Airando* (ワンダー・アイランド, "*Wonder Island*").

It's a *yomikiri* (読み切り, "one-shot," a single-chapter story) about an ex-*kamikaze* pilot in World War II who crashes into the Pacific Ocean in 1944 and washes onto the shores of Wonder Island.[23] The story reveals his hilarious attempts to get back home involving a cave man, dinosaur, fairy, vampire, angel, witch, gorilla, and a magic potion that transforms him into a chicken.

It's original, but unfortunately the public votes it as the least popular *manga* in the magazine's survey. Torishima-*san* recalls this moment in the *Tokyopop* interview, saying, "A total of 14 readers voted for him, so nobody from the editorial department believed in him." This magazine has millions of readers, so 14 votes is as bad as it gets. Toriyama remembers it being "absolute dead last."

This doesn't go as he wants, but now he's been published, and that's a motivator. He continues working hard on his craft and Torishima-*san* gives him a second chance because

---

23   *Kamikaze* (神風, "divine wind") is a term for the suicide pilots of the Japanese airforce in World War II who flew their planes into opposing naval vessels. Toriyama's ex-*kamikaze* pilot fails his mission.

he believes in his potential. He continues, "I thought his style was revolutionary. He made something new and that had never been done before in *Shōnen Jump magazine*. We also have the same kind of humor and share the same opinions about the components of good entertainment. ... So it wasn't just about convincing the other editorial staff, but also bringing the best out of the illustrator."

The second chapter of *Wandā Airando* is published in a special issue of *Weekly Shōnen Jump* on January 25, 1979. This chapter contains the cave man from the first chapter, police officer characters that he will reuse in his later works, another *Dirty Harry* look-alike, the *Star Wars* droid C-3PO on a boat, Tetsuwan Atomu, King Kong, Gojira, Urutoraman, The Statue of Liberty, and the three-headed *kaijū* dragon, Kingu Gidora (キングギドラ, "King Ghidorah"). It's eccentric and overflowing with humor. Looking back on this work we can see that Toriyama takes the different elements of what he enjoys watching on TV, puts them together, and rolls them up into a single expression that he feels other people will enjoy.

Torishima-*san* elaborates on this aspect of Toriyama's work in his Kazé interview. "One of Toriyama-*san's* biggest particularities as a *manga* artist was that he'd never read much *manga*. He was an artist without any interest in other *manga*. Even I, before I started working in the publishing business, didn't know about *Shōnen Jump*, and I'd never read any *manga*. What might happen when an editor who's never read a *manga*, and an artist who has no interest in it, meet? Well, what you get is a *manga* not bound to the existing norms. The advantage is, above anything else, that they'll create the *manga* freely. And so, in this regard, his *manga* offered something completely new."[24]

Unfortunately the readers don't like this one either. Even

---

24   Part 6 of Torishima-*san's* interview with Kazé: *https://youtu.be/ Jd0ocHDfYgg*

though he gets his break when Torishima-*san* opens the door, he has two flops in a row. Things aren't going well. Torishima-*san* recalls why in his Kazé interview. "He had never actually written any *manga* before the manuscripts I selected. He was inspired to write *manga* without understanding how to do it. I only had 2 or 3 years of experience myself. I didn't know how to make *manga*, let alone how to make them good. Over the years, I analyzed in-depth, as an editor, the art of *manga*."[25]

Toriyama continues working at his craft and submits more *manga* for publication, but they're all denied. He's low on money, but high on determination. Toriyama believes he is going to become a successful *manga-ka*.

Four months later on April 20, 1979 he gets another *yomikiri* published, titled *Honjitsu no hairai-shima* (本日のハイライ島, *"Today's Highlight Island"*). It's about a young boy who suffers a toothache and goes to see an anthropomorphic goat doctor who claims he can fix any problem. But instead of fixing the boy's tooth like a normal doctor would, he performs silly experiments that fail to relieve the pain. It receives a better reception than *Wandā Airando*, but it's not picked up for another chapter either.

Torishima-*san* still thinks Toriyama has potential and

---

25   Part 2 of Torishima-*san's* interview with Kazé: *https://youtu.be/pVdJ41YJDMs*. He says that the normal route to becoming a *manga-ka* is different from how Toriyama did it. "What does an amateur need to do in order to get published serially? Normally, the artist gets his work published in a bonus booklet (alongside the main magazine), and then in a magazine for young *manga-ka*. When the directors of the publishing house start to take notice of the artist's name, they have him draw storyboards for serialization, and if that passes, then his work gets published in the magazine." Toriyama bypassed this, and instead submitted his finished drafts to his editor. Most were rejected, but a few were published as *yomikiri*. They weren't popular, so he learned how to improve his skills through trial-by-fire until he found success.

leaves the door open for further submissions. Toriyama then gets another *yomikiri* published called *Gyaru keiji tomato* (ギャル刑事トマト, *"Tomato, Girl Detective,"* August 15, 1979). At the request of Torishima-*san* this one stars a naïve but beautiful heroine named Akai Tomato (赤いトマト, "Red Tomato"). She makes blunders on her first day at the police force as she attempts to capture a villain.

This *manga* is a success! For the first time the reader's rate it well, and Torishima-*san* is happy. He recalls in his Kazé interview, "In the end, it took about two years before he made himself a big enough name to finally get published serially. And those two years were the time limit he'd given himself. He had promised his parents he would abandon this road of trying to become a manga-*ka* if he couldn't do it in two years." So if Toriyama had given up before the finish line, then he never would have achieved success. That's the power of his determination.

This moment marks the turning point in his career. He is now considered a rising talent.

Onward and Upward

What happens when you combine the Japanese cinema of giant monsters, costumed superheroes, and artificial men, with Western cinema of aliens, adventurous heroes, and talking animals, plus Hong Kong *gōngfu* action, traditional culture, slapstick comedy, and a dash of perversion? The answer is Akira Toriyama.

The young Toriyama begins by absorbing the works of Tezuka and other *manga-ka*, playing in the countryside, and drawing his heart out. Then he views countless hours of television and movies and blends them into a cultural stew. When he sees the opportunity to win a cash prize, he pursues it. To create his *manga* he thinks back to his childhood years and combines everything together into humorous parodies that get his foot in the door. This propels him down a path that will one day change the lives of millions.

Looking back on it, Toriyama realizes that it takes the continual rejections and flops for him to improve his drawing skills, writing ability, and sense of what the reader will like. He trains in the gauntlet of real life. He says, "After I studied for about a year, I became a pro." And, "Even now, I am extremely grateful to Torishima-*san*."

Toriyama has been recognized and given the opportunity to express himself through his art for a living. His renewed confidence motivates him to create a comedic masterpiece that will dominate the 1980s *manga* scene and catapult him into fame and fortune.

Let's see how high his star can rise.

Rising Star

WHO IS THE most influential *manga-ka* alive?

According to a 2010 poll,[1] it's Akira Toriyama.

Who is the most famous *manga-ka* in history?

According to a 2014 poll,[2] Toriyama is ranked #3, after Tezuka Osamu at #1, and Fujiko Fujio, the two-man creators of *Doraemon*[3] at #2.

How does this happen?

The answer lies in the rest of our story.

---

1   Toriyama is ranked as the second most influential *manga-ka* in history after Tezuka Osamu according to a poll of 841 random Japanese citizens (from teens to 40-year-olds) conducted by Orikon Kabushiki-gaisha in 2010: *http://www.siliconera.com/2010/07/17/the-top-ten-manga-ka-that-changed-manga-history/*, and *https://web.archive.org/web/20100717193946/http://www.oricon.co.jp/news/ranking/78202/full*. This makes Toriyama the most influential *manga-ka* alive.

2   Toriyama is ranked as the third most famous *manga-ka* in history in a poll conducted by Kabushiki-gaisha Enu Ti Ti Dokomo (株式会社NTTドコモ, "NTT Docomo"), the largest mobile phone operator in Japan. Out of 24,420 votes, he receives 3,704 votes: *http://ranking.goo.ne.jp/ranking/category/999/faction_2I3aue0ReKY7_all/*

3   Fujiko Fujio (藤子不二雄) was the name of a *manga* writing duo consisting of Fujimoto Hiroshi (藤本 弘, December 1, 1933 – September 23, 1996) and Abiko Motoo (安孫子 素雄, born March 10, 1934). Their creation, *Doraemon*, is a famous *manga* and *anime* about a robotic cat that travels back in time to aid a young boy. The cat is an icon of Japan.

Dr. Slump

It's late 1979 and Torishima-*san* feels that now is the time for Toriyama to be given a weekly serialized *manga*. He also believes that the young female lead who blunders her way through life is a formula for success, so he tells Toriyama to use this formula for his next *manga*, titled *Dokutā Suranpu* (*Dr. スランプ*, "*Dr. Slump*").[4]

The story is about a 5-year-old near-sighted girl named Norimaki Arare (則巻 アラレ, often called Arare-*chan*, アラレちゃん)[5] who faces life with a naïve and innocent attitude, even though she's a super-powerful robot. Her creator, Doctor Norimaki Senbei (則巻 千兵衛), is a scientific genius, but is inept when it comes to women, and now he's got this robotic girl to take care of. The two of them live in Pengin-*mura* (ペンギン村, "Penguin Village"), a small town inhabited by characters from Toriyama's previous *manga* and a new cast of whacky people and talking animals.

The idea of using a female lead in a *shōnen manga* targeted at young boys is daring. Toriyama recalls this decision in *Daizenshū 4*, saying, "In the case of *Slump*, before the start of serialization, I drew it intending the Doctor to be the main character. But Torishima-*san* told me that he wanted me to turn Arare-*chan* into the main character, and I remember that I resisted: "What? A girl as the main character?"" Toriyama just wanted her to be one of the Doctor's many inventions, and she wasn't supposed to reappear. Torishima-*san* recalls in his *Tokyopop* interview, "Back then, Toriyama absolutely refused to draw girls, because

---

4   The title of Toriyama's *manga* is *Dr. Suranpu*, but I use *Dr. Slump* moving forward, just like *Dragon Ball* instead of *Doragon Bōru*.

5   *Chan* (ちゃん) is a Japanese suffix used to refer to young males who are your age or older in an endearing way. It can also be applied to cute girls, such as Arare-*chan*.

the *Shōnen Jump Magazine*, as you know, is primarily read by boys. But I was convinced that there has to be a female main character in *Dr. Slump*. This was Toriyama's hidden talent. His female supporting characters were simply great. So I had to pull out some tricks and offered him a deal. "You draw one chapter with a girl, and if it flops, then you won't have to draw girls ever again.'"' Toriyama has no choice. He takes the deal and makes her the lead.

The *manga* premieres in *Weekly Shōnen Jump* #5/6, inside the New Year's double-issue special in January 1980. Its unique combination of humor and scientific gadgets catapults it and Toriyama into success.

Volume 1's first edition of *Dr. Slump* has a print run of 1.9 million units. The fact that Shūeisha invests this much capital into printing and marketing the *manga* shows you that they expect it to sell. And it does, so they have to print more. The sales streak continues with each successive volume. For example, *Dr. Slump* Volume 5 (August, 1981) sells 1.3 million units, and *Dr. Slump* Volume 6 (December, 1981) sells 2.2 million units. In total the 18 volumes of the series go on to sell over 35 million copies in Japan alone.[6]

Torishima-*san* adds, "What can I say? We were successful. The series even made girls read *Jump* (grins). Yet Toriyama insisted on calling the series *Dr. Slump*. Typical..."[7]

---

6   Sales figures of *Dr. Slump* at 35 million volumes, as recorded by 2007: *http://comipress.com/article/2007/05/06/1923*

7   Torishima-*san* elaborates on Toriyama's rejected manuscripts in Part 3 of his Kazé interview: *https://youtu.be/ZJeNEJh7tZM*. "Thanks to the money Toriyama made from *Dr. Slump,* he could afford to move. By diving into his archives, he found about 500 manuscripts I had refused since he started. *Dr. Slump* was only made because of all the constant trial and error we made with those 500 previous manuscripts. What was amazing about him was that he reused gags from rejected projects in *Dr. Slump* without me noticing. I learned about that later."

Gyagu Manga

Dr. Slump is a quintessential *gyagu manga* (ギャグ漫画, "gag comic"). This is a genre of lighthearted *manga* where the author puts his characters into funny situations and makes jokes along the way. Toriyama lampoons every bit of pop culture he can think of, from *Tarzan*[8] to time travel, *Star Trek*[9] to *Superman*, with tons of poop jokes, puns, and perverted humor thrown in for good measure. There's a laugh on every page, and readers can't get enough.

Toriyama is a *gyagu manga* author at heart. He just wants the reader to have a good time. He's the opposite of a *sutōrī manga* (ストーリー漫画, "story comic") author. *Sutōrī manga* is a term coined in the 1960s to differentiate *manga* from newspaper comic strips. They feature long stories with overarching plots, such as Tezuka's more serious pieces. In the mid-'80s almost all *manga* have stories of some sort, but *Dr. Slump* has short and self-contained stories. This contrasts against the long fight scenes and story arcs found in *batoru manga* (バトル漫画, "battle comics"), of which *Dragon Ball* is the quintessential example.

As strange as this may sound in a book that's about *Dragon Ball*, if you want to better understand Toriyama's mind, you need to read *Dr. Slump*. *Dr. Slump* is a perfect example of an artist in his element. It's not a manufactured series or a cash-in. It's an artist's true expression, and that is why it is so successful and representative of Toriyama's work. It's also why his later creation of *Dragon Ball* is so entertaining.

---

8   *Tarzan* (1912) is the story of a young British boy who loses his parents and is raised in the jungle by animals. A book and film series, it premieres in the novel *Tarzan of the Apes* by Edgar Rice Burroughs.

9   *Star Trek* (1966) is a famous science fiction television and film series about the crew of a 23rd century spaceship who fly across the galaxy and engage with aliens.

To write battles that are exciting is one thing. But to make them funny at the same time? That takes talent.

This is the era where he's in his creative prime. Because think about it: The man is single, living with his parents, and working on his own. The world has taken notice of his talent, so he does everything he can to impress his readers and his editor, and ensure that his star keeps rising.

Something about Arare

Arare has a special charm that readers love—a combination of naïve innocence with curiosity and whacky idealism. She goes on to become the icon of a generation that grows up with her in the 1980s.

Part of the reason why is because Arare is an ultra-powerful robotic girl, but she's also nearsighted and needs glasses to see, just like Toriyama himself. He says in *Tetsuko no Heya* (1983), "I thought that a robot wearing glasses would be silly, and that there hadn't often been a girl who wears glasses as a protagonist, and also, when I draw girls, they all end up with the same face, so I gave her glasses in order to give her a distinguishing trait. ... I don't know that it has anything to do with my wearing glasses myself. But I'm fine with there being lots of girls who wear glasses."

Toriyama intends her glasses to be a one-time gag and says they are a pain to draw. However, readers write to him and say that the glasses make them feel less sensitive about their own glasses while at school, so he keeps the glasses on her and it becomes a signature part of her character. "There've been letters saying that they'd always been embarrassed about wearing glasses, but now it doesn't bother them so much; like that. I was pretty happy getting those." The glasses are such a distinguishing trait that any entertainer or young singer in Japanese pop culture who wears big glasses is compared to Arare-*chan*. So Toriyama has no choice but to keep drawing them on her.

Because of her incredible popularity, Toriyama receives boxes full of fan mail. It's an overwhelming amount. He says, "At most, I could handle about 10 at a time, so I wondered how I should reply to them all. They just came all at once in a cardboard box, which surprised me. Because at first, I brazenly wrote, "I will definitely reply!", so... It was tough just reading through all of them."

Arare is an example of how Toriyama is able to create memorable characters who speak to the readers, even when he's not trying to do so. There's something about his characters that resonates in our hearts. That's why fans connect with Arare, Gokū in *Dragon Ball*, and others. Some of the letters say that by looking at Arare, the fans are able to relax and forget their concerns with studying and passing tests. Toriyama thinks it's because he keeps his stories light, and that this makes it easy to read and allows the reader to go to a different world.

Of course it's not all because of Toriyama. Much of Arare's success comes from his editor, Torishima-*san*.

Toriyama and Torishima

When Toriyama first pitches the idea of writing a *manga* about a doctor to Torishima-*san*, he tells Toriyama to add a robot. Toriyama wants it to be a giant robot, but he can't draw the whole thing within the panels of the comic, so he makes it a small robot instead. Torishima-*san* rejects that idea, so Toriyama makes it a girl robot since he figures he'll think it's "cute." Torishima-*san* approves, and the character becomes a hit.

This is one of countless creative conflicts between Toriyama and his editor that will continue for the life of their relationship. Almost every idea that Toriyama has is first rejected by Torishima-*san* and then modified several times before or sometimes during the story in order to make it more to his liking. Although there are occasions when Toriyama will win or his ideas will be accepted outright.

Toriyama owes Torishima-*san* a lot and respects his professional opinions. After all, without his editor he wouldn't be where he is. Nevertheless, they argue with each other all the time, both in and out of the studio.

For example, one time they get into an argument about Toriyama not including a photograph of himself in his own *manga*. It's Shūeisha's custom for all the *Shōnen Jump manga-ka* who have their books published in a *tankōbon* volume format to include a photograph of themselves.

Toriyama refuses. He's shy and prefers to keep his face shrouded in mystery, either by drawing himself wearing a surgical mask, dressed up in mummy bandages, or in the likeness of a bird. Why a bird? The *tori* (鳥) in Toriyama's name means bird, so he decides that rather than draw his own face into his comics he's going to depict himself as an anthropomorphic bird holding a pencil. On occasion it wears human clothing and has a wind-up key in its back.

Torishima-*san* gets angry with him and turns the request into an order. Toriyama still refuses and the problem escalates into a debate over the fine lines in his contract that state he *must* provide a photograph. Toriyama agrees to send a photograph, but to spite him it will only be one that they won't be able to publish! Torishima-*san* screams back that whatever he sends is going to print!

He sends a picture of himself urinating into a toilet.

It goes to print.

That's the type of relationship we're talking about. Two people with different mentalities on how things are supposed to be done, but with a mutual goal.

Toriyama makes light of their relationship several times, such as by showing a caricatured version of Torishima-*san* screaming at Toriyama's likeness. He paints his editor as controlling and quick to dismiss his ideas, associating him with the catch phrase, *"Botsu* (ボツ, "Rejected")!!"

In short, Toriyama has a tough boss. So what does he do? Like any good artist who is suffering, he uses it to inspire his art. Torishima-*san* becomes the villainous Dr. Mashirito (博士マシリト), the archenemy of Dr. Slump and a man determined to *control everything*! Note that Mashirito has the same syllable pronunciation as Torishima, but with the order of the *kana* in reverse. Ironic as it sounds, Torishima-*san* approves of this and it goes to print.

He recalls this characters creation in the *Tokyopop* interview, "Haha. Well, almost every day we had discussions about what makes a real villain, because I had rejected Toriyama's initial suggestion. My opinion was that it should be an 'Emperor Nero,'[10] a person who enjoys the suffering of others. So I suggested him to think about someone truly mean who really gets on his nerves... It looks like he thought about me, and then he sent the manuscript in so late that I didn't have time to change it." So it's revenge on Toriyama's part, but he says, "I have to be able to withstand things like that, especially when the result is something so good. As a good editor you mustn't force anything upon your author, but instead recognize his potential and get it out somehow."

Toriyama looks back on their relationship with gratitude in *Daizenshū 4*. He says, "In my *manga* if I bring out the author's likes too strongly, it won't be very popular to begin with, so it's difficult to keep things in moderation. In other words, the hits *Dr. Slump* and *Dragon Ball* were works that I

---

10   Nero (*Nero Claudius Caesar Augustus Germanicus*, December 15, 37 – June 9, 68 A.D.) was an Emperor of Rome infamous for his torture and execution of countless people, including his own mother. So when Torishima-*san* asks Toriyama to think of someone as bad as Nero, Torishima-*san* comes to mind. The result is Dr. Mashirito.

drew while suppressing my own preferences. I really have to thank Torishima-*san*, my editor at the time, for that."

He's saying that if he's left to his own vices, the quality of his work won't be as strong as if it's tempered by an editors' vision. He needs a man like Torishima-*san* to restrict his wild creativity, to shape his work, give it direction, and make it better.[11] Torishima (鳥嶋) means "Bird Island," so it's fitting that Toriyama would rely on the foundation of Torishima-*san's* mentoring and editing as an allegorical island for the placement of his own "Bird Mountain."

Above all else, Torishima-*san* teaches Toriyama how to write professional *manga*. Toriyama recalls in his interview with *Terebaru*, "Your first editor always has an impact on you that lasts for a long time. In my case, it was 'to write *manga* that is easy to understand.'"

Tanaka Hisashi

Toriyama's acceptance into the hallowed halls of Shūeisha as a serialized author earns him the right to an assistant. He is assigned the 21-year-old Tanaka Hisashi (田中久志, born in April, 1959).

Toriyama takes an unorthodox approach to becoming a *manga-ka*. Instead of seeking apprenticeship, he teaches himself everything he needs to know. So he prefers to do things by himself, but now here he is with an assistant. A *manga-ka* will often have 4 or 5 assistants to help them meet their weekly deadline, but Toriyama doesn't want that many people around him, so he limits it to one and does most of the work himself.

---

11   By "make it better," I mean that Toriyama is a contrarian who prefers to make things less interesting than people expect. Torishima-*san* rejects his ideas and reshapes them into what people will like.

As a result, Toriyama has never worked so hard in his life. He says in *Men's Non-No*, "Before starting the serial, I hurried and drew two chapters' worth of material, but because there were too few pages or something, they ended up being run together, and all at once I was left without any stock (material prepared ahead of time). That was the start of my hell. ... Well at any rate, I couldn't sleep. At its worst, I'd be up all night for four days, sleep for 20 minutes, and then be up three more days. The style of *Dr. Slump* was that each chapter was to be self-contained as a rule, so I had to come up with a new story and punchline every time, which was tough."

The junior Tanaka-*kun* works under the now 25-year-old Toriyama, as Toriyama works under the now 28-year-old Torishima-*san*. They're young men writing *manga* for young boys, so they have a good time at it, and their hard work pays off.

An Orange Star Rises

At the end of 1980 the readers of *Weekly Shōnen Jump* submit their votes in a survey to name their favorite authors. For the first time in his career Toriyama makes it in the top 10.

As a result of working at Shūeisha, Toriyama is given the chance to meet his childhood idol, Tezuka Osamu. In a rare moment for Toriyama, he is invited to a party and goes to it. It's the debut of *manga* artist Araki Hirohiko (荒木 飛呂彦, born 1960), who wins a second place Tezuka-*shō* (手塚賞, "Tezuka Award") for his debut *manga*, *Busō pōkā* (武装ポーカー, "*Armed Poker*," 1981). Hirohiko is the later creator of the famous and best-selling *JoJo no Kimyō na Bōken* (ジョジョの奇妙な冒険, "*JoJo's Bizarre Adventure*," 1987). Toriyama's *Dr. Slump* is the ticket that gets him inside, and now he's rubbing elbows with the world's most famous *manga-ka*.

As he's writing *Dr. Slump,* he decides to write another *manga yomikiri* called *Pora ando Roido* (ポラアンドロイド, *"Pola & Roid"*), published in March, 1981 in *Weekly Shōnen Jump* #17. Named after the famous self-processing camera film called Polaroid, this *manga* tells the story of a young space taxi driver named Roido who lands on a planet and fights against an alien king with the so-called assistance of a sly girl named Pora. With this *manga,* Toriyama wins the *Readers Award* prize and a trip to Switzerland. He earns his vacation the hard way.

In 1981, *Dr. Slump* ranks in the top 10 once again, and goes on to win the 27th Shōgakukan *Manga-shō* (小学館漫画賞, "Shōgakukan *Manga* Award") for "best *shōnen / shōjo manga* of the year."[12] This is a prestigious annual award that begins in 1956, and is a great honor to receive. It's especially surprising that Toriyama wins it so quickly in his career, given his young age and that he does not dedicate his life to the craft beforehand.[13] He jumps from being a small fish in a big pond to winning the highest honor in his industry and being perceived as a huge star. What is that like for him? In *Tetsuko no Heya* he says, "It really did make me happy." Likewise in the *Dragon Ball: Bōken Special* he recalls that the happiest moment in his life, "Is when my *manga* became a hit, and I could finally put food on the table doing *manga.*"

Suffice to say, Toriyama no longer needs to borrow money from his parents to visit the café.

---

12   *Shōjo* (少女, "young girls") is *manga* written for young girls. The counterpart of *shōnen* for young boys.

13   Toriyama does not win any major awards after his prestigious 1981 award for *Dr. Slump,* despite the incredible popularity of his work. Torishima-*san* elaborates in his Kazé interview by saying, "In Japan we call him the *mukan no teiō* (無冠の帝王, "Uncrowned Emperor")." So Toriyama is popular with the people, but has not received the recognition and awards that he is arguably due.

Dr. Slump Anime

Toriyama receives an offer from Tōei Animation to adapt *Dr. Slump* into an *anime*. The offer comes half a year after serialization begins, and is the fastest offer ever received by a *manga-ka*.

The show is called *Dr. Slump Arare-chan* (*Dr.スランプ アラレちゃん*), and it airs one year later on April 8, 1981 on Fuji Terebi (フジテレビ, "Fuji Television").[14] The series becomes a smash hit and dominates the ratings. It broadcasts a total of 243 episodes and outlives the *manga*, airing its last episode on February 19, 1986.

The series is such a hit that Tōei creates 5 animated films for it. The first is titled *Dr. Suranpu Arare-chan Harō! Wandā Airando* (*Dr.スランプ アラレちゃん ハロー! 不思議島, "Dr. Slump and Arare-chan: Hello! Wonder Island"*). It premieres on July 7, 1981 at the Tōei Anime Fea (東映アニメフェア, "Tōei Anime Fair"), an annual event that has taken place since the 1960s and occurs in both the spring and summer in several major cities across Japan, backed by a huge marketing effort. The film is a success, so they make a new one each year.

The *anime*, films, and merchandise that accompany Toriyama's *manga* cement *Dr. Slump* and Arare into the minds of millions of young children and create what's called the "*Dr. Slump* Generation." They grow up with Arare in the same way that *Dragon Ball* fans grow up with Gokū.

---

14   Kabushiki-gaisha Fuji Terebijon (株式会社フジテレビジョン, "Fuji Television Network, Inc.," or Fuji Terebi (フジテレビ, "Fuji Television"), founded 1957), is one of the largest television networks in Japan. The *anime* adaptations of Toriyama's work are broadcast on Fuji Terebi.

Merchandizing

The merchandise machine kicks into high gear to capitalize on *Dr. Slump's* success. You name it, they make it, from action figures and dolls, to school supplies, backpacks, hats, clothing, and furniture. If there's a product format that exists, they slap a picture of Arare-*chan* on it and ship it to stores. By early 1983 there are about 800 different items, with more being added all the time.

In terms of licensing his work he says in *Tetsuko no Heya*, "I've got my hands full just drawing the *manga*, so that sort of thing I leave up to people like my editor, Torishima-*san*." This gives us insight into their business relationship. Toriyama focuses on being creative while Torishima-*san* does double duty as business manager.

In addition to the financial gain, Toriyama receives samples of the items, and he gets so many of them that he runs out of room in his house. He is forced to rent a second house just to store all the stuff. He has so much Arare-*chan* merchandise that it's, "To the point that whenever I have a child, I won't have to buy any school supplies. But just looking at it makes me uncomfortable."

His solution? Build a bigger house.

Matsuyama Takashi

Almost two years into *Dr. Slump*, Toriyama's assistant, Tanaka-*san*, is replaced by Matsuyama Takashi (まつやまたかし, born November 17, 1957).[15] Toriyama has an affinity

---

15   Toriyama (鳥山, "Bird Mountain"), plus Torishima (鳥嶋, "Bird Island), and now Matsuyama (まつやま, or 松山, "Pine Mountain"). An island with a mountain full of pine trees that supports the life of birds?

for him because they both love modeling. Matsuyama-*kun* wins the Tamiya Figure Remodeling Award every year from 1979 to 1989. This is a contest held by the famous modeling company Kabushiki-gaisha Tamiya (株式会社タミヤ, "Tamiya Incorporated," founded 1946), where you have to remodel a 5cm miniature soldier to look like a different person. So he and Toriyama have a lot to geek out about.

Matsuyama-*kun* says on his official website,[16] "In 1981 I met Akira Toriyama ... and [later] joined his company Bird Studio as a partner and second assistant. I was in charge of drawing the buildings and the scene of *Dr. Slump's* Pengin-*mura* and the house of Kame-*sennin* or the background scene on Namekku-*sei* (ナメック星, "Planet Namek") in *Dragon Ball*." They work together for the next 13 years.

Bird Land Press

Toriyama's success makes him one of the most recognized *manga-ka* in Japan. An unofficial fan club springs up called the Toriyama Akira Hozon-kai, (鳥山明保存会, "Toriyama Akira Preservation Society"). This is an unofficial fan club, but Toriyama decides to send them original sketches, stickers, buttons, key chains, and toys.

It becomes so large that on April 30, 1982, Shūeisha makes it the Toriyama Akira Kōshiki Fankurabu (鳥山明公式ファンクラブ, "Toriyama Akira Official Fan Club"), complete with numbered ID cards for its over 10,000 members.

In July, 1982 they publish the first issue of a bi-monthly 26 page magazine to discuss his works called *Bird Land*

---

16   Matsuyama Takashi's official website: *http://art-front.com/*. See */workshop.html* for the source of the cited quote where he describes his partnering with Toriyama. It's unknown if he is a "partner" in the genuine business sense or just the figurative sense.

Press (the title is written in English), in honor of Toriyama's name and persona. A bird holding a pencil is on the cover of issue #1, representing their idol. The magazine contains original illustrations, interviews about Toriyama's work and daily life, prints of his previous *manga*, photographs of his studio, and his model collection.

So in addition to his weekly deadline for *Dr. Slump*, he draws original work for this magazine and provides content that is never found anywhere else. *Bird Land Press* continues being published for 5 years until the autumn of 1987, producing a total of 25 issues. They are rare collectibles that have never been republished or translated.

Wealthiest in Japan

The *Asahi Shimbun* (朝日新聞, *"Morning Sun Newspaper,"* founded January 25, 1879) is the second largest national newspaper in Japan. Every year they publish a list called "Japan's Wealthiest." Guess who makes the list?

The *Asahi Shimbun* releases their annual report in May of each year, tallying up the earnings during the Japanese fiscal year of April to March. It says in 1980 that Toriyama earns 55,410,000 *yen* (~$542,506 USD (in 2014 exchange rates)).[17] This shoots up almost ten-fold in 1981 when he earns 539,240,000 *yen* (~$5,279,574 USD) and becomes the #1 wealthiest person in the "other" category, ranking 35th in the country for overall earnings. This is a catch-all category for fields outside of politicians in parliament, authors, actors, and professional athletes. He earns more than anyone in those categories, and is only eclipsed by company executives and real estate moguls (listed in their

---

17   The listings of Toriyama's earnings, reported by the *Asahi Shimbun*: *http://motoken.na.coocan.jp/material/choja/choja_81.html*

own category). His #1 streak continues in 1982 when he earns 647,450,000 *yen* (~$6,339,034 USD). So in only 3 years at Shūeisha he earns 1,242,100,000 *yen* (~$12,147,092 USD).

How does a young artist without a college degree become so wealthy? By being creative. It's his rise to fame and sales of the *Dr. Slump manga, anime,* and merchandise that fill his bank account with piles of cash.

But the funny thing is, he's aloof to his own wealth.

In the *Tetsuko no Heya* interview the host says his new-found wealth is amazing, and Toriyama replies, "I suppose so? Well, things like money, I can't quite picture, so..." The way he says this sounds like he is oblivious to his own success, and the financial numbers are so large that they don't 'click' in his mind.

Because he lives in Nagoya, he doesn't realize that his *manga* is selling like crazy in the cities. "So when I come to Tōkyō, times like that, seeing the bookshops stacked with copies, I think, 'Well I guess it really is selling, huh.'" When told that *Dr. Slump* Volumes 1 through 9 sold a combined total of 22,480,000 copies he says, "Really? That much?"

In his mind he's not rich, and he's shocked when he hears the numbers or is treated as a celebrity. "After all, when I look at the book store in my neighborhood, I'll think, 'I bet they're just selling it because they feel obligated to.'"

Perhaps Toriyama is unattached to his wealth because he grows up in a poor family living in the countryside, and therefore finds other things to value. As a child his parents are unable to afford to buy him toys, so he learns to appreciate nature and have fun with his friends. Now he has more toys than he knows what to do with, but it doesn't concern him. He has his mind on other things.

Like love.

Birds of a Feather

The titular *Dr. Slump* is not smooth with the ladies, but in 1982 he gets his dream woman to marry him. It's Arare's school teacher, the beautiful and blonde-haired Yamabuki Midori (山吹みどり). Perhaps it's no coincidence that while Toriyama draws this wedding into the 104th Chapter of his *manga*, titled "*Today is Truly a Day for Celebration!*," he also draws up his own plans to get married.

Like the Doctor, Toriyama's an introvert. He likes to be alone, draw his art, and put together intricate models. That means he doesn't get out much and doesn't have the ladies banging down his door. So how in the world is he going to meet a woman and go on dates?

Fortunately there is a lady who works for Shūeisha as a fellow *manga-ka*. She is Mikami Nachi (みかみなち), the author of *shōjo manga* titles *Ue o shita e no rokkunrōru* (下へのロックンロール, "*The Top and Bottom of Rock and Roll*," 1977) and *Hijiri mefisuto konran-den* (聖メフィスト混乱伝, "*The Confusing Legend of St. Mephisto*," 1985).

Toriyama says in *Tetsuko no Heya*, "I thought I'd try and meet someone in the same line of work. So five of us in the same field met up, that first time." He references this on the title page of *Dr. Slump* Chapter 64, titled *Yoake no Bōsōzoku no Maki* (夜明けの暴走族の巻, "*Riders at Dawn*," April, 1981). Excluding himself in the count, he goes out to eat dinner with five other *manga-ka*, including Mikami-*san*. It's telling that they're all *shōjo manga-ka*, as he says, "Most people who draw *shōnen manga* go off to Tōkyō, but people who draw *shōjo manga* are women, after all, so there are many people who work from afar." So as luck would have it, she happens to live and work in Nagoya and prefers the countryside just like him.

Sometime between Chapter 64 and Chapter 104, Toriyama becomes smitten. He says in the *Dragon Ball: Bōken*

Special, "I admired her for her adult personality and her attention to other people's needs. I like efficient people. I'm pretty impatient, so I can't stand people who putter around. Efficient, sexy women are great." He also says that he likes women with short hair and glasses, and wouldn't you know it, Mikami-*san's* got both.

Toriyama doesn't have much experience with women, and the interviewer in *Tetsuko no Heya* says, "You yourself are of course truly pure, but perhaps, especially when you met, did you try to take that purity, and..." He interjects, "Of course! After all, she's older than I am." She continues, "I see. So, you played up that pureness a bit, then?" "No, it's not that I played it up or anything. I had hardly ever spoken to women, after all. I'm a serious person, (laughs)." Toriyama's awkwardness, lack of experience, and "purity" works in his favor here to create chemistry.

Unlikely as it seems, Toriyama gets himself a wife.

When you think about it, how else could it have happened? He says, "That's right. A relative of my wife's just happened to live in the same town as me, so we got in touch. Something like that hardly ever happens, after all..."

If he hadn't bumped into that relative in town, then he wouldn't have gone on the group date with Mikami-*san* and wouldn't have fallen in love.

Wedding Bells

In *Dr. Slump*, it's an ordinary day like any other when Midori decides to visit Senbei. Senbei stands up to make some tea; meanwhile Midori goes to the bathroom. Unaware of this, he stops nearby the bathroom during his return and practices his wedding proposal out loud. Midori hears him ask the question, exits the bathroom, and says she'll marry him!

Toriyama's real-life proposal is just as smooth. He pops

the question: "Marry me, pleeeeeaase."

She says yes!

They arrange to get married on May 2, 1982. The bride and groom will wear traditional Shintō wedding attire, and they'll cut through a multi-tiered cake at the local Nagoya Reception House.

Toriyama plans for his wedding to be a quiet and private affair. But there's one little catch.

Media Blitz

By sheer coincidence the *Asahi Shimbun* publishes their list of "Japan's Wealthiest" during 1981 on May 1, 1982, the day before his wedding ceremony. This causes a flurry of media buzz about Toriyama's great wealth, and the next day reporters rush over to his home to ask him questions. It just so happens that he's having a wedding!

Media attention is the thing Toriyama likes least because he doesn't want people to invade his personal life. Now all of a sudden, on the biggest day in his life, media reporters show up at his house and start asking him questions about, "Money this, money that..." He says, "I didn't think my wedding would be such a big deal, though. It's tough [being in the media]. And I didn't think the mass media, *manga-ka*, were viewed like that." He continues, "I just figured one of the neighbors had stopped by to ask about the wedding, so I said, "What, is this about my wedding?" And it seems like that's how they found out."

Fortunately the wedding goes off without incident. But now Toriyama's marriage and personal life are displayed as national news.

This is the straw that breaks the camel's back.

Toriyama decides to never show his face in public again.

Tetsuko no Heya

Another year rolls by and Toriyama is the talk of the town, even though he doesn't want to be. Despite his preference, on May 4, 1983, he is broadcast to the nation on his first televised interview as a guest on *Tetsuko no Heya* (徹子の部屋, *"Tetsuko's Room"*). This is Japan's first and most famous talk show, hosted by the actress and host, Kuroyanagi Tetsuko (黒柳 徹子, born August 9, 1933). It airs on the largest television channel in Japan, Kabushiki-gaisha Terebi Asahi (株式会社テレビ朝日, commonly called "asahi tv," founded November 1, 1957), owned by the Asahi Shimbun newspaper conglomerate and by Tōei Animation.

Tetsuko introduces him to the audience: "To be honest, I actually wanted him to come here sooner, but last year, the announcements of his wedding and his coming in first in the ranking of Japan's wealthiest came at the same time, and things were thrown into confusion, and this very pure individual became quite shy of other people, and wouldn't show his face up until now; today, we have finally got him here. My guest today: Akira Toriyama-*san*."

I don't know what superhuman force convinces him to come onto the show. Maybe Torishima-*san*? Or maybe he feels pressure to do the interview by Tōei and the Asahi Shimbun, since they own this channel. *Dr. Slump* is the biggest series in Japan, so they no doubt want to capitalize on its success. And if the creator doesn't engage with people, how can they sell more *manga*, *anime*, and merchandise?

But just because he's on TV doesn't mean he becomes an extrovert. He says on air, "It's my first time. I didn't think there would be this many people who could see me. Man, it makes me nervous. It's embarrassing."

Toriyama appears uncomfortable while Tetsuko talks and tries to bring him out of his shell. There's even a period of dead air as he just stares at her, unsure of how to respond.

But to be fair, he does open up as they continue. Then he tells some good anecdotes and laughs.

This appearance makes "Akira Toriyama" a household name. And that's the last thing he wants.

It's the longest interview in Toriyama's life and the only televised interview where he allows his face to be recorded. The other interview occurs in 2013 (30 years later), but it's only a minute long and he forbids the camera from filming above his neckline. Forget about blurring the face afterward; they're not even allowed to film it.

Toriyama and Mikami

During the interview, Toriyama's new wife, Mikami-*san*, is shown sitting in the audience, and he often glances over to her for reassurance. Tetsuko asks about his wife and her *manga* career. He says, "Well, it seems that she can't draw that much anymore now. We've gotten married, and she doesn't have a career anymore, so she's busy keeping house. She says that she can't do it properly." Tetsuko laughs and says, "I'm amazed; you're quite [traditional]. Your wife draws *manga*, but she abandons her career after getting married, so your [views] toward marriage [must be]... That now, she's focused on [housekeeping], that she immediately can't draw *manga*. That she can't do it properly." Toriyama says, "Yes. Sometimes she helps me [with my work], though. She's a lifesaver in that respect."

As much as Toriyama is a child of the 60s, rebels against the standard lifestyle of the degree-holding salary man in a suit, and is a creative artist, he also has traditional views on marriage. As soon as his wife gets married, she stops her successful career as a *manga-ka*. They don't even have kids yet, but tradition dictates that she becomes a housewife, and that's evidently what one or the both of them wants.

Even though he's creative and breaks new ground in his *manga*, in his personal life he is conservative.

Despite her career coming to an abrupt end, she's still a talented woman, so she helps with Toriyama's *manga*. "For instance, when I'm coming up with a story and such, she starts talking to me without reservation. That point—since she drew herself, as well—it seems she knows what parts are hard for me." Tetsuko says, "In that case, you've married the right person." He says, "Yes, I did. (laughs)."

He also says he consults with his wife, "about clothes, that sort of thing." He asks her if the clothes he draws are *naui* (ナウい, "now-y," or "hip"). "And she'll tell me, 'They're not *naui* at all.'" So a lot of the fashion designs we see in *Dr. Slump* and *Dragon Ball*, especially with the female characters, are influenced or designed by Mikami-*san*, supporting her husband behind the scenes.

Bird Studio

Toriyama has been working for Shūeisha for 3 years, and *Dr. Slump* pulls in millions of *yen*. Toriyama decides he wants to take control of the rights to his work and have more independence, so he founds his own company called Bird Studio (バードスタジオ, *Bādo sutajio*). This is another play on the *tori* (鳥, "bird") in his name. Toriyama likely does this because of the cultural importance of the family name in Japan. But instead of naming it Tori Studios he changes it to the literal meaning and writes it in English.

He bases his studio in Nagoya so that it is nearer to his home and he does not have to go into Tōkyō as much. In the *Dragon Ball: Bōken Special* he says he prefers to work here because otherwise, "It's just too much of a pain. Plus, I'm a real country boy, and I can't stand how crowded Tōkyō is." This may also be because he wants to be closer to his new wife. So instead of going to Tōkyō, his assistant comes to this lab and works with him.

In Bird Studio, Toriyama and Matsuyama, these two creative "mountains" (山, *yama*) of men, create some of the most famous *manga* in the world. It's also where they build models, with mountains of boxes on the shelves, as they build their futures.

The business relationship between Bird Studio, Shūeisha, and Tōei has never been explained. But it can be surmised that Bird Studio provides him with greater rights to his own work, rather than it being solely owned by the publisher who then licenses it out to *anime* production studios, toy manufacturers, and video game companies for a fee. Whenever you read Toriyama's *manga* or watch his *anime* you'll see "Bird Studio" in the licensing information, showing that the rights belong to him.

This is a bold move for a *manga-ka* to take, but it allows Toriyama to gain independence from his publisher and to establish his financial future as an artist.

Toriyama's Art Style

Toriyama isn't a professionally trained *manga-ka*, nor does he go to school for story-telling or animation. He's just a boy who likes to draw. His only real job before becoming a *manga-ka* is as a designer of still life and advertising fliers. After this he learns everything through hard effort. He's skilled in the art of illustration because he has to be.

Toriyama's art style is hard to define, but a few words come to mind: Simple, bright, clean, and energetic.

He favors an abstract style, meaning that characters are humanoid in appearance but can come in different shapes. They can also stand next to talking dogs and insect monsters and hold a conversation. Yet his representational art can be realistic, such as the structure of Gokū's muscles.

Toriyama's main focus is on the details of the central target of the illustration, and not in background art. This is why most of his backgrounds are simple or sparse while his characters are richly detailed. Yet the backgrounds do not suffer any, and I would argue their simplicity is their strength, adding to the value of the composition as a whole by allowing the standouts to stand out.

His characters are easy to understand, with simple lines, distinguishing colors and features, yet not boring. He says in the *Battle of Gods Animanga* (2013) interview, "My style is to first tear down the image, then think up the contents." Whatever stereotypical image you're expecting to see, he'll give you the opposite. In this manner he combines opposite qualities together to create a single unified being, such as how his monsters appear cute and silly while still being diabolical or scheming.

Toriyama's illustrations have no disagreeable aspects. They're attractive, fun, and filled with energy.

Toriyama's Writing Style

Toriyama is praised for his drawings, but he should be equally praised for his intelligent, witty, and multi-layered writing that anyone can relate to and enjoy. He's a linguistics genius, and this is noticeable in the Japanese originals where each character has their own way of speaking, a witty origin to their name, and says hilarious puns.

How does Toriyama write? In the *American Shonen Jump* #3 interview (2003) he says, "Obviously I was an adult at that time, but whenever I got stuck in a storyline I would try and imagine myself when I was a child. I'd think to myself, 'Okay, what did I enjoy or what did I want to read or to see when I was a kid?' That's how I thought up my storylines."

He tends to procrastinate on the job until the deadline approaches for publication. As a result, he lets his ideas percolate. In *Daizenshū 4* he says, "With me, I think up the story in advance, then come up with the world's background information to be consistent with it. I guess that if I was a normal *manga-ka* who did things properly, I'd think up the background information first and then come up with the story. Saying that, you'd think that I don't really think through anything. There's a vague image, even before I create the story." Instead of working he spends most of his time putting together models or playing video games. "I'm relatively serious about them, or rather, I'm the kind of person who can only do one thing at a time. So I'll end up doing just that one thing." Then as the clock ticks toward the cutoff date he receives inspiration and puts the story together on the spot, drawing the pages into the midnight hours.

This leads to a lot of happenstance. Events that occur next in the story are only possible because of the previous events that are only possible because of previous events before these. So he paints himself into corners that can only be resolved by creating more of such events. He says in *Daizenshū 6*, "But, just as I've been driven into a corner, it's like my brain waves go taut, and some sort of idea bubbles up." This builds on itself again and again to outrageous proportions, where events in the early parts of the story end up altering the story decades later.

You'll see examples throughout Gokū's story, and I'll take those moments to describe his writing style in more detail.

Creating Art

Whenever he's not in Bird Studio or at Shūeisha, he works at home. In *Daizenshū 4* he says, "My way of working has ended up being while sitting at a *kotatsu* table watching TV." A *kotatsu* (炬燵, "heated table") is a low table with a blanket draped down all four sides with an electric heater attached to the underside. You sit in a low chair and stick your legs under the table, where it keeps you cozy.

Toriyama shows idiosyncrasies while working under a deadline. He smokes cigarettes like a maniac. "I know that it's best to quit, but without them I can't relax. Before a deadline I'll smoke about 100 in a day." He also picks his ears with a swab. "This is just because I have a peculiarity where I can't quite relax if I don't periodically clean my ears." So his lungs are dirty, but his ears are clean.

In terms of tools, he keeps it simple. He uses a mechanical pencil or 2B pencil, drawing brush, and Zebra G-Pen with replaceable nibs, along with documentary ink, waterproof color ink, and Kent paper.

Toriyama is raised on TV and it makes him feel comfortable. While he sits at the *kotatsu* and draws, smokes, and cleans his ears, he watches programs. Even if he's not paying attention, he likes to hear the background noise, and the sound effects inspire the action noises in his *manga*.

He has an odd strategy to avoid being visually distracted. Toriyama wears glasses because he is nearsighted, "But for my job I use weak ones, about 0.7. It's hard to draw if I can see too much." So he wears glasses that limit his vision so that he will focus on the page in front of him. That's dedication. Nevertheless, the constant noise soaks into his mind and influences the art that pours out of his hands.

Crummy Manga Lab

Toriyama is now a recognized expert in the *manga* industry. Not only by millions of readers, but by professionals.

To share his hard-earned knowledge and expertise on

art and writing with the world he partners with freelance writer Sakuma Akira (さくま あきら, born July 29, 1952) to co-author a new *manga* called *Toriyama Akira's Hetappi manga kenkyūjo* (鳥山明のヘタッピマンガ研究所, *"Akira Toriyama's Crummy Manga Lab,"* October, 1982 – March, 1984).

This is a *manga* about how to draw and write *manga* in the Toriyama style. It uses comedic illustrations combined with valuable techniques to provide an entertaining guide to aspiring *manga-ka*. It advises the *manga-ka* to draw characters with simple lines, have people face one another when talking, and make dialogue easy to understand. It offers practical step-by-step tutorials on drawing clothing, weapons, and other aspects of a characters design. Though humorous, it presents a thorough tutorial on how to write *manga* that readers will enjoy.

The two authors publish 12 small lessons in *Fresh Jump* (*Furesshu janpu*, フレッシュジャンプ) magazine over these 2 years and then bring the lessons together into a single volume with additional content in May, 1985. For many aspiring *manga-ka* it becomes their bible. The next generation of authors in the late-'90s and 2000s who grow up with this book and his *manga* will go on to state that Toriyama is their mentor and greatest source of inspiration.

It's in this book that Toriyama uses his new likeness that he calls "Robotoriyama."

Robotoriyama

Toriyama is reclusive, so instead of drawing himself as the teacher that gives advice, he uses a stand-in likeness. This is in keeping with his preference to hide his face. In *Dr. Slump* Volumes 1 and 2 he uses a bird alter ego, but starting in Volume 3 he prefers to use a robotic miniaturized stand-in.

The character looks like a small humanoid robot wearing

a World War II gas mask. Why a gas mask? In the *Dragon Ball: Bōken Special* he says, "Because it's embarrassing to draw my own face." It also wears human clothing, such as a suit and tie, lab coat, casual day wear, a running tracksuit, and in later depictions, the iconic Kame-*sen-ryū dōgi* from *Dragon Ball*, just like Gokū's. It often wears a baseball cap with the word "TORI" written across the front.

Toriyama gives it a name in *Dr. Slump* Volume 5 (1981), calling it "Robotoriyama" (ろぼとりやま). He writes the name in *hiragana*, rather than in a combination of *katakana* for *robo* (ロボ), for it being a foreign term, and *kanji* for Toriyama (鳥山), as his name is written. This is similar to how he signs his signature, written in *hiragana* as "Toriyama Akira" (とりやまあきら).

Few fans are aware of the character's real name, as it's never mentioned in *Dragon Ball* and only appears in *Dr. Slump* Volumes 5 and 8 as one-word entries in additional content outside of the serialized story. It's a name so rarely known that even in the official *Daizenshū 7* guidebook the character is called "Toriyama Akira" (鳥山 明).

As a result of international *Dragon Ball* fans not knowing the real name when the series was localized, they instead referred to it as the Tori-bot; a portmanteau of "Toriyama" plus "robot." This name began to be used in 1997 and is a far more common name for the character outside of Japan.[18]

Since Toriyama doesn't like to draw his face or be photographed, he uses the Robotoriyama when he wants to represent his presence in his *manga*. When you see this little robot with a gas mask, you know it's supposed to be him. He says that he's happy to have created this character so early in his career, because without it he couldn't settle down and would be overrun by hundreds of fans while shopping.

---

18   Read about my discovery of Robotoriyama's real name: http://thedaoofdragonball.com/blog/history/tori-bot-real-name-discovered/

Famous Introvert

Toriyama is now one of the most famous men in Japan, but it's not because of his outgoing personality. He avoids the limelight like it's the plague and says in *Daizenshū 1*, "I'm just a *manga-ka*, so I can't stand being scrutinized. I just want to loiter around. So now I seldom go to places where I might be discovered."

He chooses not to appear on TV, teach classes, or do lengthy interviews. "I don't go for mass communication or lectures. I've always hated those anyway. Well, now I've got a face that can't go out in public. ... When I'm out and about, it's rare for me to be recognized, but for some reason every now and then someone will know who I am."

He then makes the explicit choice to not include photographs that show his face, saying, "Sorry. I think this way I won't have to put up with even more of this." And in the *Dragon Ball: Bōken Special* he says the one thing he'd like most right now is, "to move out to an even quieter part of the sticks." He's famous, despite his best efforts.

What's Next?

It's now 1984. *Dr. Slump* is a hit and Toriyama has all the success he could have imagined 10 years earlier when he graduated high school. Not bad for a kid who never went to college. Toriyama knew that sitting through another 4 years of school just to get a piece of paper with his name on it wasn't the right choice for him. His choice was to use his own paper and write his own name on it. Now he's a millionaire with money to spare and has so much fame that he finally has a legitimate reason to avoid crowds. And on top of that he's got a wife. Everything is perfect.

However, he's exhausted.

Toriyama recalls this period in *Chō-zenshū 4*,[19] saying, "I had exhausted my material for *Dr. Slump* and wanted to end it, but it was popular so I couldn't. At that rough point, Torishima-*san*, who had learned that I liked *kanfū* (カンフー, "kung fu") movies and often watched them, suggested to me, "If you like them that much, why don't you draw a *kanfu manga*? If it's interesting, I'll even let you end *Dr. Slump*." That was a lifesaver as it was, but it was on the condition that, "You have to start right on it in three months.""[20]

Toriyama is desperate and accepts the offer.

Then they both wonder, 'What's next?'

---

19   *Chō-zenshū* (超全集, "*Super Complete Collections*") are the second largest group of *Dragon Ball* guidebooks, following the *Daizenshū*.

20   Torishima-*san* elaborates on Toriyama's exhaustion in Part 4 of his Kazé interview: *https://youtu.be/WtHLjIYOF1s*.

Dragon Ball's Origin

THE STORY OF *Dragon Ball's* origin is just as captivating as the story of *Dragon Ball*. In this chapter you'll learn about the true reason for *Dragon Ball's* existence, and hear how Toriyama comes up with the idea, names it, and creates it.

Working Vacation

Shūeisha's reader surveys show that *Dr. Slump* is as popular as ever and they know it's a money maker. However, the author is out of material and needs a break. So after 5 years of continual effort, Toriyama earns some time off.

His editor gives him a vacation. But not a real one.

The selling of *manga* is big business and Torishima-*san* isn't going to let his star *manga-ka* sit around and twiddle his thumbs until he feels like writing again. He gives him 3 months to come up with a new story.

But, to be fair, Toriyama does take a two-week long trip to China with his wife. And Torishima-*san*.

Yeah, his editor travels with them.

A New Story Begins

I can picture it now. Toriyama says something like, 'My wife and I have been wanting to take a trip to China for years,' and Torishima-*san* says, 'Great! I'll buy us some tickets. It'll give us a chance to see the real thing.' And then the happy trio begin their adventure.

Little is known of their trip, of where they go, or their experiences, but Toriyama's wife takes photographs that will soon serve as reference material for his *manga*.

When they come back, Toriyama remembers what he calls the "painstaking meetings" with his editor to try and create a new story. The two of them speak every day on the phone, but they struggle to come up with good ideas that can replace *Dr. Slump*. So Torishima-*san* travels from Tōkyō to Nagoya to meet with him face-to-face. He says in his Kazé interview, "We talked about what to do, but we still didn't get any good ideas. I was about to go back to Tōkyō empty-handed when his wife brought us tea. His wife was also a *manga-ka*. She said a phrase that bounced around in my head. What she said was that she found her husband to be an atypical *manga-ka*. See, a *manga-ka* usually listens to the radio or music while he's inking, because it lets him stay relaxed while he concentrates on his hand. But Toriyama, he had a video playing while he was working! That shouldn't be possible, right? How can anyone draw while watching a movie? But he said that, yes, he did. I asked him why he did that, and he said, "Well, there's this movie I like. I just listen to the dialogue, and I know when the best scenes of the movie happen." Then he stopped to watch. I asked him what this movie was. He told me it was a Jackie Chan *kanfū* movie. Then I asked him how many times he'd seen it. He answered between 50 and 100 times! If he liked it that much, I asked, why not make a *manga* based on it?"

Toriyama recalls, "I told him, "The things I like and the things that I can draw in *manga* are different, so I don't want to." But then he went ahead and set up a schedule for me, saying, 'Finish it up by such-and-such a date,' and it was this sort of, 'Whaaaat?!' feeling, you know."[1]

If Toriyama's wife hadn't said what she said at this criti-

---

1   "I told him..." comes from the *TV Anime Guide: Dragon Ball Z Son Gokū Densetsu* (2003) interview.

cal moment, then Torishima-*san* wouldn't have asked about the movie and discovered Toriyama's obsession with Jackie Chan films. Recognizing his passion for the genre, and in a pinch to come up with a new story to replace *Dr. Slump*, Torishima-*san* seizes on this opportunity and forces Toriyama to do it. But he later confesses, "That was very laborious, and he admits to cursing at me for it."

Dragon Ball Prototypes

Here's where things get layered. Throughout his years of serialization on *Dr. Slump*, Toriyama is tasked with the additional labor of creating a *yomikiri manga*. These independent *manga* serve as a creative outlet for other ideas.

Two *yomikiri* have the greatest influence on the as-yet-uncreated *Dragon Ball*.

The first of these is a *gōngfu manga* called *Doragon Bōi*.

Doragon Bōi

Doragon Bōi (written and pronounced in *katakana* as "Dragon Boy," ドラゴンボーイ, but also written in *kanji* as *Kiryū shōnen*, 騎竜少年, literally "Dragon Cavalry Young Boy," 1983) is a 2-chapter *yomikiri* published in *Fresh Jump* magazine from August to October.

It's intended to be a test prototype for a *gōngfu manga* in general, not specifically for what would become *Dragon Ball*, but in retrospect this is how it can be perceived. It's like a time capsule of Toriyama's mind from 1983.

The main character of *Doragon Bōi* is Tanton (唐童, or たんとん, "Táng Dynasty Boy"). He lives in the mountains of the *Sen no kuni* (仙の国, "Hermit Country") and is taught by a martial arts master named *go-Rōshi-sama* (ご老師様, "Elder Master").[2]

One day the master decides that Tanton is to escort a *hime-sama* (姫様, "princess") from the war-torn *Ka no kuni* (華の国, "Flower Country," a poetic name for China) back to her home, since the war is over. To aid Tanton in his quest his master gives him a magical *ronpao* (竜宝, "dragon jewel") that he can call upon when in need.

Doragon Bōi uses designs, details, jokes, and character types that are reused later in *Dragon Ball*. The first and most obvious being that they both have "dragon balls" in them. For another, both *manga* take place in a Chinese fantasy land. I'll draw more parallels throughout *Dragon Ball Culture* when relevant, but the main point for now is that *Doragon Bōi* is a success. Toriyama says, "That got an incredibly positive response from the readers, so I decided to go that route for my next serialized work."

It's because of *Doragon Bōi* that we have *Dragon Ball*, and it is Tanton that seeds the creation of Son Gokū.

Tonpū Daibōken

Just as *Doragon Bōi* establishes the Chinese fantasy world that we find in *Dragon Ball*, *Tonpū Daibōken* establishes the science fiction technology that gives it a modern twist.

Tonpū Daibōken (トンプー大冒険, *"Tonpū's Great Adventure,"* November, 1983) is about a young space traveling boy

---

2   Tanton is the ancient *on'yomi* pronunciation of the *hànzì* of Tángtóng (唐童, "Táng Boy") referring to the Táng Dynasty, the height of Chinese civilization and synonymous with China. Tanton escorts the princess back to the "flower country," an epithet for China. So the boy named after China takes the nameless girl back to China. This is an early example of Toriyama's finesse with names.

named Tonpū (トンプー) who lands on an unknown planet and meets a human girl named Puramo (プラモ).[3]

This creative science fiction adventure introduces character types, designs, and objects that will later appear in *Dragon Ball*. For example, the boy uses capsule objects to summon a speeder bike and a house out of thin air. Like Tanton and Gokū, he is super strong, fights with martial arts, and grows stronger through anger. The girl likewise uses guns and her sexiness as a weapon, just as Buruma does in *Dragon Ball*.

Dragon Ball is Born

Back to 1984. Toriyama's running out of time on his vacation and still doesn't have anything solid. Writing *Dragon Ball* is the last thing he wants to do. He says in the *TV Anime Guide: Dragon Ball Z Son Gokū Densetsu*, "From the very beginning I was drawing *Dragon Ball* going, "I don't wanna'," (laughs)." He adds, "I spent my time building plastic models and such until almost right up to the deadline. By the time I got down to work on the storyboards, it was already two days before the deadline, or thereabouts."

This story is going to be serialized in the biggest weekly *manga* publication in Japan and be read by millions of people. It's going to be the follow up to the ultra-successful *Dr. Slump*. The next work of a superstar! But he doesn't start working on it until two days before the deadline. What a guy. I can't imagine doing the same thing myself, can you?

Fortunately he has the general idea in his head. He says

---

3   I theorize that Puramo (プラモ) is a portmanteau of *purasuchikku* (プラスチック, "plastic") and *moderu* (モデル, "model"). Toriyama loves models, so he uses them as a name for this girl. The name of Tonpū may also be derived from a similar concept.

in the *TV Anime Guide*, "When I came up with *Dragon Ball* I thought I would try to combine the *kanfū* movies of Jackie Chan and Bruce Lee, which I loved so much that I'd watch them on video even while I was working, with the classic *Saiyūki* to make an enjoyable *manga*."

The Jackie Chan film that affects him the most is *Zuì-quán* ("*Drunken Master*"). He recalls in an interview in *Daizenshū 2: Story Guide* (June 25, 1995), that, "If I hadn't seen this movie, I would never have come up with *Dragon Ball*."

Like they say: "Write what you know." Toriyama's obsession with watching the same *gōngfu* films hundreds of times enables him to create the Chinese culture inspired *Doragon Bōi*. Its success motivates him to write his next *manga*. So he takes what he knows and combines it with what everybody else knows; the pop culture popularity of the *gōngfu* masters and the traditional culture of *Saiyūki*.

With that, *Dragon Ball* is born!

Saiyūki in Brief

You might be wondering, 'What's *Saiyūki*?' I dedicate the next chapter of this book to explaining *Saiyūki*, but here's a brief explanation.

Saiyūki (西遊記, Chinese: *Xīyóujì*, "*Journey to the West*") is the Japanese translation of a Chinese novel that tells the story of a Buddhist monk who travels to India to retrieve scriptures and return with them to China. Along the way he's aided by mystical forces, including his companions of the Monkey King, a pig man, a river demon, and a dragon prince that is transformed into their white horse. The story is interwoven with Buddhist, Dàoist, and Confucian culture, and has been a classic for over 400 years.

As a result of its incredible popularity, the novel has been turned into films, television series, *manga*, *anime*, and been

discussed by philosophers, scholars, and poets for generations. If you live in China, Korea, or Japan, then you likely
grow up hearing the story or seeing it on TV.

Toriyama decides to base his new *gōngfu manga* on this
story because it will be recognized by his audience. Combining this with the *gōngfu* action and humor that has been
popular in cinema for the previous decade and a half is the
recipe for *Dragon Ball's* success.

Why "Dragon Ball"?

Why does Toriyama name his series *Dragon Ball*?

Toriyama says in the *TV Anime Guide* that the title of
Dragon Ball is inspired by the use of the word "Dragon"
in *gōngfu* movies coming out of Hong Kong in the mid-to-
late '70s after Bruce Lee's death following *Enter the Dragon*
(1973). These films capitalize on the word association of
"Dragon" with Bruce's blockbuster so fans will be excited
(or duped) into buying a ticket. They star Bruce Lee look-
alikes in what comes to be known as "Bruceploitation." But
Jackie Chan and other stars use this naming convention as
well. It's "Dragon" this and "Dragon" that for years.

"Everything had "Dragon" tacked on to it. But I thought,
'Something's different. It has the feel of a cheap knock-
off.' Anyway, something *kanfū* has to have "Dragon" in it.
Because, I thought, 'If it doesn't, then it's not *kanfū*, eh?' Ah,
I'm just like all those cheap knockoff movies."

Toriyama loves these movies, they're popular, and Dragons are "Eastern," cool, and make you think of fighting and
fantasy. *Enter the Dragon* starts the trend, but the rest of
them make it meaningful. So he borrows this convention
for his first word, as an homage to his favorite films.

The "Ball" in *Dragon Ball* comes from Toriyama's desire
to give his adventurers something to search for, in homage

to *Saiyūki.* He says in this same interview, "In the original *Saiyūki* they're heading for India, but for *Dragon Ball* I changed the ultimate objective to the easier-to-understand, "gather seven orbs called 'dragon balls' in order to grant a wish," when starting the serialization."

Toriyama compares the dragon balls to the Buddhist *sūtra* (Sanskrit: सूत्र, pronounced 'soo-trah,' Chinese: *jīng*, 經, "sacred scriptures") of the original quest and uses them for the same purpose in his story, but in a non-religious way that kids can understand. A ball is a straightforward object but it becomes interesting when you ask, 'What's a "dragon" ball?' That makes you curious. So it's mysterious yet playful and makes you want to learn more. The dragon balls 'get the ball rolling' in the story.

With the two words of "Dragon" as a traditional homage to the modern *gōngfu* films, and "Ball" as a modern homage to the traditional *sūtra*, we have the title of our work: "DRAGON BALL."

Dragon Ball is a perfect title for this series because it's traditional, modern, foreign and cool, yet domestic all at once. It's a title that appeals to everyone.

Etymology of Dragon Ball

On the front of the *Dragon Ball manga* you'll see both an English and Japanese title. But Toriyama writes for a Japanese audience, so why have both?

The larger of the two titles are the English words of "DRAGON BALL" in capital letters. This is because English words give your project a hip "foreign" feel. The *gōngfu* film producers add "Dragon" to the titles of their works for the same reason: It makes a project more marketable.

Underneath this title you'll see the Japanese approximation of the English, pronounced as *Doragonbōru* (ドラゴン

ボール) in *katakana*. The *katakana*, rather than *hiragana*, helps further express this foreign feel, yet is still domestic.

So the title is a fusion of East and West. It's right there on the cover of every book. We haven't even opened it yet and we're already experiencing Toriyama's style.

This is something worth thinking about, because he could have chosen to stay true to the series' traditional Chinese roots and used Chinese *hànzì* or Japanese *kanji*. In this case "DRAGON BALL" would be pronounced *Ron Dama* (龙球, or *Ryū Kyū*) in Japanese to approximate the Chinese *Lóng Qiú* (龍球). But he doesn't do it this way despite doing similar things with characters' names and other elements in the series. Instead he titles his work in English.[4-5] So at first glance the content appears to be based on Chinese culture, yet it has an English title. Intriguing, no?[6]

"DRAGON BALL" encapsulates the mindset of Toriyama and establishes the groundwork for everything to come.

---

4   Toriyama writes the title with English words, so that's why I refer to the series as *Dragon Ball* rather than *Doragonbōru*.

5   Is the title "DRAGON BALL", "Dragon Ball", "Dragonball", or "DragonBall"? The official title is written as two separate words in all caps ("DRAGON BALL"), but it's easier to read as "Dragon Ball".

6   I argue that "DRAGON BALL" in English is the official title of the series, even in Japan. "DRAGON BALL" is the larger of the two titles on the cover, and the Japanese *Doragonbōru* (ドラゴンボール) is just an approximation for the Japanese audience to pronounce. In fact, for the premiere of *Dragon Ball* Chapter 1 in *Weekly Shōnen Jump* #51, November 20, 1984, Toriyama designs the cover of the magazine, and it says "Dragon Ball" in English above "Toriyama Akira" in Japanese, but *Doragonbōru* (ドラゴンボール) does not appear. It's only on the inside once you get to the chapter. So the marketers at Shūeisha advertise the series with an English title right from the start.

Toriyama's Method

Toriyama's "vacation" has come to an end and he only has two days remaining to start and finish the first chapter of *Dragon Ball*. He says in *Chō-zenshū 4: Dragon Ball Super Encyclopedia* (2013), "I had almost no break, since I had other work and such, and I had no choice but to start drawing without clearly deciding on the contents."

Of course, you and I both know that he spends his free time watching TV and building models. So you can see that Toriyama's method is to procrastinate until the deadline is near and then make a mad dash to the finish line.

This is his routine, not a one time event. He says in the *TV Anime Guide*, "I'd start at around midnight, finish up the storyboard around 6 in the morning, then spend until the evening of the next day inking everything... so I probably finished up everything in about a day and a half."

How can such a master as Toriyama follow this method and yet still produce high quality work? This is the part of his genius that I described in the "Akira Toriyama" chapter. He's an inspired man. It's when deadlines approach that ideas pour out of his hand. "Well, it was telling a story, so it was pretty easy. When a new character would appear, or something like that, it would take a little bit more time, but once the design concepts and the story were decided, it was about a day and a half." That anyone could call writing and inking at least 14 pages of a *manga* by hand in a day and a half of work "easy" is astounding.[7] Only a true master who has honed his craft through continual practice, or a savant, can achieve such feats. Toriyama does it in his first week and every week thereafter.

Part of why he can do this is because he makes it up as he goes. He says in *Daizenshū 2*, "I hadn't thought it up at

---

7   An average chapter of *Dragon Ball* is 14 pages, plus 1 title page.

all. I figured it would probably end in about a year, and I had only really prepared storyboards for three chapters."

Because the stories are rushed, so too are the illustrations. To save time on his drawings he skips the rough draft process altogether. He pencils the storyboards and then applies pen and ink directly on top of these.

He works like this for the next 10 years.

Dragon Ball Premieres

Applying this method, Toriyama finishes the first chapter of his *manga* and delivers it before the deadline. It goes to print and premieres in *Weekly Shōnen Jump* #51 on November 20, 1984 (with a publication date of December 3, 1984). He writes a note inside that says, "Here I am again, and without having had any time to rest! I'm happy, but sad too. Still, I'll do my best!"

Upon its arrival the gates of heaven open and the people of the world stare in awe at Toriyama's creation!!

Hmm, wait a minute. No, that's not how it goes.

Instead of this dragon being a roaring success right out of the gate, it doesn't meet readers' expectations. They think that Son Gokū is boring and there's not enough action. This comes as a surprise not only because of Toriyama's talent and reputation, but because the first five chapters are in color, which should have added to its impact.

In normal terms the *manga* can be considered a success because it helps sell millions of copies of *Weekly Shōnen Jump*. But this is Toriyama we're talking about. Compared to the benchmark set by *Dr. Slump*, it's a disappointment.

Undaunted, Toriyama continues to work his magic and publish a new chapter each week.

Then, it happens.

The Dragon Soars

After the first story arc is complete at Chapter 23,[8] he takes some advice from Torishima-*san*, makes some changes, and *then* it becomes a hit.

And I mean a *big* hit. *Dragon Ball* becomes the best-selling *manga* in history by the time it concludes its 10 and a half year run in 1995, having sold over 200 million volumes, 230 million volumes in Japan by 2014, and 300 million volumes in total worldwide.[9] In so doing it solidifies itself as the most popular *manga* on Earth.

Dragon Ball catapults Toriyama into superstardom and he becomes a "living god" to the following generations of *manga-ka*. The series goes on to become the quintessential *shōnen manga*, that then influences the creation of *manga* such as *Naruto*, *Wan Pīsu* ("*One Piece*"), and *Burī-chi* ("*Bleach*").[10, 11, 12] It becomes a billion-dollar franchise.

---

8   *Dragon Ball* Chapter 23 is titled *Doragon Chīmu Kaisan* (ドラゴンチーム解散, "*The Dragon Team Parts Ways*") and premieres in *Weekly Shōnen Jump* #23, on May 4, 1985.

9   *Dragon Ball* becomes the best-selling *manga* in history in 1995. *Wan Pīsu* (ワンピース, "*One Piece*") took the #1 spot in 2008. As of 2013, *Wan Pisu* sold over 300 million volumes in Japan, and over 345 million worldwide: *http://goo.gl/DYGnXz*. But in terms of global popularity and recognition, *Dragon Ball* is still the king. *http://goo.gl/Oj0uu0*

10   *Naruto* (ナルト, 1997) is a best-selling *shōnen manga* written by Kishimoto Masashi (岸本 斉史, born November 8, 1974), about a young *ninja* who follows his "*ninja* way." Kishimoto idolizes Akira Toriyama.

11   *Wan Pīsu* (ワンピース, "*One Piece*," 1997) is the world's best-selling *shōnen manga*, written by Oda Eiichirō (尾田 栄一郎, born January 1, 1975), about a young pirate and his traveling crew.

12   *Burīchi* (ブリーチ, "*Bleach*," 2001) is a *shōnen manga* written by Kubo Tite (久保 帯人, born June 26, 1977), about a young man who dies and is reborn as a death god.

It turns Toriyama into the most influential *manga-ka* alive. It generates hundreds of parodies, inspires countless millions to follow their dreams, and as far as I'm concerned, becomes the greatest *manga* ever made.

All of this from a man who says, "I was prepared for it to end after 10 weeks if it wasn't a hit."

Lucky for us, it was.

Origin of Dragon Ball

There is no straight path to *Dragon Ball*. It requires a lifetime of cultural influences, a borderline obsession with watching movies, and a creative artist who writes about what he loves.

But the real spark of the series is when Toriyama's wife makes her astute comment about her atypical husband. This causes Torishima-*san* to capitalize on the idea of a *kanfū manga* and force Toriyama to take action. Our young author isn't fond of that arrangement, but he does the work, stays determined, and through years of effort creates a series that changes the world.

That's the origin of *Dragon Ball*.

Xīyóujì

"I'M THE GREAT Sage equal to heaven!!" declares Sūn Wùkōng before he is slammed under a mountain by the Buddhā. Thus begins the legend of *Xīyóujì* (西遊記, 'shee-yoh-jee,' Japanese: *Saiyūki*, 'sigh-yoo-key,' *"Journey to the West,"* 1592). This is the story that inspires Akira Toriyama's creation of *Dragon Ball* almost 400 years later.

Toriyama uses *Xīyóujì* as the basis of the first story arc of *Dragon Ball*, for the characters, their quest, and the world they adventure through. Some fans think this only applies to the beginning of *Dragon Ball* and that Toriyama then leaves it in the dust, but that's not the case. He borrows bits and pieces at whim, including new characters, settings, martial arts techniques, and spiritual concepts more than 160 chapters into it, including in *"Dragon Ball Z."* So if you lack the knowledge of the story he borrows these concepts from, you won't catch the cultural connections.

That's the problem this chapter solves. We'll explore the parts of *Xīyóujì* that give you a better cultural context in which it's written, how it becomes a huge phenomenon, and then serves as the model for Toriyama's masterpiece. It may feel like a history lesson, but I'd wager that about 99% of *Dragon Ball* fans have never read *Xīyóujì*. I say that because out of the thousands of fans I've met, I only know of one who ever has.

Dragon Ball is a fusion of ancient and modern, and its traditional content is inspired by this Chinese legend. So to understand *Dragon Ball* we first have to understand *Xīyóujì*. Along the way you'll learn about the ancient belief systems that make this story and *Dragon Ball* possible. Most of the deeper aspects and spiritual content of *Dragon Ball* originate here.

Journey to the West

Xīyóujì's origin begins with the Táng Dynasty monk named Xuánzàng (玄奘, 'shoo-en-zahng,' "Great Mystery," 602 – 664 A.D.). He travels to India in the pursuit of *sūtra* ("sacred scriptures"), and in the act of doing so changes the world. Without Xuánzàng there'd be no *Xīyóujì*, and without *Xīyóujì* there'd be no *Dragon Ball*.

It's important to note that he's a monk of the Táng Dynasty (唐朝, Táng-*cháo*, 'tahng chow,' "Boastful Pestle Dynasty," 618 – 907 A.D.). The Táng is considered the height of Chinese civilization and a golden age of culture. Most of what we now call "Japanese culture" is imported from China during this period of time.

Why does he travel to India? Xuánzàng enters a Buddhist monastery at the age of 5, studies the teachings for 15 years, and becomes an ordained monk at the age of 20. He studies both Mahāyāna (Sanskrit: महायान, Chinese: Dàchéng, 大乘, "Great Vehicle") and Hīnayāna (Sanskrit: हीनयान, Chinese: Xiǎochéng, 小乘, "Small Vehicle") Buddhist ideologies, but leans more toward the Mahāyāna concepts because they profess the salvation of all beings and the promulgation of faith to those who wish to learn, rather than just monks. He believes in compassion and feels that it is his duty to help other people become enlightened.

During his years of study he determines that the Chinese translations of the *sūtra* are inadequate, garbled, or misconstrued. In addition, abbots of different monasteries each claim to have the true version of the Buddhā's words, yet their texts have conflicting ideologies or are of dubious origin. Xuánzàng is confused and unable to determine which principles are acceptable.

The only conclusion is that the texts are lacking. So he makes up his mind to return to the source and retrieve the complete and canonical Sanskrit text of the *sūtra*.[1]

He begins his journey to India at the age of 27. Despite his youth it is a difficult trip. The young man requests permission from Chinese authorities to travel into foreign lands, but he is not given clearance because the trip is deemed too dangerous on account of recent attacks on China's western borders by the Turks.

Xuánzàng decides to travel onward after being inspired by a vision from Guānyīn Bodhisattva (Chinese: Guānyīn-*púsà*, 觀音菩薩, 'gwahn-yin poo-sah,' Japanese: Kannon, 観音, Sanskrit: Avalokiteśvara, अवलोकितिश्वर, "the enlightened being who hears your cries").

A *bodhisattva* (Sanskrit: बोधसित्त्व, 'boh-dee-saht-vah,' Chinese: *púsà*, 菩薩, "enlightened existence") is a being who interacts with the world of men to lead people to the Buddhā (Sanskrit: बुद्ध, 'boo-dah,' Chinese: *fó*, 佛, Japanese: *hotoke*, 仏, "enlightened being," or "awakened one").[2] It's common for Westerners to compare Guānyīn Bodhisattva to Saint Mary in the Christian faith, as they both lead people to eternal salvation, and because Guānyīn is depicted as a compassionate woman.

---

1   There are two other well-known monks who make the trek. The first is Fǎxiǎn (法顯, "Manifest Law," 337 – 422 A.D.), who travels west from China to India. The second is Pútídámó (菩提達摩, Japanese: Daruma, 達磨, "Bodhidharma," circa 5th to 6th century A.D.), the patriarch of Chán (禪, Japanese: Zen, 禅, Sanskrit: Dhyāna, ध्यान) Buddhism, who travels east from India to China. Both are difficult journeys made by foot, but neither is as grand as Xuánzàng's.

2   The word *fó* (佛, Japanese: hotoke, "Buddhā") depicts a man (亻) who is not (弗) a man. That is to say, 'a being who looks like a man, but isn't.' The Japanese use this *kanji* until 1947 when *shinjitai* (新字体, "simplified *kanji*") start to be used across the country. Then it's replaced with *hotoke* (仏). The *kanji* used prior to 1947 is called *kyūjitai* (旧字体, "old *kanji*"), and I prefer to use this style because it retains the deeper meaning, like the traditional Chinese *hànzì*.

Since Xuánzàng does not receive the approval of Emperor Táng Tàizōng (唐太宗, January 28, 598 – July 10, 649 A.D.), he leaves China as a fugitive in the darkness of night. Unfortunately, his horse dies at the start of the journey. Then he gets another horse, but he has to trade that one for an old one so he can sneak past the gateways disguised as a man in rags. If that isn't bad enough, he has a travel guide who tries to assassinate him as he sleeps.

When he passes the Yùmén-*guān* (玉門關, "Jade Gate Pass"), the western border of the Táng Empire, he reaches a point of no return. On one side is the well-known and civilized world with its cultural tradition and familiarity, on the other is a foreboding sense of the unknown, the dangers of nature, beast, and man. And this is just in his own country. Can you imagine what happens after he leaves?

For now you're going to have to do that, because I'm skipping it. But throughout *Dragon Ball Culture* I'll detail Xuánzàng's journey as it parallels Toriyama's adaptation.

Return Home

Xuánzàng traverses more than 10,000 kilometers (6,213 miles) on a quest for Buddhist scriptures. He scales three of Asia's highest mountain ranges, survives deserts, dodges bandits, meets with kings, tribal leaders and luminaries, engages in philosophical debates, serves as an unofficial diplomat of China, and does all of this while wearing the humble sandals of a pilgrim.

Upon his return to the ancient capital of Cháng'ān (長安, "Perpetual Peace") he delivers 657 volumes of *sūtra* and seven Buddhā statues into the Báimǎ-*sì* (白馬寺, "White Horse Temple"). His 16 years of adventures are transcribed by one of his disciples in 646 A.D. at the request of the Emperor. They're titled *Dàtáng Xīyóujì* (大唐西遊記, Japanese: *Ōkara Saiyūki*, "*The Journey to the West in the Great Táng*"). This record reveals his journey in meticulous detail and still serves as a historical map and record of the ages. It also provides the name of his adventure that will be elaborated on for centuries to come.[3]

Even though he betrays the imperial restrictions on travel, the Táng Emperor Tàizōng welcomes Xuánzàng home as a scholar and diplomat. He supports his scriptural efforts and has scholars portray him as the iconic monk, and likewise referred to as Táng Sānzàng (唐三藏, "The Three Baskets Monk of Táng"). Because of Imperial support of Buddhism and Xuánzàng's high degree of intellect and fame, the practice flourishes throughout the nation. Xuánzàng spends the remaining years of his life at the Báimǎ-*sì* where he passes away in 664 A.D.

His return home with fresh scriptures leaves a permanent mark on East Asian society. But it's his cultural influence and fame that inspires *Xīyóujì* and *Dragon Ball*.

Xuánzàng's Influence

Xuánzàng's story is both true as well as legendary, and he is lauded as the quintessential monk—responsible for the surviving continuity and spread of Buddhism into China, preserving it as a major faith. Without Xuánzàng, Buddhist thought in India would have been lost forever, replaced by the growing resurgence of Hinduism and the invasion of Islam. Buddhism is ultimately lost in India, but a renewed Buddhism lives on in China, Korea, and Japan thanks to

---

3   Cháng'ān (長安, "Perpetual Peace") is the ancient name of Xī'ān (西安, "Western Peace"). At the time of Xuánzàng's journey, Cháng'ān is a capital city and gateway to the western regions. This is why he leaves from, and returns to, this city.

Xuánzàng and other Buddhist adventurers and teachers.

Xuánzàng is heralded as one of the greatest scholars in China's history. His translations are considered authoritative because of his mastery of the language and the intricacies of the finer esoteric principles that he gained while studying under the Indian masters.[4] His translations serve as models for other monks and lead to the establishment or revitalization of new schools of Buddhist thought in China and Japan. These new philosophies reinvigorate Chinese Buddhism. So not only is he a scholar, but one of the greatest Buddhā Law (Sanskrit: *dhárma*, धर्म, Chinese: *fófǎ*, 佛法, Japanese: *buppō*) masters of his age. Monks from Korea and Japan hear of his expertise and travel great distances to become one of his disciples.

In addition to bringing back the 657 volumes, he brings Buddhist artworks that are emulated by artisans and monks. The likenesses founded upon these arts establish the groundwork for Sino-Japanese artistic representations of the Buddhā, Bodhisattvas, and their heavenly realms for over one thousand years to come. These illustrations define

---

4   By the end of Xuánzàng's life, he and his team of disciples are credited with the transcription of over 1,000 scrolls from Sanskrit to Chinese, and the training of countless monks in the Yogācāra (Sanskrit: योगाचार, "one whose practice is *yoga*," Chinese: Wéishí-*zōng*, 唯識宗 "Consciousness-Only School," Japanese: Yuishiki, 唯識, "Consciousness-Only") system of cultivation and Indian logic. *Yoga* (Sanskrit: योग, Chinese: *yújiā*, 瑜伽, "to yoke") is the practice of unifying the mind and body to attain liberation. His translation of these texts comes to be called the *Yújiā shī de lùn* (瑜伽師地論, *"Treatise on the Stages of Yoga Practice"*). He also translates an unabridged version of the *Mahāprajñāpāramitā Sūtra* (Sanskrit: प्रज्ञापारमिता, Chinese: *Dà bōrě bōluómì duō xīnjīng*, 大般若波羅蜜多心經, *"Great Heart Sūtra"*), that is eighty-four times the length of the Bible, the *Saddharma Puṇḍarīka Sūtra* (Chinese: *Miàofǎ liánhuá jīng*, 妙法蓮華經, *"Lotus Sūtra of the Marvelous Law"*), and countless others which would have been lost in India.

the look and feel of the depictions of these beings for all the monks, lay believers, playwrights, and poets to follow, including Toriyama. Buddhist culture as we know it would not exist without *Xuánzàng*.

Xuánzàng's Fame

You can't write stuff this good; you can only elaborate on it. So that's what poets, artists, and playwrights do.

In the book *Xuanzang: A Buddhist Pilgrim on the Silk Road* (1997) by Salley Hovey Wriggins, she quotes the British archeologist and explorer Aurel Stein (1862 – 1943) as saying, "The dangers and quasi-miraculous escape that marked the beginning of Xuánzàng's travels were neither exaggerated nor fictionalized. Both his memorable desert crossing and his vision (of Guānyīn Bodhisattva) at the beginning of his 10,000-kilometer journey in search of truth embody the universal elements of a hero's quest. The Buddhist monk was not simply traveling over thousands of miles of dangerous deserts and mountains as if he were a Chinese Marco Polo;[5] he was on a pilgrimage of the soul. His was both an inward and an outward journey; therefore, it carried an aura of special value."

Xuánzàng's real-life hero's quest serves to inspire future adventurers and becomes a timeless part of popular culture. He is considered a genuine hero of a spiritual epic while alive, and his legend grows greater after his death. His name can be heard among denizens at bars, in folktales, and in bedtime stories told to children.

---

5   Marco Polo (September 15, 1254 – January 8, 1324) is an Italian adventurer who traveled to China and back, among other places, helping to establish cultural exchange between the East and West. His journey is similar to Xuánzàng's, but in the opposite direction.

The Buddhism that Xuánzàng strives to save becomes the springboard for wild fancy and additions to his life story. Like a century's-long game of telephone where something new gets added at every telling, his fame becomes embellished and turned into a larger than life folktale. Buddhist and Dàoist magic, deities in heaven and hell, mystical creatures and talking animals, you name it. That's because at the same time this is happening there are tales being passed around about a Monkey King, his violent rise to power, and his mischievous antics. So having completed his journey in the 7th century, Xuánzàng has gained a group of humanoid animal companions by the 10th century. And it grows more outlandish from there.

From the 13th century onward there is evidence that theatrical plays and narrative poems are written about Xuánzàng's journey to entertain the masses. For example, *Dàtáng sānzàng qǔjīng shīhuà* (大唐三藏取經詩話, "*Tripiṭaka of the Great Táng Seeks the Scriptures, a Tale with Verse*," circa 1280), *Xīyóujì zájù* (西遊記雜劇, "*Journey to the West Drama*," circa the 14th century), and *Qítiān-dàshèng zájù* (齊天大聖雜劇, "*Variety Drama on The Great Sage Equal to Heaven*," circa 1450). This material parallels much of what we find in *Xīyóujì*, so it allows us to see the progression from actual events in Xuánzàng's life to the fanciful and theatrical additions that make it more dramatic, both on stage and in books. It's the pop culture entertainment of medieval China just as *Dragon Ball* is the pop culture entertainment of late 20th century Japan.

By the late 16th century when the *Xīyóujì* novel is written, Xuánzàng's journey is well established and these countless fables aid the authors endeavor.

Writing Xīyóujì

This story about a traveling monk and his companions circulates around China for almost 1,000 years before an author decides to write it down in the form that we know today as *Xīyóujì*. This author's identity has been debated for centuries, but is most often credited to Wú Chéng'ēn (吳承恩, c. 1500 – 1582 A.D.). It's a book that just about everybody in China and Japan is familiar with, but who is the man who wrote it?

Wú Chéng'ēn is born in Liánshuǐ-*xiàn* (漣水縣, "Rippling Water County"), Jiāngsū (江苏, "River Province"), in the east of China during the Míng Dynasty (Dà Míng, 大明, "Great Brightness," 1368 – 1644 A.D.).[6] He is born into an unsuccessful merchant family but receives a traditional Confucian education at the prestigious Nánjīng Dàxué (南京大學, "Nánjīng University"). There he studies the Confucian classics, such as *Lúnyǔ* (論語, "*Analects*," circa 476 – 221 B.C.), and becomes a poet and master of classical prose. He then earns a job as a provincial level civil servant. However, despite his writing talents and education he repeatedly fails the higher level civil service exams that would lead to a greater career. It isn't until his career is over that he dedicates himself to writing *Xīyóujì*. He doesn't finish the story until he's in his 60s. It requires around 10 years of his life to complete, is one of the last things he ever does, and is considered his greatest accomplishment. The complete *Xīyóujì* consists of 100 chapters spread across approximately 2,500 pages when translated into English.

The book remains relatively unknown for decades because it's fashionable in these times for an author to first

---

6   Wú Chéng'ēn is born in Liánshuǐ-*xiàn*, the northernmost county of Huái'ān (淮安, "Huái River of Peace") in Jiāngsū, China. For this reason Huái'ān is often called his hometown.

share a written work among friends and other educated writers for amusement. But the technological advances of the Míng period in the 16th century lead to a boom in printing, and *Xīyóujì* becomes one of the first books printed in great numbers. Nevertheless, the book's first edition isn't published until 10 years after his death, in 1592.

Afterward, *Xīyóujì* becomes one of the *sìdà míngzhù* (四大名著, "four great masterpieces") of Chinese literature alongside *Shuǐhǔ Zhuàn* (水滸傳, "*Water Margin,*" 1589 A.D.), *Sānguó Yǎnyì* (三國演義, "*Romance of the Three Kingdoms,*" circa 14th century), and *Hóng Lóu Mèng* (紅樓夢, "*Dream of the Red Chamber,*" circa 16th century). Each of these novels cultivates a man's soul by reading them, and for the next 300 years it is held that you are not educated until you have studied each of them to the point where you can debate them in a scholarly manner. Indeed, soon after *Xīyóujì* is published it becomes an integral part of the imperial examinations in the Confucian order. That is to say, you can't get a government job in China without reading this book!

Xīyóujì is iconic within China as a representation of both traditional Chinese culture as well as an extended analogy of the journey toward enlightenment. It is regarded as one of the world's first novels and stands as one of the most important literary works ever created.

But the key point to understand here is that *Xīyóujì* is not the product of one man. It's the culmination of thousands of years of culture, real life events, and dramatic additions that become the pop culture of its time. Wú Chéng'ēn wasn't the first to come up with the idea, but he did do the hard work of combining these ideas together in a written narrative structure told in an episodic format. Toriyama does the same thing with *Dragon Ball* 400 years later.

Three Belief Systems

Before we get into *Xīyóujì's* story we need to discuss the belief systems that add mysticism to Xuánzàng's journey, because the cultural content of *Xīyóujì* establishes the cultural framework of *Dragon Ball*.

The three major belief systems in China are Buddhism, Dàoism, and Confucianism. They are syncretized together into a cultural milieu that produces countless works of art, language, and metaphysical thought. The culture of China is synonymous with its belief systems.

Buddhism

Buddhism (Chinese: *fó-jiā*, 佛家, "School of the Enlightened") is a belief system comprised of the teachings of Śākyamuni (Sanskrit: सिद्धार्थबुद्ध, 'sahkyah-moonee,' Chinese: Shì-jiāmóuní, 釋迦牟尼, Japanese: Shakamuni, 563 – 483 B.C.), an Indian prince who leaves the secular world and enlightens to the Buddhā Law, becoming a Buddhā and offering salvation to others.

It's primary focus is *shàn* (善, "compassion") and *cíbēi* (慈悲, "mercy"). The principle tenet is that all beings experience suffering because of ignorance; there is a way to end this suffering; and this way is by following the Buddhā Law. When the cessation of ignorance and desires has been accomplished, the practitioner attains enlightenment and becomes a Buddhā.

Buddhism is an export of India that is promulgated in China, flourishes, and transforms Chinese culture.

Dàoism

Dàoism (Chinese: *dào-jiā*, 道家, "School of the Way") is the native belief system of China. The patriarch of Dàoist thought is Lǎozi (老子, 'low-zuh,' "Old One," circa the Zhōu Dynasty (周朝, Zhōu-*cháo*, "Circumference Dynasty," 1046 – 256 B.C.). He teaches the Dào (道, 'dow,' "way," or "path") that leads to immortality. The *hànzì* of *dào* is comprised of *shǒu* (首, "head") above a radical of *chuò* (辶, "walking"), and suggests a person walking down a road.

Its primary focus is *zhēn* (真, 'zhun,' "truth"). The principle tenet is that this world is a false reality and our human notions are nothing but illusory constructs formed by living in society. Dàoists believe that the purpose of being human is to return to our original, true self, and attain the Dào, becoming a *zhēnrén* (真人, "true man"). We do so by living in accordance with the way of nature and following the truth. We go beyond the dualism of *yīn* (陰, "darkness") and *yáng* (陽, "brightness") and return to the void of nothingness.

Confucianism

Confucianism (Chinese: 儒家, *rú-jiā*, "School of Scholars") is a modified subset of Dàoism. Its founder is Kǒngfūzǐ (孔夫子, "Confucius," 551 – 479 B.C.).

Its primary focus is *yì* (義, "righteousness," or "justice"). The principle tenet is that when the individual is perfect, society will be perfect. Societal harmony is established by living in accordance with human nature, improving moral character, following customs, and maintaining relationships. Upon mastery of these concepts a man becomes a sage. Confucianism is the foundation of East Asian society.

Separate but United

Each of these three belief systems can stand alone, but what's unique about China is that they mix the three of them together over the course of 2,500 years of civilization. The result is a society so interwoven with its belief systems that you cannot separate one from the other. This means that a person can believe in the Buddhā Law, ascribe to the Dàoist principles of truth and be unattached to society, while at the same time have an ideal Confucian family and be a productive member of society. *Xīyóujì* writes about these belief systems in a way that makes them seem like one unified faith. Even though Buddhists often oppose Dàoists, and vice versa, they're still part of the same cosmos. It's this dynamic interplay between the belief systems that enlivens the story.

Wú Chéng'ēn isn't an ordained Buddhist or a Dàoist ascetic; he's a Confucian scholar. Yet he manages to understand both of the other faiths so well that he can write them into his story with precise detail. He fills his book with quotes from the Buddhist *sūtra* and Dàoist poetry.

Part of the reason why he can do this is because he's well-read. But the other part is because he, like Toriyama, is a product of his environment. The Buddho-Dàoist-Confucian synthesis contained within *Xīyóujì* is a reflection of how Chinese people view the world at this period of time. Wú grows up in this environment and his worldview is shaped by it. He grows up hearing these stories about Xuánzàng and his animal companions and then makes the monumental effort to write them down in a book. Toriyama experiences the same thing 400 years later by watching movies and TV series based on *Xīyóujì* and then makes the monumental effort to write his own version in a *manga*.

Three Realms

The syncretism of the three belief systems creates a cosmological framework where the deities of each system coexist alongside one another in three distinct yet interwoven realms. These are called the *sānjiè* (三界, Japanese: *sankai*, "three realms"), and refer to heaven, earth, and hell.[7]

Each of the three realms is its own dimension of space and time consisting of different sized particles. The lighter and more refined the particles, the higher the realm and the beings within it; and vice versa. So the beings in heaven are more beautiful and lighter than the coarse and heavy beings in hell, with mankind in-between.

The beings that live within these realms are the *tiānrén* (天人, Japanese: *tennin*, "heavenly people"), *rén* (人, Japanese: *ren*, or *nin*, "people," or "mankind"), and *dìyùrén* (地狱人, Japanese: *jigokunin*, "hell people"). "Mankind" refers to Earth-born humans, aliens, animals, and all life forms made of molecules within this dimensional plane; not just those on Earth. Toriyama uses this idea in *Dragon Ball*, with Earthlings and aliens who die and go to a universal afterlife, and then to heaven or hell.

Depending on different sectarian beliefs, there are either 27 levels of heaven in Buddhism or 81 levels of heaven in Dàoism, along with 18 levels of hell. Each level is sub-divided into upper, middle, and lower. Beyond these three realms are empty realms consisting of formless and eternal beings. The levels increase in magnitude and beauty with every step upward. Toriyama uses this idea to ensure there is always a higher level to ascend to in Gokū's adventure, with gods above gods.

---

7   The Buddhist hell is not an eternal damnation, but a lower realm in which beings reincarnate in order to repay their *karma*, and then reincarnate in another realm.

According to Buddhist beliefs the three realms are created by higher level beings beyond the three realms in order to give sentient beings one last chance to awaken. It's held by Buddhists and Dàoists that the cosmos has deviated over time from the higher standards held at its creation, with the myriad forms of existence losing their virtue and heading toward destruction. Likewise that each of us either falls into this maze from higher realms due to ignorance and poor choices, or we choose to come here in order to enlighten to these higher standards. Therefore our suffering is our opportunity to awaken to the truth and return to our original selves and positions in higher realms.

This world is an illusion and it's time for you to wake up and return to your home.

Saṃsāra

As a result of being trapped within the three realms, we experience *saṃsāra* (Sanskrit: संसार, Chinese: *lúnhuí*, 輪迴, Japanese: *rinne*, "transmigration"), the cycle of reincarnation from one body to the next as we die and are reborn.[8]

---

8   Our spirits go through *saṃsāra* within the *liùdào* (Chinese: 六道, Japanese: *rokudō*, "six paths"). This Buddhist concept maintains that all beings are suffering within one of six states of existence. These six *gati* (Sanskrit: गति, "movements") within the wheel of the *liùdào* are: beings in hell (Sanskrit: *naraka-gati*, नरक, Chinese: *dìyùdào*, 地獄道, Japanese: *jigokudō*), hungry ghosts (Sanskrit: *preta-gati*, प्रेतगति, Chinese: *èguǐdào*, 餓鬼道, Japanese: *gakidō*), animals (Sanskrit: *tiryagyōni-gati*, तिर्यग्योनिगति, Chinese: *chùshēngdào*, 畜生道, Japanese, *chikushōdō*), *ásura* (Sanskrit: *ásura-gati*, असुरगति, Chinese: *āxiūluódào*, 阿修羅道, Japanese: *ashuradō*, "demons"), humans (Sanskrit: *manusya-gati*, मनुष्यगति, Chinese: *réndào*, 人道, Japanese: *nindō*), and *deva* (Sanskrit: *deva-gati*, Sanskrit: देवगति, Chinese: *tiāndào*, 天道, Japanese: *tendō*, "gods").

Your *karma* (Sanskrit: करम, Chinese: *yèlì*, 業力), an accumulation of metaphysical and spiritual debt, determines the realm into which you are reborn, the type of being you become, and your fortune in each life. The lower the level and the more *karma* you carry on your consciousness, the more suffering you experience and the shorter your life, in accordance with the retribution of your *karma*. In contrast, the more *dé* (德, 'duh,' "virtue") you carry, the more blessings and the longer your life.

However, even the vast multitude of gods within heaven are subject to eventual death and rebirth, including the celestial kings. You can live for millions of years and have every desire fulfilled, but you'll still die. And without hardships, there is no way to pay off *karma*. The only way out of this cycle of suffering is to have a human body and attain enlightenment by either following the Buddhā Law or the Dào and escape the system of life and death. Therefore, the only beings who are beyond the three realms, the six paths, and life and death, are the Buddhās, Dàos, and gods of higher levels. And the only way to get there is to first jump into the world of delusion. This is why it's best to be reborn as a human.

This belief creates a rich tapestry for humans, deities, demons, animals, and ghosts, to interact. If you want to escape the cycle of suffering and exist forever, then you'll need to seek the Buddhā Law or the Dào. This means you have to find a way to cultivate your mind and body, and that means facing both inner and outer demons. At the heart of this is conflicts with yourself or others. And conflicts are at the heart of every great story.

This is the worldview of the Chinese people that is held for thousands of years. It's why Xuánzàng travels to India. He returns to the source to recover the canonical *sūtra* that will save mankind.

Xīyóujì's Story

Imagine a world filled with *gōngfu* masters, beautiful Chinese landscapes, dragons, talking animals, magic, gods, demons, and an epic quest that brings a band of adventurers together. Sounds like *Dragon Ball*, right?

Xīyóujì is an illustration of the pilgrimage of the individual soul toward enlightenment in the Buddhā Law system of cultivation. Along the way the pilgrims defeat monsters, help the common people, and learn right from wrong. It combines Buddhist, Dàoist, and Confucian ideals into a story built on reality but fused with creative cultural tales.

Oddly enough the story does not begin with Xuánzàng; It begins with Sūn Wùkōng (孫悟空, 'soon woo-kong,' Japanese: Son Gokū, "Monkey Grandchild Aware of Emptiness"). He is also called the Měihóu-*wáng* (美猴王, 'may-hoh-wahng,' Japanese: Bikō-ō, "Handsome Monkey King") and Qítiān-*dàshèng* (齊天大聖, 'chee-tee-en dah-shuhng,' "Great Sage Equal to Heaven"). This is the character that inspires Son Gokū in *Dragon Ball*.

The start of the story reveals Sūn Wùkōng's origin, rise to power, quest for immortality, and ascension into heaven where he causes chaos by fighting the gods. The forces of heaven try to stop him, but he is too powerful. They have no choice but to call upon Buddhā for help. Buddhā arrives, out tricks the trickster, and slams Sūn underneath a mountain. He is forced to stay there for 500 years and to eat a hot iron pellet each day as penance for his crimes until a Buddhist monk comes to relieve him of his suffering.

Five hundred years later we are introduced to Xuánzàng, the Táng Monk. He receives a vision of his true identity in a dream. Then, while holding a religious ceremony he is approached by Guānyīn Bodhisattva who reveals that he has been chosen by Buddhā to embark on a great journey.

Xuánzàng has experienced several rounds of reincarnation up to this point, and it is in this life that he is deemed fit to take on this divine mission. Guānyīn gives him the name Sānzàng, which is the Chinese translation of the *tripiṭaka* (Sanskrit: त्रिपिटक, Chinese: *sānzàng*, 三藏, Japanese: *sanzō*, "three baskets") of *sūtra* he is sent to recover.

Tripiṭaka refers to the *sūtra* lectures, the monastic precepts, and the systematic philosophy written down by the Indian monks hundreds of years after Śākyamuni Buddhā's death.[9] Since the pilgrim's quest is to retrieve the *tripiṭaka*, he is given the same honorary name in Chinese.

Xuánzàng is the character that inspires Buruma in *Dragon Ball*, the girl who meets Son Gokū in Chapter 1 and takes him on her adventure to retrieve the dragon balls, just as the monk does with Sūn Wùkōng to retrieve the *sūtra*.

Sānzàng tells the Táng Emperor of his providence. The Emperor declares that Sānzàng is now his sworn younger brother and gives him the surname Táng (唐), after the Dynasty itself. Táng Sānzàng (唐三藏, "The Three Baskets Monk of Táng"), as he's likewise known, is compelled by the spirit of Guānyīn to leave the safety of China and thrust himself into harm's way for the sake of others.

You can see how parts of the story are based on the genuine history of Xuánzàng's life, while others are embellished or fanciful. But in both cases the monk believes that if the Buddhā Law can take root in China, then it will bring enlightenment to sentient beings throughout the world.

---

9   Śākyamuni Buddhā's teachings are not written down until hundreds of years after his death because his teachings are passed down verbally, from heart to heart. It is with the establishment of religions and philosophies based on these teachings that they are codified into a canonical text. So the texts in India are the most authoritative versions of his original words, but these are likewise abstracted through word of mouth and the passage of time. It is from these texts that the majority of Buddhist teachings are derived.

Gathering Disciples

The monk now has three names, but that's not going to help him on the journey. He needs muscle. That's why he is given heavenly aid in the form of four guardians who swear to protect him from demons and other foul creatures.

Of course, he doesn't know he's going to receive these companions, and they forget that he's ever going to visit them, after being told of his impending arrival by Guānyīn.

Along the way he encounters Sūn Wùkōng trapped under the mountain. He frees the Monkey King from his *karmic* prison, but he is violent, wild, and unmanageable. In order to control him, Guānyīn gives Xuánzàng a magical diadem that the Monkey King is tricked into wearing. A diadem is a circular band that is worn around the head. This one is called the *jīngāng-lún* (金刚轮, Japanese: *kongō-rin*, "thunderbolt ring," "lightning bolt circle," or "*vajra* diadem").[10] After Sūn puts on the diadem it binds itself around his head and tightens whenever the monk chants *sūtra*, causing such intense and instantaneous pain that it's like being struck by lightning. The external tool forces him to control his inner mind by changing his behavior to avoid suffering. After some conflicts and conversations about proper Buddhist non-violence, Xuánzàng makes him his first disciple. The two are now Buddhist pilgrims on a sacred mission, and Sūn Wùkōng becomes his sworn bodyguard to protect the monk in order to repay his *karmic* debt against heaven.

After this they meet Zhū Bājiè (豬八戒, 'zhoo bah-jieh,' Japanese: Cho-hakkai, "Pig of Eight Restraints"), the man-pig. He is a former field marshal of the heavenly army who is exiled from heaven because of his drunken and lustful

---

10   Sūn Wùkōng's *jīngāng-lún* is shaped as a diadem made of metal. It is often designed as a simple metal bar with the two ends meeting in the front of the forehead and then curling back onto themselves.

actions against the moon goddess at a party. Then during the reincarnation process on Earth there is a bureaucratic error and he ends up inside of a mother pig instead of a woman. Despite his bad luck, he still wishes to repay his *karmic* debts and return to his origin. He becomes the monks' second disciple. This is the character that inspires Ūron in *Dragon Ball*.

Next the pilgrims are attacked by Shā Wùjìng (沙悟淨, 'shah woo-jing,' Japanese: Sa-gojō, "Sand Aware of Purity"), a demon who lives in a sand-filled river and attempts to eat the monk. He is a former general in heaven who breaks a crystal bowl by accident and is condemned to Earth to repay his *karmic* debt. He becomes the monks' third disciple. This is the character that inspires Yamucha in *Dragon Ball*.

Often forgotten but still important is the Táng Monks' white horse. He is Bái Lóngmǎ (白龍馬, 'buy lohng-mah,' Japanese: Shiro-ryūma, "White Dragon Horse"), a dragon prince who commits sins in a previous life by disobeying his father. He also wishes to return to his original, true self. In order to do so he becomes the monks' beast of burden and carries him and his luggage to their destination and back. It's my belief that this character inspires Buruma's white motorcycle in the first chapter of *Dragon Ball*. But this is a loose connection and he otherwise does not play a role in Toriyama's story.

Toriyama confirms that these characters are the inspiration for the characters in *Dragon Ball* in *Daizenshū 2*. He says, "Buruma was Xuánzàng, Ūron was Zhū Bājiè, and Yamucha was Shā Wùjìng."

Xuánzàng's life story appears to be about his solo adventure and how he overcomes the challenges by himself, but in *Xīyóujì* it's about a group of people with a similar cause. Sūn Wùkōng is powerful but is nevertheless bound to protect his master and can't complete the journey without the others. Zhū, Shā, and Bái are also supernormal, but they rely on one another and tackle challenges together. With that said, Sūn Wùkōng still loves to fight on his own, in the same way that Son Gokū prefers to fight his opponents by himself but will rely on his friends when he has to.

This assemblage marks the start of their adventure.

Hardship and Liberation

These five pilgrims accrued *karma* in previous lives and are trapped in the maze of life on Earth. In order to pay back their debts and attain liberation they must endure 81 hardships as they head west.[11]

There are exactly 81 hardships because the number 9 in Chinese implies a looping circuit or boundlessness. To complete the '9 times 9' implies a full circuit and return to your origin, in the process transcending the space and time boundaries of the three realms. Failure to pass a single trial means the pilgrims cannot escape the cycle of *saṃsāra* and reach the other shore of *nirvāṇa* (Sanskrit: निर्वाण, Chinese: *nièpán*, 涅槃, Japanese: *nehan*, "liberation," "extinguishing," or "blown out").[12]

With these four converted Buddhist guardians at his side, Xuánzàng overcomes wild animals, demon kings, a devil

---

11   One of the reasons the pilgrims head west, in addition to the geographical logic, is that in Chinese culture the Buddhā and his paradise are located in the west. "*Dàodōng fóxī* (道東佛西, "Dào to the east, Buddhā to the west")." This creates a poetic parallel between their physical journey and their spiritual journey, in that the closer they move toward the *sūtra*, the closer they move toward heaven. When they retrieve the *sūtra*, they achieve enlightenment.

12   *Nirvāṇa* is the Buddhist concept of extinguishing desires and attachments to achieve a state of non-dual bliss, or enlightenment. Liberation from the cycle of *saṃsāra*.

tiger, sexy ladies, corrupt politicians, foul weather, con-artists, pirates, super-humans, shapeshifters, evil miasmas, and inner nightmares on his way toward the *sūtra*.

When they finally make it to the monastery in India they receive the *sūtra*, but the documents are blank. That's because they had only undergone 80 of the trials. However, they are unaware that the *sūtra* are blank and unaware of this holy requirement. Then on the way back to China they are attacked by a giant golden eagle that is a manifestation of the Buddhā. The Buddhā does this to gauge their emotional reaction and see if they will be willing to travel all the way *back* to the monastery. When they show their conviction and willingness to return, he teleports them back in an instant and gives them the real *sūtra*. It is because of their determination and resilience that they complete the 81st hardship, repay their *karmic* debt, and complete their mission on Earth.

Having fulfilled their destiny and improved their moral character, they now meet the standard of heaven and can return to their original positions. At this point there is nothing left to learn because they learned their lessons in the journey of life. It is only through the perils and struggles, lies, deception, mistrust, mortal dangers, temptation, and reconciliation that the pilgrims become mature. The external situations allow for internal improvements.

The travelers are liberated and transcend life and death as Buddhās and gods. Xuánzàng becomes the *tán-gōngdé-fó* (檀功德佛, Sanskrit: *Candana-puṇya* Buddhā, चंदनपुण्यबुद्ध, "Sandalwood Buddhā," or "Buddhā of Virtue"),[13] in accordance with his virtuous merits.

Sūn Wùkōng raises his hands to feel for the *jīngāng-lún* that restrains his violent tendencies, but finds that it has vanished from his brow. He transforms his inner mind

---

13   Sandalwood is a symbol of virtue and merit in Buddhism, so Xuánzàng's title refers to the virtue that he accrues during his journey.

along the journey, so the external tool disappears. At this moment he ascends as the *dòu-zhànshèng-fó* (鬥戰勝佛, "Buddhā Victorious in Fighting").[14]

Because Zhū Bājiè has not thoroughly removed his lust or hunger, but still performs good deeds and accrues virtue, he is honored as the sacred *jìngtán-shǐzhě* (淨壇使者, "Altar Cleanser Envoy") who travels to sacrificial altars across the world and eats the food.

Shā Wùjìng is raised to the level of *jīnshēn-luóhàn* (金身羅漢, "Golden-bodied Arhat"),[15] escaping the cycle of *saṃsāra*.

And Bái Lóngmǎ transforms into a *wèibābù-tiānlóngmǎ* (為八部天龍馬, "Heavenly Dragon Horse of the Eight Classes") and soars into the skies.

In the end they recover the *sūtra* and gain enlightenment, return to their origin, and forever provide assistance to the people of the world. These are the Buddhist, Dàoist, and Confucian ideals rolled into one perfect ending.

Analogy of Life

The reason the story of *Xīyóujì* is so popular is because it is an analogy of life.

Xīyóujì serves as a fantastic representation of Xuánzàng's historical quest mixed with Chinese fables, popular beliefs, and religious overtones. It's this combination of religion and reality that makes it appealing. But beyond the adventure itself, the underlying message of the story is that the

---

14 Sūn Wùkōng's ascended title is also written as *dòu-zhàn-fó* (鬥戰佛, "War Fighting Buddhā"). This name has clear parallels with Son Gokū in *Dragon Ball*, with his love of fighting.

15 An Arhat (Sanskrit: अर्हत्, Chinese: *luóhàn*, 羅漢, Japanese: *arakan*, 阿羅漢, "worthy one") is an awakened being who transcends life and death. The first level of enlightenment, below Bodhisattva.

characters improve themselves amid ever-increasing hardships. It's the same idea in *Dragon Ball*, and this is why the series is so popular. *Dragon Ball* makes us want to believe that we are inherently good and can improve ourselves. That even if we make mistakes, we can find redemption and salvation. We have to lose in order to gain, and these stories remind us that it's okay to suffer for a nobler cause.

Readers are taken on a pilgrimage of the mind. Each sub-story within the book's 100 chapters has analogies and ethical lessons on how to overcome hatred, greed, lust, desire, and how to learn humility, mercy, honesty, and bravery against the difficulties of human existence. The story contains profound wisdom and pragmatic concepts as well as complete nonsense and unrealism, balanced through poetry, physical combat, and satire. Each of the animalistic characters appears human, with their own frailties and passions. They shine light on our weaknesses and provide insights into our humanity. Through seeing their hypocrisy as they fall short of their ideals, we reflect on our shortcomings and strive to make our ideals real.

The story is an epic treatise on mankind's position in our world and the meaning of life. It teaches by example that we can unlearn our vices and learn virtues. Or as I like to put it, stop doing the bad things and keep doing the good things. The external progress of the pilgrims is dependent upon their internal spiritual progress and ability to align themselves with the higher standards of their faith. When they comply with the ethics of their belief systems, they make breakthroughs.

This is an important concept to understand, because in previous era's of Chinese thought a man could not repay all of his *karma* in one lifetime: you had to go through several rounds of reincarnation. But as these belief systems evolved over time they lead to the popular idea in Wú Chéng'ēn's era that self-enlightenment can be achieved in a single lifetime by learning the principle of cause and effect. Selfish acts lead to increased suffering while sacrifice leads to the cessation of suffering and the attainment of liberation. There is cyclical retribution or reward for your deeds, words, and thoughts, until you learn what you need to learn and improve your character. It's the process of retribution that brings miracles.

This becomes a common theme in Buddhist stories of the later Míng Dynasty, such as *Xīyóujì* and another novel called *Jīnpíngméi* (金瓶梅, *"Golden Lotus,"* 1610).[16] Now it is possible to pay back your debts and receive blessings by walking the arduous path of self-cultivation. And it's the widespread distribution of these stories to the masses that helps spread the message that a person can attain self-liberation if they have both a will and a way. The characters in the stories get to heaven by walking the pilgrim's path through hell. That means the reader can too.

The closest parallel *Xīyóujì* has in the West is *The Pilgrim's Progress* (1678) by John Bunyan (November 28, 1628 – August 31, 1688 A.D.). This is a story of a man named Christian who experiences a dream and travels from the "City of Destruction" (i.e. Earth) to the "Celestial City" (i.e. heaven) to repent for his sins and attain salvation in Christ. The Italian poet Dante Alighieri's (1265 – 1321 A.D.) *Le Comedia* (*"Divine Comedy,"* ~1321) is another iconic example. Here Dante tells the story of a man who seeks beauty and finds it by traversing through hell, purgatory, and heaven.

These are both similar to the *Xīyóujì* story, with the difference being that the pilgrims in *Xīyóujì* attain *self*-realization and liberation. This is owing to the differences in culture, with the Eastern culture focused on inward, self-realization, and the Western culture focused on outward salvation through a higher power. It's the difference between target-

---

16 *Jīnpíngméi* (金瓶梅, *"Golden Lotus"*) is a masterpiece alongside *Xīyóujì* and the other classics mentioned above. It tells a tale of the lurid sexual affairs of a nobleman and his consorts.

ing the 'soul' or targeting the 'mind.' The elevation of the mind and heart through enlightenment is at the core of the three belief systems of China. But even in *Xīyóujì* the adventurers receive external assistance from the divine and are spurred on by happenstance and providence in pursuit of external objects.

This idea of self-realization from within combined with divine intervention from without is weaved into *Xīyóujì*. It's no surprise then that Toriyama's version of *Xīyóujì* should share these traits and have such an inspirational impact on its readers. For while Gokū is on his quest he often receives external assistance from the gods, but it's his own efforts that allow him to get there in the first place and to overcome the challenges at hand. This causes you to adopt a similar worldview in your own struggles in life.

The authors of such stories mix historical truths with fantasy and moral ethics to instill a set of true principles in the hopes of waking the reader up and helping them correct their incorrect ways.

Now let's discover why Toriyama chooses *Xīyóujì* as his model for *Dragon Ball*, and see how he adapts the story in his own style.

Toriyama's Xīyóujì

ARTISTS LOOK TO the past for inspiration. The Táng Monk is inspired to take his journey because of Buddhist teachings and artwork created by men who lived before him. His journey then inspires artists to exaggerate his life and turn it into a legend. This legend becomes one of the most popular tales in Asia, and then 400 years later Toriyama grows up with this story and repeats the process by creating *Dragon Ball*. This further inspires hundreds of millions of people to live to the fullest, become artists, and follow their dreams. *Xīyóujì* is the bridge that connects the real-life Xuánzàng with the fanciful *Dragon Ball*.

Why does Toriyama choose to use *Xīyóujì* as a model? He says in *Daizenshū 2*, "Since *Dr. Slump* had been in a Western scenery, I decided to change that impression and make my new work have a Chinese scenery. And if I was going to give it a Chinese feel, I thought I would make the story based on *Saiyūki*. *Saiyūki* is absurd and has adventurous elements, so I guess I decided to make a slightly modernized *Saiyūki*. I thought it would be easy if that story served as the basis, since all I would have to do would be to arrange things."

Using *Xīyóujì* (*Saiyūki*) seems easy because of the 5,000 years of Chinese culture baked into the story. It seems easy because this culture permeates every aspect of East Asian society, and the book's title, content, and characters are common knowledge. And it seems easy because even though it has a moral lesson and a lot of spirituality, it's also "absurd" and has fighting and supernormal powers.

If you're going to do something "Chinese," then you might as well use the most well-known Chinese story in Japan as your model. By basing his story on *Xīyóujì* he gains the power to tap into a collective consciousness that recognizes the work. The audience feels a positive sensation for the *manga* before they read it because they already love the original. They grow up with *Xīyóujì*, so they are primed to feel the same way about Toriyama's version.

While *Dragon Ball* is not a clone of *Xīyóujì*, the parallels are abundant. Sometimes these are obvious, such as with Son Gokū and Sūn Wùkōng, but in other cases they're left to the viewer's recognition of the source material.

Let's take a look at how *Xīyóujì* inspires Toriyama's masterpiece, and how it then inspires fans across the world.

Xīyóujì or Saiyūki?

I switch between the use of *Xīyóujì* and *Saiyūki* because *Xīyóujì* is the original Chinese name of the story, while *Saiyūki* is the Japanese equivalent translated in the mid-17th to early 18th century.[1] It's a Chinese story filled with Chinese culture, so it makes more sense to refer to it in its original Chinese. The exception to this rule is when Toriyama or one of the other staff members behind *Dragon Ball* refer to the story as *Saiyūki*. In this case I quote them verbatim, because

---

1   According to *The Indiana Companion to Traditional Chinese Literature: Volume 1* (1986, by William H. Nienhauser, Jr., p. 304), the proper translation of *Xīyóujì* into Japanese began in 1758, with several installments from 1758 – 1831, likely involving several translators. The work on a proper translation, rather than short derivatives, was started by a group of intellectuals in Edo founded by Ogyū Sorai (荻生徂徠, March 21, 1666 – February 28, 1728). This is telling of the closed door policy of the Tokugawa government, showing that it required 235 years for *Xīyóujì* to receive a full translation into Japanese, despite its fame and importance in China during the 17th and 18th centuries. Given this late arrival in Japan, it's likewise telling of *Saiyūki's* quality that it becomes so popular so quickly.

in Japanese culture *Saiyūki* is considered a Japanese story.

Come again? Yes, similar to how there are people who watch *Dragon Ball* and don't realize it is Japanese, there are Japanese people who don't realize that *Saiyūki* is Chinese. *Saiyūki* is such a constant part of Japanese culture that to them, Monkey and the others are Japanese characters. They don't realize that it comes from China, takes place in China, and is filled with Chinese characters.

For example, in 2013 I met a young Japanese lady in her 20s living in New York City who had this understanding. As we walked through Central Park I tried to politely tell her that it's a Chinese story, but after a couple of attempts I felt it would be best to stop. It's so ingrained as part of Japanese culture that it was difficult for her to accept that it was anything but Japanese. In the end I think she understood, but it took a moment to get past that notion.

Another reason for using the Chinese names is because of the Sūn Wùkōng and Son Gokū dynamic. Son Gokū in *Dragon Ball* is inspired by Sūn Wùkōng in *Xīyóujì*, but in the Japanese equivalent of *Saiyūki*, Sūn Wùkōng's name is Son Gokū. So if I use Son Gokū for both characters it will be unclear which one I'm talking about, except through context. By using different names it's easier to understand.

Growing up with Saiyūki

Like most Japanese children, Akira Toriyama grows up hearing the *Saiyūki* story.

Toriyama is a fan of the *manga-ka* Tezuka Osamu, and Tezuka creates a *manga* version of the story called *Boku no Son Gokū* (ぼくのそんごくう, "My Son Gokū," 1953). This successful *manga* is then turned into an animated feature film titled *Saiyūki* (西游记, 1960, known in the United States as *"Alakazam the Great,"* 1961).[2] It's produced by Tōei, the same company that creates the *Dragon Ball anime* 25 years later. Toriyama is 6 years old when this comes out, and he likely watches it on TV or reads the *manga* as a child.

He might see other versions of *Saiyūki* as well, because this story has been repurposed countless times in movies, video games, TV shows, *anime, manga*, and plays.

For example, one of the Chinese versions of *Xīyóujì* that becomes popular in East Asia is developed by the "Shaw Brothers," creators of classic Hong Kong *gōngfu* cinema, entitled *Xīyóujì* (西游记, *"Monkey Goes West,"* 1966). This 4-part series of live-action films uses costumes, vivid scenery, musical numbers, special effects, and camera tricks to depict several selections from the original story. Following

---

2   *Saiyūki* (西游记, *"Journey to the West,"* 1960) is retitled *"Alakazam the Great"* (1961) in the United States because there's too much Eastern culture for a Western audience to accept. Or so the production studio, American International Pictures (AIP, founded 1954), believes at the time they localize it. They change all of the Eastern culture into its Western equivalent. For example, Son Gokū's name is changed to Alakazam, and instead of learning the immortal Dàoist arts under a Buddho-Dàoist master named Xūpútí, he learns magic under "Merlin the Magician." Rather than cause chaos in heaven, he causes disorder in "Majutsu Land," and instead of challenging the Buddhā, he is defeated by the human "King Amo." Then he is sentenced to become the bodyguard of "Prince Amat," instead of a Buddhist monk, and is assisted by "Queen Amass," instead of Guānyīn Bodhisattva. The changes don't stop there, with Zhū Bājiè renamed as "Sir Quigley Broken Bottom." The film is not a success, despite its impressive Japanese animation, long-established plot, and star-studded Hollywood voiceovers, such as the 1960s American teen heartthrob, Frankie Avalon (born September 18, 1940) providing Gokū's singing voice. I feel it serves as an example of how a foreign cultural product is localized while stripping it of its essence. Nevertheless, it's fun to watch, especially when you compare it to the story it's supposed to be telling.

this there's a Japanese television series titled *Saiyūki* that runs during the 1970s.

This trend of new releases of *Xīyóujì* continues throughout the '70s, '80s, '90s, and up to today. Every couple of years a new version of the story is made somewhere in the world. For example, there's the film titled *Xīyóu Jiàngmó-piān* (西遊·降魔篇, *"Journey to the West: Conquering the Demons,"* 2013) by Hong Kong martial arts actor, writer, and director, Stephen Chow (Chinese: Chow Sing-Chi, 周星馳, born June 22, 1962).[3]

Chow's film is a humorous retelling of Xuánzàng's life, with liberal changes for comedic effect. Not only does it become the highest-grossing film in Chinese history at $215 million USD in global box-office receipts,[4] but Toriyama loves it. To accompany the film's release in Japanese theaters he draws an illustration of Sūn Wùkōng in his traditional armor as depicted in the film, along with a message overflowing with praise for its humor and brilliant direction. *"This* is the pinnacle of my ideal in popcorn-movies!"[5] In particular he admires how it does the opposite of what every other adaptation has done, calling it a "wonderful betrayal." For example, it makes Sūn Wùkōng the villain. As you'll read about in this chapter, Toriyama always tries to do the opposite of what you expect, so he appreciates when another artist does so as well, and especially with this story. He continues, "It was just the greatest *Saiyūki*, so much so that I don't even know how to express it!!"

The point being that *Xīyóujì* and *Saiyūki* are impossible

---

3   Chow Sing-Chi (周星馳) is Stephen Chow's name in Cantonese. In Mandarin it is pronounced Zhōu Xīngchí.

4   The box-office receipts for *Xīyóu Jiàngmó-piān*: *http://www.box-officemojo.com/movies/?page=intl&id=journeytothewest.htm*

5   Toriyama's illustration of Sūn Wùkōng and praise for Stephen Chow's film: *http://www.kanzenshuu.com/2014/11/07/akira-toriyama-draws-sun-wukong-in-support-of-chow-film/*

to avoid seeing if you grow up in Japan or China.[6] Everyone knows and loves the story. This is to Toriyama's advantage when he decides to create his own version.

Toriyama's Version

Toriyama thinks it will be easy to use *Xīyóujì* as the model for his story because all he has to do is arrange things. But it turns out this isn't the case because his artistic mindset gets the better of him.

He chooses *Xīyóujì* so he can tap into a collective consciousness familiar with the story, but he believes that following the original story verbatim will make it too serious and boring, and nobody will read it since it'd be the same thing as the original. So he takes the spirit of the story, the environment that makes the adventure possible (such as the fighting, deities, and cultural content), and drafts his own story with those elements mixed in. As an artist he wants to be innovative, so while the beginning of our adventure starts on familiar territory, he then takes it in new directions. That's why *Dragon Ball* feels like *Xīyóujì* if you're familiar with the story, but it's still original and stands on its own if you're not.

Toriyama chooses characters, settings, and personalities from *Xīyóujì* in a manner that suits his evolving story. Making things up as he goes along, he borrows bits and pieces from different chapters of the original. Characters

---

6   A popular version of *Xīyóujì* in film outside of East Asia is *Gōngfu zhīwáng* (功夫之王, "*The Forbidden Kingdom*," 2008) starring Jackie Chan and Jet Li (Chinese: Lǐ Liánjié, 李连杰, born April 26, 1963). This American-Chinese joint production is the first film to star both of these martial arts superstars, and is an America-centric adaptation of the story made to appeal to Western audiences.

that are originally men become women, the wicked become kind-hearted, and stereotypes are inverted for the sake of a joke or moving the story along. He borrows less from the source material as the series progresses, but still stays true to it in theme and worldview.

The spirit of Toriyama's version is that it's familiar, yet different, and the same as the old, but new.

Simplified Over Time

Xīyóujì is a serious adventure that is undercut by jokes. *Dragon Ball* is a joke-filled adventure that is undercut by even more jokes. But underneath the jokes is a meaningful story. That's because the storytelling trend over time is toward simplification and humor, and away from a serious and religious tone. With each transformation the story becomes more endearing to the common man and more widespread in its readership. However, this comes at a cost. Toriyama's version of *Xīyóujì* is so simplified and far removed from the source in its appearance that if you aren't familiar with the original, you may not recognize it.

When the real-life Xuánzàng receives a divine vision and call to adventure, he answers it with utmost seriousness. Compassion swells in his heart and he feels that if he can bring the original words of Śākyamuni Buddhā back to China, that countless people can escape the cycle of *saṃsāra*. In his mind there is no greater purpose in life.

As the fame of Xuánzàng's trip gains renown it receives more fanciful additions, such as the talking animal companions, the demons, gods, and jokes. It's these jokes and humor added in for additional entertainment that make the fables, plays, and eventual book of *Xīyóujì* so attractive to commoners and such a big phenomenon. The book uses a divine mission as the vehicle to tell the story, but the comedic coating makes it attractive and worth repeating.

Then when Toriyama does his own version of *Xīyóujì*, he does the opposite of what the reader expects. He makes it way less serious, removes the usual visual cues that film directors include, and focuses on telling jokes, having a good time, creating a lighthearted adventure, and making it up as he goes along. This is why it's more popular than *Xīyóujì* is when first published and more well-known across the world than Xuánzàng's real-life adventure.

Like other authors of the Míng Dynasty, Wú Chéng'ēn expects his readers to be educated and have a general knowledge of philosophical and religious texts, literary history, awareness of their country and political system, current popular culture and recent events, and be willing to read a lengthy narrative in episodic format. That's a tall order in our day and age. Toriyama can't make those assumptions for his young audience of Japanese boys in the 1980s, so he lowers the barrier to entry by making it simple, "easy to understand," and fun.

By looking back we can see that the trend is away from religious content and toward humor. The traditional culture is still there under the surface, but by removing the doctrine and speaking in a less formal manner with simplified visuals and more jokes it enables a wider audience to enjoy the story. Nevertheless, by choosing to use *Xīyóujì* as the model for *Dragon Ball*, Toriyama unwittingly incorporates 5,000 years of Chinese culture into his story, and if you have the eyes to see it, you'll see it on every page.

Many fans of *Dragon Ball* are only able to see the surface level content. After you read *Dragon Ball Culture*, the jokes will still be funny and the fights will still be exciting, but you'll be able to see past the superficial appearances and into the heart of its hidden spirituality.

Hidden Spirituality

What's easier to accept and understand? A 2,500 page tome written in Chinese several hundred years ago; a *manga* aimed at children; an *anime* aimed at children; or a Hollywood blockbuster where handsome men and beautiful women use martial arts to kill robots that fight back with guns and explosions? Probably the latter, right? Here I'm referring to the *Matrix* (1999), one of the most spiritual films ever made, even though on the surface it's about a computer programmer fighting against machines.

Many fans who watch *Dragon Ball* may not realize it contains spirituality. This is for three reasons.

First, because Toriyama avoids mentioning religion or sectarian spirituality unless it's for the sake of a joke. He has characters and personalities from various faiths or worldviews, but the religious and historical topics found in *Xīyóujì*, while present, are never explained.

Second, because spirituality in art has simplified over time and become hidden; so the messages are introduced in a more subdued or covert fashion to make them more acceptable to a wider audience. Even though Toriyama says he has no theme and has no message to his work, it's there all the same.

Third, because *Dragon Ball* is filled with spiritual concepts such as internal life energy, supernormal powers, gods, demons, heaven, hell, and other topics you might attribute to religion. Yet even though these are in there, Toriyama doesn't discuss them. He just uses them as fuel to propel the plot forward.

Each of the above-mentioned artistic vehicles involve fighting. Xuánzàng's original spiritual pilgrimage doesn't involve much fighting except to save his own life from bandits. He's a Buddhist, after all. Yet over the centuries that follow his return, more fighting and supernormal powers are added in. His spiritual quest is then only possible because of the mighty warriors who kill the demons that try to stop him. As the centuries pass by the emphasis becomes more focused on the fighting and less on the spiritual quest. Ultimately it gets to the point we're at today in *Dragon Ball* and in cinema where the emphasis is almost 100% on the fighting and humor, and the spiritual message is hidden within the subtext of the story.

The martial arts are the medium of the message. This is because the martial arts are inherently spiritual and connected to the mind-body paradigm. The normal self-cultivation process of a spiritualist occurs internally, but the movements of the martial arts are visible, showy, and cool. You don't need to understand the internal to appreciate the external. And it just so happens that there is an audience of people outside the religious and spiritual realms who find enjoyment in the same themes found within those realms. They enjoy it because it's presented in a different mode that speaks to them in a non-religious way. The martial arts bridge the gap between secular and non-secular.

The fighting, excitement, and jokes are like a party piñata that you allow inside your mind because it's so attractive, and then it bursts open and reveals its content. The spiritual and ethical aspects were always there, but they might not have been as noticeable in your youth. As you mature along with it, your life experiences cause you to pause, reflect on what you see in the series, and draw parallels between the two. Then you to start to realize that the choices you're making in life can be altered for the better by thinking about how a character in your favorite series makes their choices. Eventually the line between the show and your life becomes blurred and you start to take the characters and their actions as ideals. The moment when you are influenced to change your life in the direction of those ideals is the moment where the spirituality in your heart comes to the surface.

When Gokū pushes himself hard, endures suffering, and comes out the victor in a long battle, he gives you an ideal to strive for. He's powerful but kind, fights to protect others, and is always improving himself. He makes people want to be better and persevere through hardship.

Each of the characters in *Dragon Ball* represents an ideal internal trait. The humor is that Toriyama makes their external self the opposite, or often undercuts their hidden nature. So it's only when you become a long-time fan of the series and see these characters for who they are on the inside that it starts to become clear just how powerful this series is. Then when you apply those ideals to your own life, you change.

I've received hundreds of stories from fans across the world telling me how important *Dragon Ball* is to them, and I know they're not alone.

For example, Michael, in the United States, shared with me that during his teenage years, "I had fallen into dark times, and the opportunity to see Gokū and his friends persevere through even the most difficult of situations filled me with hope and inspired me to keep pushing forward; always looking to better myself. Gokū was a huge role model and his worldview stays with me to this day."

Jed, in the Philippines, said, "This show inspired me to be strong. Not in fighting with others, but in being strong to myself. In my opinion, *Dragon Ball* is a representation of how to go through your daily life; to never give up and keep on training to get strong. If you achieve your goal through your hard work, you'll keep training even harder because you know there will always be a stronger obstacle in the course of your life. Then when you meet it, get excited, because that challenge will be the greatest fight you'll ever face. That is how Son Gokū would do it."

When Jed was 14 years old his father took him on a trip to Fuji-*san* (富士山, "Mount Fuji"), in Japan. As the two of them climbed the mountain with heavy backpacks, Jed became tired and his legs ached. His father told him it was okay for him to stop climbing or to go back down, but Jed remembered how Gokū persevered through his training with a heavy turtle shell on his back, and continued to put one foot in front of the other. Like Gokū, Jed kept going until he reached the top of the mountain. "This experience made me feel so proud of myself. *Dragon Ball* was the inspiration for me to be strong; not in strength of muscle, but in strength of will. My life has always been hard and will continue to be so. I can't hide or run away from it, so I will continue to face it head-on."[7]

As you can see, the martial arts is the medium through which this message is transmitted. As Jed said, it's not about conquering others, but about conquering yourself.

Xīyóujì is a pop-cultural simplification of these cultural beliefs. Once the esoteric secrets of monks and noble elites, the Buddhist, Dàoist, and Confucian perspective of *Xīyóujì* represents a culmination of thousands of years of cultural development in an epic made suitable for the masses. The deep philosophies and aspects of personal refinement toward an ultimate spiritual ascension are transformed into an external journey filled with martial conflicts and tests of desire. These external manifestations are reflections of the internal, and are written in a way that's relatable to an everyday person, no matter how fantastic they may seem.

Dragon Ball inherits and transforms this legend into an even more simplified epic, with a stronger focus on the martial arts and comical relationships. The result is an explosion of popularity that continues to reverberate around the world and inspire millions. The esoteric principles are made shallow for the masses and popularized, yet at its core the heart of spirituality still beats strong. That's *Dragon Ball's* hidden spirituality.

---

7   Michael and Jed's full stories, along with over 100 more, are in my book *Dragon Soul: 30 Years of Dragon Ball Fandom* (2015).

Míng and Qīng

The primary source of culture for *Dragon Ball* is a combination of Míng and Qīng era China. This is because Wú Chéng'ēn writes *Xīyóujì* during the Míng Dynasty (1368 – 1644 A.D.) while most *gōngfu* films take place in the Qīng Dynasty (Qīng-*cháo*, 清朝, "Clarity Dynasty," 1644 – 1912). Toriyama borrows from wherever he feels like it, so throughout *Dragon Ball* you'll see elements from both.

These dynasties have distinct cultures and appearances. The main reason for this is because the Míng Dynasty was founded by native ethnic Hàn (漢, "Dry Riverbed") Chinese, while the Qīng Dynasty is a foreign empire founded by Jurchen invaders from Manchuria in Northeast China. Despite the fact they rule for three centuries, the Hàn Chinese always perceive their rulers as foreigners without legitimate claim to the country. This leads to rebellions, and with the combined external pressure from the British, French, Americans, Russians, and other nations, the eventual collapse of China's last dynasty in 1912.

The perception of the Qīng as being ruthless and selfish makes for a perfect villain in *gōngfu* cinema in the 1970s and '80s when the producers make the films that Toriyama grows up watching. So you'll see that some of the villainous characters in *Dragon Ball* look like Qīng elites dressed in their finest attire, or bandits dressed in military clothing, while the good guys look like the commoners who struggle against them. For example, Tao Paipai (桃白白, "Peach White White"), who we'll meet in Part 2 of Gokū's adventure, is taken straight out of a Jackie Chan film.

This is also the era when martial arts flourish and the fame of the Shàolín-*sì* (少林寺, "Young Forest Temple") becomes synonymous with *gōngfu*. The Hong Kong filmmakers draw from traditional culture and depict the Shàolín monks' incredible skills. Then Toriyama draws inspiration from the films and mimics the various techniques that look good on paper, while exaggerating their effect. He takes these cinematic concepts inspired by Chinese history and ramps them up to the next level of entertainment. He also uses their appearance and history as the basis for Kuririn, who we'll meet in Part 1.

Easy to Understand

Dragon Ball is easy to understand, but the easier a book is to understand, the harder it is to write.

Toriyama's easy-to-read *manga* requires a lot of effort. In the *Dragon Ball Full Color Comics Volume 5* (2013) interview he says, "I consistently drew it with the desire for elementary and junior-high schoolers to read it. I remember consciously making it as easy to understand as possible, and altering it when it seemed like plot developments would get difficult to understand." He says in his interview with *Terebaru*, "I planned for *Dragon Ball* to be aimed more at older readers than *Dr. Slump* was. I discussed the storyline with my editor and we actually created some stories. But the new storylines are the same as *Dr. Slump* in the sense that it should be 'easy to understand.'"

This is a difficult feat to achieve given his complicated source material. Toriyama achieves it by focusing on the action. He tells the story through his characters' actions, supported by just enough dialogue to connect the next sequence of events together. Because the action moves the plot forward, you feel a continual sense of escalation. Even when they're just standing and talking you get a sense of motion and that something big is about to happen.

He says in his *Wired* (1997) Japanese edition interview, "I don't waste much time blathering on about useless things. As a rule, you can understand the content to a certain extent with just the pictures, and words are nothing more than a supplement to them. I had that drilled into me by my first editor: If you're going to come out and say something, then make it something that will strengthen the characterization even further."

Because the action does the talking, you don't get weighed down with prose. In most chapters you can understand the story without reading the dialogue, so even if you don't speak the language, you can still understand the events on the page. A single punch speaks volumes.

One of the greatest challenges for an author is to write like people talk. There's a tendency to write complicated dialogue to make things seem interesting, but real conversations are simple and direct. The more an author can be simple and direct, the easier it will be to understand. The fewer words used, the faster the plot moves forward.

Toriyama writes for his audience. The dialogue has a conversational tone and feels natural, with common words that don't take time to understand. By writing efficient dialogue and action-oriented images, Toriyama avoids the common traps of most writers and creates something that everyone can enjoy. This makes it seem like the characters are talking with you, which allows you to stay focused on the actions they take. It also makes sense within the story because most of these characters are uneducated martial artists who have taken blows to the head. But even the scientists sound like real people and not too smart for the readers' own good.

Four hundred years prior, Wú Chéng'ēn does the same thing when he writes *Xīyóujì* for the common people instead of the elites. Since he's an educated man he can write it in an imperial style or a scholar's style, but he chooses to use the *báihuà* (白話, "plain speech") style instead. *Báihuà* is an informal way of writing that is closer to how people talk in person. *Xīyóujì* is a story based on spoken word and dramatic live theater, so when you take this story that everyone knows and transfer it to the written word, it needs to maintain that spoken word quality. To do this he uses everyday expressions that are common for the Huái'ān region where he grows up. Since more people can read it, more people do, and it becomes a popular classic.

Toriyama likewise uses informal expressions from where he grows up in Aichi that appeal to young boys. His conversational and homegrown way of writing is noticeable in the Japanese version, where each character has a distinct voice, accent, and behaviors. Each of these voices comes from a different region of Japan or a specific age group or gender. So when the reader hears each voice in their head, they associate it with a stereotype. Stereotypes help the reader understand who each character is, whether they are a country hick or a political leader.

Toriyama uses the shortcut of stereotypes, but he doesn't fall into the trap that is so common among cartoonists of relying on this for novelty. For example, he doesn't make an alien have an Australian accent just for the sake of giving them a unique voice, when in the story they're from outer space where there is no such thing as Australia. He only adds accents when it's logical and expresses those characters' personalities. Hundreds of characters in the *manga* have a unique voice and personality, so instead of coming off as lazy, this makes it seem like he put a lot of thought and effort into their expressions.

The dialogue is simple, but it still has depth. Because each of the characters has their own accent and personality, their expressions can either be obvious in their external actions or subtle and between the lines. This is an advantage to the reader because it makes each character more relatable and contributes to the richness of the world. Some of them are countryside farmers, while others are kings, truckers, or office workers.

The end result is a low barrier to entry with a high value. *Dragon Ball* can be read by children yet still be enjoyed by adults. By making it accessible to everyone, including the educated, he lowers the barrier to entry even further than Wú Chéng'ēn does in his time. That's why so many people across the world enter through *Dragon Ball's* door, and it remains the world's most recognized *anime* and *manga*.

"Recent *anime* have gotten to have pretty complex character relationships, but in that area I developed things simply while leaving in a whiff of *Shōwa*, so I'll be happiest if I can get them to understand the fun of the characters. Something this simple and pure isn't depicted all that much, so I'd like for them to enjoy simply seeing something that's easy to understand!!"

Entertaining

Toriyama writes *Dragon Ball* to entertain you.

And nothing more.

He says in the *Dragon Ball Full Color Comics Volume 4* (2013) interview, "As a rule, there is no such thing as a theme in my work. I want to make it exclusively a piece of "entertainment" that's easy to understand for anyone who watches. There are a lot of other *manga* written in a complex style, so I suppose I'd like all the more for it to be pure entertainment." He reiterates in the *Asahi Shimbun Digital* (2013) interview, "I believe the mission of my *manga* is to be entertainment exclusively. I even feel that as long as I can allow the reader to have an enjoyable time once, I don't mind if nothing remains, so I've never deliberately drawn it with the intention of sending a message. Messages and moving scenes are things that other *manga-ka* already draw."

Wait a second. No theme? No message? This seems at odds with the story's rich cultural content and profound inner message that so many receive, doesn't it?

"The theme is that there is no theme! ... I wrote it, not to make people emotional, but to cherish the feeling of refreshment after having finished watching. I've aimed to have simple developments that will be as easy as possible for small children to understand, and I feel that being exclusively devoted to entertainment is my role and my distinguishing trait. I try to avoid teaching some kind of heavy-handed lesson."[8]

This is the strange thing about *Dragon Ball*, because even though it's beloved across the world for its inner qualities and the way it makes people feel, Toriyama doesn't intend for this to happen. He makes it up as he goes along and denies that there is a theme or message in his work. He wants lighthearted, not deep. He wants simple, plain, and unemotional. Whenever events lead to a scenario that seems like it will be emotional, he goes the other way with it to keep that from happening. He wants you to laugh, feel a more positive attitude, and go on with your day. Everything else comes as a result of happenstance.

In the original script for *Dragon Ball Z: Kami to Kami* (2013) that's written by another author and given to Toriyama for his input, there are what he calls "moving scenes." So he rewrites those scenes and then continues to rewrite the rest of the script. He says in the *V-Jump Akira Toriyama Special Interview* (2013), "There are already plenty of people in the world who are good at doing stuff like "making people cry," and "moving people." Really, I think simply being devoted exclusively to entertainment is probably 'my style.'" He then says that when the audience creates an emotional connection with his characters, it's only as a result of his relentless pursuit of entertainment.

---

8   "I'd like for them to enjoy simply seeing something that's easy to understand!!" and "The theme is that there is no theme!" are quoted from the *Official Battle of Gods Website Interview - Akira Toriyama × Shōko Nakagawa Interview* (2013).

The truth is that Toriyama is just a guy who likes to have fun as he nerds out and watches TV and builds models. In his heart he's a geeky introvert who likes to mix sci-fi and fantasy elements together and make corny jokes. He goes out of his way to avoid emotions, wholesomeness, or lessons. Instead he focuses on lighthearted entertainment.

And that's fine. But despite his best efforts to avoid emotions, *Dragon Ball* is an emotional experience. It's a series that causes you to become excited, cry, feel nervous, or jump with joy. And for many readers it carries a deep message. You connect with it in a way that becomes part of your being and changes your worldview. There's a quality to it that the author doesn't want to be in there, but is. Despite his best efforts to avoid delivering a message, he delivers a big one. Some fans see *Dragon Ball* as a way of life.

This is the irony of his masterpiece. It's the opposite of what he intends it to be.

Opposites

Toriyama always does the opposite of what you expect. When asked in the *Son Gokū Densetsu* interview how he developed his story, he says, "I always approached it as, 'do the opposite of the readers' expectations.' ... That's my bad habit."

You expect the story to be emotional? He makes it shallow. You expect Son Gokū to look like Sūn Wùkōng? He makes him a happy-faced boy without any fur, armor, or crown. You expect the Táng Monk to be dressed in Buddhist robes and riding a horse? He makes him a young girl dressed in a skirt and riding a motorcycle. You expect Gokū to win the fight? He has him lose it. You expect your favorite character to survive a fierce battle? He kills him. Whatever you're expecting, you will get the opposite.

Another thing Toriyama does is present each character with a certain image and then subvert that and show you the opposite image hidden within their personality. He loves having characters with multiple sides and personalities. For example, Gokū appears to be cute and innocent, but he has a raging and murderous beast hidden within his subconscious. Ranchi appears to be a demure and feminine lady who cooks food for her friends, but her alternate personality is a psychopath with a machine gun. Kuririn is a Buddhist monk and martial artist, but his reason for training hard is so he can get a pretty girlfriend.

He puts the qualities and images of his characters in contrast to themselves and to one another. Stark opposites unify into one character and then square off against others with different types of opposites in contrast. This is part of their charm and ease of understanding for the audience, because every character has two sides and they can show either one at any time.

Each character is either the opposite of what you expect them to be for the sake of downplaying what you do expect them to be, or they're the opposite of who they seem to be on the surface. They then bounce between these two states of 'black' and 'white' throughout the story. By doing it this way his characters become dynamic and interesting, yet also easy to understand at a glance. When Toriyama shows you black, it allows you to see the hidden white.

Why does Toriyama prefer to do the opposite? He goes on to say, "A basic tenet of being a *manga-ka* is, as much as possible, to avoid imitating others." People expect whatever they've seen or heard before in a story. But Toriyama doesn't want to give them that, so despite his initial desire to do a simple arrangement of the *Xīyóujì* story, he immediately does something different. This mentality carries him through the story from beginning to end.

I'm not sure where he receives this idea. It may have been from Torishima-*san*, or it could have been his own.

Though we do find this same thing in *Xīyóujì*, where Buddhist monks and Dàoist sages use violence to solve their problems and the deities have human flaws. If Toriyama adopts the idea from seeing such things in *Xīyóujì*, then it's no surprise that he takes to the idea like a duck to water.

He applies this same mentality of opposites to his own life. He pushes himself harder to get out of his comfort zone, and ups his level of creativity in his writing and plot development just like his characters push themselves harder to reach the next level of their training. The reason his characters have this mentality is because Toriyama himself has this mentality. If his readers expect that a character will do something, he makes them do the opposite, even if he wants what the readers want. And if he doesn't like something or finds it painful, then he'll do that exact thing. So he pushes himself to introduce scenarios that he hasn't used before, and this ensures there are no repeat events. The exception is where it makes his life more difficult or wastes time. Then he'll take the path that's easier. Or if he forgets that he already used a joke, then he'll use it again.

In short, when others expect a zig, he zags. When others want big, he goes subtle. It doesn't matter if your expectation might 'help' the story. Toriyama blazes his own trail, and it's what allows his storytelling to remain special. It's part of why he has so many fans, and personally, I love it. The result is that you're always on your toes and the story stays fresh.

Touching back on the idea of *Dragon Ball* being mere entertainment: It's ironic that by always doing the opposite within his work, and by trying to make it the opposite of meaningful, he creates the opposite effect in the readers' mind. His fans consider it to be one of the most meaningful stories ever told.

It's similar to how he went out of his way to not become famous, and in the process of doing so became the most famous *manga-ka* in Japan. Opposites rule Toriyama's life.

Flaws

The characters of *Xīyóujì* have flaws, and so do the characters of *Dragon Ball*.

For example, Sūn Wùkōng is consumed by rage and egotistical pride. He causes a ruckus in heaven and smashes people to death with his magic staff. The Táng Monk falls prey to his own naivety and the illusions created by demons. Zhū Bājiè is consumed by lust, hunger, and laziness. These character flaws are reflective of their imperfections and the reason why they cannot return to heaven.

Toriyama continues this storytelling paradigm by ensuring that every character in *Dragon Ball* has a psychological weakness, incorrect notion, or trait that undercuts their strength. For example, the world's greatest martial artist is a skirt chaser and attached to comfort. Buruma is overly emotional despite being based on a Buddhist monk that is supposed to be free of emotions. Others are fueled by ego and self-validation, are afraid of death, or choose to walk down the path of darkness instead of light.

Toriyama says that giving them flaws makes it more fun and brings more laughs to the story. It's also because nobody is perfect, and he wants to show that even though everyone has their flaws, they're not so bad.

It's the same for the bad guys. Toriyama describes his approach to creating villains in the *Mando Kobayashi* (2013) interview, saying, "What I wanted was to give them flaws in amongst that fearsomeness, or rather, to make them characters where you could feel their humanity." So they can play the role of villains, but if they have flaws, then that means they're human. And human beings can change, so they may not be villains forever.

Likewise, the heroes of *Xīyóujì* are anti-heroic. They don't put their hands on their hips and declare that "justice is here to vanquish evil." They're ambivalent characters who live their lives according to their own personalities, and their meaning as individuals is defined by their relationships to the other characters around them. Same for the deities, who have just as many flaws as the people on Earth. They're supposed to be holy figures, but Wú Chéng'ēn makes them have weaknesses like us. This makes them relatable and opens up opportunities for humor.

Therefore the character flaws of each so-called hero or villain in *Dragon Ball* only has meaning in context of the others involved. It's more like a theatrical play, in that the 'good guy' or 'bad guy' depends on perspective and which part of the story you see them act.

Flaws are what allow for character development. As the story progresses you see how the characters either overcome their flaws or stay the same as others change. That's where the meaning comes from, because it's the same for each of us in our own lives. Some people change, while others stay the same. Which character do you relate to?

Throughout *Dragon Ball* we can see the strongest and weakest parts of ourselves.

Illustrations

The big difference between *Xīyóujì* and *Dragon Ball* is that one is a prose novel and the other is an illustrated *manga*.

Toriyama is a graphic artist and designer by trade before he becomes a *manga-ka*. He loves to express himself through his art and capture the real world in his pen. This explains why his designs are so striking, including the creation of vehicles, weapons, clothing, armor, and logos.

Xīyóujì has had illustrations added to it, but the artistry always pales in comparison to Toriyama's. His illustrations make the story more accessible because you don't need to read the words to follow the plot. And as far I'm concerned, his modern and more realistic (yet still abstract) take on the characters is more believable than any of the *Xīyóujì*-based films created before or afterward.

It's Toriyama's incredible art that captivates people and draws them into the adventure. And his wide-eyed and innocent Gokū is recognized throughout the world. Arguably more than Sūn Wùkōng himself.

Humor

Dragon Ball is one of the funniest *manga* ever written. This is because of Toriyama's sense of humor and the humor of *Xīyóujì* that provides a foundation for his gags.

When Toriyama refers to *Xīyóujì* as "absurd," I believe he's referring to its jokes, slapstick, and situational humor. Laughter and humor play a large role in traditional Chinese culture, such as by poking fun of societal conventions, highlighting the futility of man's pursuits, or as a reminder to take things lightly and put your faith in the gods. For example, the comedic interplay between Buddhist monks and Dàoist sages in the imperial court is a common theme in the story. They repeatedly try to one-up the other and gain favor with the Emperor. Meanwhile the pilgrims have to put their faith in Guānyīn's master plan, despite all the hardships and near-death scenarios they encounter. I suspect that many of the comedic situations in the story are added in during the theatrical renditions to create a humorous feeling in the audience. And then there's the brotherly dialogue between Sūn Wùkōng, Zhū Bājiè, and the other pilgrims. They become comrades over the long journey and use shorthand insults as they roughhouse around. Each of these adds charm to an otherwise repetitive and verbose text.

When Tezuka creates his version of the story in 1953 he veers off from the standard formula by adding more humor and making it more colloquial. This allows it to be more accepted by the modern Japanese society of the 1950s. Toriyama continues this trend by making it even funnier and even more colloquial and accepted by the modern Japanese society of the 1980s. This is why the worldwide audience that likely doesn't know the culture that it's founded upon can still get most of the jokes and appreciate the action.

That said, Toriyama does use some jokes intended specifically for young Japanese boys. These are often inspired by his own childhood. These parts are usually edited out during localization because they're too difficult to translate, so throughout this book I'll explain each of those jokes for you. You'll finally be able to laugh at the jokes that the Japanese audience has been laughing at for decades.

For Wú Chéng'ēn's audience the appeal of *Xīyóujì* is the moral guidelines followed by the fighting and social commentary, with humor to liven it up. For Toriyama's young audience it's the opposite: the jokes, fights, and adventures are what matter, so he makes it as funny as he can.

Subversion

Another part of *Xīyóujì's* humor is how it subverts the expectations of a proper Confucian society. Consider that there's a Buddhist monk traveling with animal-men who smash their opponents into bloody pulps. Right from the start you have something that makes you scratch your head. Then there are the often repeated sexual seduction scenes, where the Táng Monk or Zhū Bājiè is tempted by a beautiful woman or demon in disguise. They become lured by their desires and fall into a trap, and just as they're about to be eaten alive, Sūn Wùkōng busts down the door and slams his staff onto the demon's brains. Four hundred years ago these scenes would seem risqué or 'off-kilter' of society's expectations of proper conduct. A 'good' Buddhist would never have fallen into such a trap, nor would he have solved the problem with violence. But it happens a lot in *Xīyóujì*. That's because *Xīyóujì* has an outward appearance of a serious quest, but is subverted internally by the main characters' mischief.

Toriyama loves this stuff. Wherever there's a chance to subvert your expectations, he takes it. He uses the more serious tropes and characters in *Xīyóujì*, but then subverts them to make them funny. For example, he makes the all-powerful hero a little boy. He transforms the men into women. He turns wise men into dirty old men. And he adds in perverted humor for its own sake. So his characters play similar roles as those in the original, but their seriousness is undercut by their personalities.

Xuánzàng and the other pilgrims revere the Buddhā and Bodhisattvas, but Sūn Wùkōng has the habit of undercutting everybody's ego. Just by the virtue of being himself he pops their ego-filled balloons, throws his monkey wrench into the gears of their minds, and forces people to face reality. He's the one that points out the emperor is wearing no clothes. Toriyama does this same thing with his Son Gokū, in that he stands as the innocent and naïve foil that subverts everybody's self-image, just by being himself. Toriyama uses Gokū to ensure that nothing is sacred and no one is holy.

Perversion

Toriyama is a self-declared pervert. In the *American Shonen Jump* Vol. 1, #1 interview he is asked who his favorite *Dragon Ball* character is, and he says, "It's Gokū, naturally. For one thing, I'm a very perverse person, so I'm drawn to a pure, innocent character like him."

That sounds like a bad thing, but it's actually a good thing because his perverted jokes are hilarious. Even though he later denies that he is a pervert in several interviews, when you read his *manga*, it comes through loud and clear in his characters' actions and words. Toriyama's humorous style of debauchery is especially noticeable in the early chapters of *Dragon Ball* when he's following up on *Dr. Slump*.

Toriyama's perversion has three causes. The first is that he writes for young boys who have dirty minds. I was once a young boy, so I can attest. Telling dirty jokes isn't appropriate inside the home, but when you're out with friends you let them fly. You rip on your friend, he rips you back, you talk about things you wouldn't dare do elsewhere, and through that you bond. These kinds of jokes, which are often situational or at someone else's expense, are crude and funny, but they're taken with a grain of salt. Toriyama's perverted jokes follow that playful nature. They are profane, but they don't stop you in your tracks in disgust. On the contrary, they make you laugh and carry on with the story. It's another part of *Dragon Ball's* charm.

The second reason for Toriyama's perversion is because he's a product of modern Japanese society. This society has questionable aspects that cause me to cringe. I don't want to judge, so I'll just present them as they arrive in the story and let you come to your own conclusions. Hint: they involve young girls' panties.

The third reason is because of *gōngfu* films. In the research for this book I watched hundreds of *gōngfu* films, and there are a surprising amount of naked women in these movies. I don't know if the creators feel like adding boobs to the movie advances the plot, but maybe it enhances the ambiance? Or perhaps this is a result of the 1970s progressive mentality on sexuality? In any case, there are sexy ladies in these movies just for the sake of being sexy, and given that Toriyama watches countless *gōngfu* films, I can't help but feel that he's affected by them. Or it could be the case that these movies are intended for a young male audience to begin with, and young males like looking at naked women and hearing dirty jokes. So Toriyama adopts this mentality and includes these same things in his work.

Even though it's in there, *Dragon Ball* never becomes overtly sexual and Toriyama doesn't try to entice you like the demons that seduce Xuánzàng in *Xīyóujì*. If anything, *Xīyóujì's* words are more internally seductive than Toriyama's external illustrations and humor could ever be. But hey, when boobs are in your face you can't help but notice.

Censoring Perversion

This perverted content isn't a problem in Japanese society. Toriyama intends his *manga* to be read by young boys, his jokes and illustrations are approved by his editors, go to print, and are read by millions of children each week. Nothing happens. Nobody cries or suffers mental damage. They laugh and carry on, because that's Japanese society.

One place Toriyama's perverted sense of humor poses a problem is in the United States. For example, in 1999 the toy store chain Toys "R" Us drops the *Dragon Ball manga* after a complaint by a father in Dallas, Texas, about these lewd aspects. He calls it "borderline soft porn," and says, "I don't want it to get to the point that when I'm at Toys "R" Us I have to put everything through a porn-scanner."[9]

Another example occurs in October, 2009, in Wicomico, Maryland, when the *manga* is pulled from the elementary, middle, and high school libraries after a complaint from a parent.[10] Why? Because Volume 1 of the *manga* shows the innocent nakedness of a young Gokū, a rear-view angle

---

9   Toys "R" Us article: *https://goo.gl/GR18kZ*

10   Maryland school decision: *http://goo.gl/IV0ejr*, and *http://www.wboc.com/Global/story.asp?S=11321353*

of a panty-less Buruma, and perverted humor courtesy of Kame-*sennin*. The mother complains after seeing these illustrations in her 9-year-old son's reading material.

A committee is gathered to discuss the decision. Joe Holloway, a Wicomico County Council member gives a presentation of the photocopied illustrations in question back-to-back and says, "the drawings and story lines are disgusting." He then calls it "smut." School board president Mark Thompson says, "The pictures I saw, if it was meant for adults, it crosses the line for child pornography. If it's for a child, why show these for children?"[11–12]

Yes, *Dragon Ball* is "smut," "child pornography," and inappropriate for children, despite being made for children.[13]

What does this mean? It's not that Japanese society is a godless land of depraved adolescents and hedonistic adults. It's that a few people in American society have a problem with juvenile humor intended for boys in Japan.

Is Toriyama a horrible man who draws child pornography? No. Should his work be censored for juveniles in America?[14] That's up for debate, but my opinion is still no. I don't believe in censorship of an artist's work. Either accept it 100% or don't buy it and display it. It isn't rational to equate children's *manga* with hardcore pornography just because of ignorance and intolerance.

It's easy to point the finger and say that this is just 'Puritanical America' being afraid of everything they deem is

---

11   Quotes from Maryland school board: *http://www.delmarvanow. com/article/20091008/NEWS01/910080338/*

12   Article on Maryland news website: *http://goo.gl/wTzv7k*

13   Viz, the American *Dragon Ball manga* localization company and subsidiary of Shūeisha, rated the *manga* that was in the Wicomico school system as Teen (ages 13+). It arguably should not have been in the elementary school. However, *manga* are often marketed to young children, so it causes confusion among library staff and parents.

14   Viz also publishes a censored version of *Dragon Ball*.

inappropriate. But I think a more nuanced understanding is that there's a culture clash going on. It's a conflict between the disparate worldviews of Japanese society and American society, and the importing of foreign artwork into school libraries for children to read. American parents don't want their children reading something that they themselves don't understand.

It's a good thing for parents to get involved with what their children are reading. But the real cause of this decision is ignorance of and intolerance for another culture, combined with a lack of respect for their children's ability to accept and appreciate things as they are. Kids are not the ones who have a problem with the *manga*. It's the parents who have the problem.

I suppose if you take Toriyama's jokes out of context or just look at the illustrations by themselves like the Wicomico County Council members do, that they might seem inappropriate. But they make sense within the context of the story.

Is it the right decision or the wrong decision? I'll let you be the judge. My point is that it's a result of culture.

It can't be denied that the content is there. Throughout this book I'll show you why it's there.

Episodic

Shōnen manga are created and distributed in a weekly, bi-weekly, or monthly chapter format that is similar to episodes in a serialized TV show. *Dragon Ball* is created in a format called *shūkan* (週刊, "weekly"), consisting of 14 pages a week, plus a title page, and then distributed in *Weekly Shōnen Jump*. It's not the first series to do this, but given *Dragon Ball's* long story arc it's interesting that we find a similar episodic format in *Xīyóujì* centuries prior.

Wú Chéng'ēn writes *Xīyóujì* with interwoven elements that connect each chapter together or reference previous chapters. This is because Late Míng Dynasty novels share a set of similar creation and distribution characteristics: They are over 100 chapters long, divided into 10-chapter narrative blocks, and with each block further divided into 2-to-4-chapter episodic sub-stories.

The sub-stories have their own story arcs called *biān* (編, Japanese: *hen*, "arc," "part of a book," "compilation," "composition," "arrangement," or "volume"). These *biān* are introduced and concluded by narration at the front and end of each chapter, along with occasional poetry or commentary. The part that connects them together is the hook, where the narrator gets you excited to read the next chapter, such as by leaving you on a cliffhanger ending.

So that's the popular format of Wú Chéng'ēn's era and Toriyama uses this same format for *Dragon Ball*, where each *hen* ("arc") is one part of a larger story and he connects them together by using a narrator and a hook.

This makes it feel like you're being told a grand story that carries on where it leaves off. It's like a modern serial TV drama and makes for an ideal framework to follow when releasing a weekly *manga* or *anime*.

Narrator

Do you remember what it's like to be told a story you've heard so many times that you could tell it yourself but you prefer to sit and listen? That's how *Xīyóujì* is for a lot of fans. And that's because the story is told by a narrator.

A simulated oral narrative establishes a human connection with the audience and makes the content appear genuine even when it's outlandish. This 'storytellers' manner' gets the reader to participate in the story and make them experience what's happening in the pages. Writing prose this way doesn't add to the progression of the story's plot, and in some sense detracts from it, but it does add to the readers' enjoyment and contemplation of the text.

Toriyama copies this storytelling style in *Dragon Ball* by using his own narrator. Their name? Narēshon (ナレーション, "Narration"). We don't know anything about this Narēshon because we never get to see them, but they have the same all-knowing, all-seeing mind of the narrator in *Xīyóujì*. And because the narrator in both versions starts each chapter and ends each chapter, we get the feeling that the narrator is the one running the show.

These narrators know everything about the story from beginning to end. They know every character and event. They know the motives and the backstory of the different deities and their complicated bureaucracy, as well as the lives of the common people, from their birth to death, previous lives and reincarnations. They're like the storyteller who sits at a campfire and tells your favorite fable, or a parent who reads their child a bedtime story. They are the comfortable voice that guides you through the adventure.

It's the narrators role to tell you the story and comment as it develops by using prose or verse, such as poetry, to express the mood of each chapter. They also provide a continual voice that helps point out the jokes, parodies, and characterizations that the author wants to highlight. This is a novel idea for Wú Chéng'ēn's era, because it's the opposite of a scholarly writing style. By speaking directly to you and using easy to understand expressions, the book becomes more enjoyable and gains a wider audience.

Toriyama uses it for fun when he tries to hook you into reading the next chapter.

Hook

The narrators of both stories use the hook. This is when a chapter ends on a cliffhanger or exciting jump-off point and you're left wondering what's going to happen next.

For example, in *Xīyóujì* a chapter ends with, 'Want to discover how the monkey and pig escape from this deadly situation? Let's read on!'

Toriyama uses this technique in *Dragon Ball* in the early chapters and sporadically throughout the rest. As a chapter concludes he has a tiny scroll with ancient-looking writing on it that has the Narēshon's thoughts on the ending or what will soon unfold. The same thing happens in the *anime* when the Narēshon says in the episodes, "The world is finally at peace... however...!" And then you have to tune in next time to see what danger awaits. This is ramped up in the American version of *Dragon Ball* when he shouts his signature line, "Find out what happens next time... on the next exciting episode of *Dragon Ball*!"

If nothing else, the Narēshon uses the phrase *tsuzuku* (つづく, "it continues") to get you to come back. This is a standardized way to finish a chapter of a serialized *manga*, and stands in contrast to the conclusive endings of a *yomikiri* ("one-shot").

The narrator in *Xīyóujì* knows everything, but still sometimes acts like they're unsure of what will happen next. This is even more the case in *Dragon Ball*. When the Narēshon is surprised by what just happened or is curious about the next chapter it's because Toriyama is surprised by his own story and is making it up as he goes. You can see how Toriyama has fun by speaking through the Narēshon, since in reality Toriyama is the one telling you the story and creating every page, and he's the clueless one.

The hook is a perfect way to connect the reader back to the source material of *Xīyóujì*, while being fresh and fun.

Vehicle for the Author

Art reflects the artist. Wú Chéng'ēn and Toriyama are artists of different natures and times, but their masterpieces serve as vehicles to reflect the artist's mind and worldview.

A big part of Wú's version of the story is satire and commentary on society's ills. His *Xīyóujì* shows how the rich socialites of the Míng Dynasty squander food, have biases against the poor, and how the central leaders are incompetent. Likewise the deities in heaven carry a great air of pomp and circumstance about them, yet are powerless to defend themselves against the savage Monkey. Above all else, he provides a portrait of what it's like to be human.

Wú uses the vehicle of the already established Xuánzàng-based fairy tales and religions to express his unhappiness with his life and society at large. It's through the story that examples of his perspective shine through. Wú expresses himself as a product of poverty, having grown up in a poor merchant family during the rise of capitalism. He cautions against it by showing how society's focus on financial externals and on political nonsense will lead men astray. Far better to follow the Buddhā Law and Dào, he seems to say.

Toriyama does a similar thing with *Dragon Ball* where it's not as much about the religious or moral teachings as it is about using this vehicle of an already established framework as a medium for his own artistic expression through jokes and adventures. He wants to tell a story and entertain the audience, yet throughout the piece we see his humor, his perversion, his fascination with model toys, with *gōngfu* films, action stars, aliens, and science fiction. Rather than criticize society's ills, Toriyama seems to say, 'this is the ideal world in my mind.'

Reading *Dragon Ball* is our chance to see inside.

Life, Art, Legends

Life inspires art, art gives life to legends, and legends give life to further art. It's because of Xuánzàng's life and his impact on Chinese society that Wú Chéng'ēn creates *Xīyóujì*, and it's because of *Xīyóujì* and its impact on Japanese society that Toriyama creates *Dragon Ball*.

You can now see that *Dragon Ball* is a story thousands of years in the making. Xuánzàng is inspired by Buddhist artwork and culture. Then his real-life adventures lead to folktales in China that become plays, drama's, and camp-fire stories. This popular culture leads to *Xīyóujì*, a new form of storytelling with old Buddho-Dàoist elements that speaks to the masses in a simplified way. This then leads to *Dragon Ball* 400 years later, with an even more simplified and accessible story made in an illustrated popular culture format that uses the martial arts as the medium for its message; whether intentional or not. In the process, Toriyama gives life to a new work of art, and it becomes a legendary source of inspiration and entertainment.

What will we discover in the next exciting chapter? Come with me as we explore Toriyama's Dragon World!

Dragon World

THE SETTING OF *Dragon Ball* is called the *doragon wārudo* (ドラゴンワールド, "Dragon World").[1] It's Toriyama's ideal environment: A place where adventurous teenagers travel through a miraculous land filled with talking animals, dinosaurs, dragons, demons, gods, flying cars, and romance.

If a Dàoist painting and *Star Wars* mated, the Dragon World would be its baby. A fusion of old and new, rooted in a *Xīyóujì*-inspired framework combined with science fiction and pop culture. Part *Blade Runner*, *Alien*, *The Flintstones* (1960), and Chinese martial arts legend, the Dragon World has as much personality as the main cast.

Yet as wondrous as this setting is, Toriyama says, "If you could please enjoy that Dragon World without thinking about anything, I'll be happy."[2]

Sorry Toriyama, but we're going to do a lot of thinking about it. Because even though it would have been easier for him to use the world of *Xīyóujì* and leave it at that, he chose to create a fusion world of East and West with cinematic influences. And even though he makes up the story as he goes, his world has endless detail and allure.

The Dragon World is the story's greatest strength, because it is the stage upon which the drama of lives is set.

---

1   For an in-universe example of the term, *Dragon Ball* Chapter #519 is titled *Baibai Doragon Wārudo* (バイバイ ドラゴンワールド, "Bye Bye, Dragon World") and premieres in issue #25 of *Weekly Shōnen Jump*, on August 4, 1995. It is also the title of Volume 42.

2   "If you could please..." is from the *Special Booklet Message* in the *Dragon Ball Z: Battle of Gods Special Limited Edition Box* (2013).

Origin of the Dragon World

At the dawn of time the cosmos is created by an all-powerful and all-knowing being called "Akira Toriyama." But it happened so long ago that nobody, not even Toriyama, can remember if this is true. Could just be a rumor.

This being forms the cosmos as a particle in the shape of a ball, divided in two. The upper half is the afterlife where souls arrive after losing their physical bodies to death. The lower half is the mortal world, itself consisting of two parts: the upper portion ruled by the laws of science, and the lower portion ruled by the laws of magic.

Within this cosmos there is a planet much like our own, and it's also called Earth, but it's not the Earth we know. This Earth has its own geography, society, timeline, and culture. Why does Toriyama create a world so similar to our own yet different? He says, "In the end, because it's easy. Basically with everything, I choose my criteria based on what can be easy. If I made the real world the setting, I'd have to draw looking at reference materials, for stuff like buildings and vehicles. When you do that, people complain even if it's just a little bit off." By creating an Earth that isn't Earth as we know it, Toriyama makes an environment that is relatable yet provides artistic freedom.

It's a world where he can do whatever he likes, and it serves as a playground to recreate the lighthearted and adventurous stories he gravitates to as a child. Toriyama is a man with a young heart; an idealist who imagines things as different from how they are. The Dragon World is a wild place that runs counter to the rigid values of Japanese society. His *manga* creations are his own world that he shares with others for the sake of entertainment. It's his mind, put on paper.

Speaking of which, the Dragon World is a collective cosmos that includes all of Toriyama's other *manga*, such as *Dr. Slump*. Toriyama makes up his stories as he goes, and he then provides retroactive rationale for the events that follow previous stories. Smaller worlds thus fit inside larger worlds, like Russian *matrëška* dolls.[3] With each new *manga* he publishes, these individual worlds become part of a greater interwoven whole, which in turn becomes the collective Dragon World.

Etymology

In Japanese the planet Earth is referred to as *chikyū* (地球, "earth ball," or "soil sphere"). By referring to the Earth as a ball it strengthens the connotation of being a single particle in a vast sea of planet-sized particles, all of which are part of a grander cosmos. Since *Dragon Ball* is written in Japan, the characters within the story refer to their Earth as *chikyū*, but the Earth in *Dragon Ball* isn't a clone of the real world, so "Dragon World" is first used by Toriyama, the *Dragon Ball* license holders, and by fans to refer to the Earth within *Dragon Ball* as a distinct entity.

As the story expands beyond the Earth, Dragon World grows to encompass the multiple planets and dimensions that Gokū and the other characters visit. So the term can refer to the in-universe Earth, or the entire cosmos. In turn, to the cultural milieu of *Dragon Ball* as an entity, including its characters, terms, places, and mythos, similar to the "Marvel Universe" or "DC Universe" in Western comics.

---

3   Russian *matrëška* ("*matryoshka*") are a series of hollow dolls with a similar appearance and shape, but different size, that you place inside one another.

Appearance

Because *Dragon Ball* is inspired by *Xīyóujì* and traditional Chinese culture, the world's appearance reflects this—pine trees, bamboo, curvy mountains, and flowing streams are rendered in rounded strokes and soft tones as if painted on a Dàoist scroll. This creates a mystical appearance and tone for the adventure.

Toriyama refers to his artistic style in *Daizenshū 4*, saying, "I wanted to change tempos and structures so as to draw a clear line between the old and new series. For example, I drew *Dr. Slump* in an American-like style and am writing *Dragon Ball* in a Chinese-like style."

He uses *Xīyóujì* as his starting point, but doesn't feel constrained by it. Toriyama writes the following on the first page of *Dragon Ball manga*: "The setting of *Dragon Ball* has a sort of Chinese feel to it, but it's not necessarily China. Exactly where it takes place is uncertain. The overall story is very simple, but I'd like to keep making up more details and illustrations as I go along. This way, I can draw anything I want to and enjoy the tension and excitement of figuring out what I'll draw next."

As the series evolves from a child-like fantasy to a fighting-focused epic, the soft art style becomes sharper. But the established settings do not vanish, they get added upon as the scope expands. So the bedrock of mystical Asian landscapes continue to remind the reader of where it all began.

Geography

The geography of Dragon World is a single Pangaea-like supercontinent. Pangaea ("whole Earth") is the giant land mass that formed 300 million years ago on our own planet, when all the continents combined together as a supercontinent and dinosaurs ruled the Earth. The continental plates started to split 100 million years ago and gradually shifted to where they are today. Since the Dragon World is running wild with dinosaurs, it's appropriate that Toriyama's Earth is the shape of a supercontinent.

It is difficult to know with precision how large this continent is, but there is a world map in *Daizenshū 4* that makes it appear to be several thousand kilometers long and wide. This is because the geological structure of mountain chains, rivers, and forests tend to be this large in our own world, and we can presume the same types of distance would be required to create such variety in the Dragon World. These variances include tundras, scorching deserts, tropical islands, jungles, and temperate zones.

Just like his characters, the settings for Toriyama's world are inspired by other sources. For example, Paozu-*yama* (パオズ山, "Paozu Mountain"), where Gokū lives, is inspired by Guìlín (桂林, "Laurel Trees"), China, and its karst mountains. Toriyama says, "At that time my wife was interested in China, and I drew looking at the books of Chinese photographs that she bought."

He leads the characters to new environments in order to shape the world and provide new settings for Gokū to explore. He says, "I'm not persisting with frameworks. *Dragon Ball* was originally a story of China, but these days I draw places such as Bali, Siberia, and western-like places, whatever I feel like. If you think of the story as occurring on a big continent, you can create such stories logically."

He's inspired to draw most of these environments by watching films, but also his travels across the world. He says, "I've been to many places, but Australia, with what I felt was a pleasant balance between its cities and its magnificent natural spaces, moved me very much." Australia is the inspiration for Minami-*no-miyako* (南の都, "South City"), one of several metropolises.

Culture

The Dragon World is spiritual without being religious. Toriyama bases his story on *Xīyóujì*, so it is founded upon a Buddho-Dàoist worldview, but he doesn't reference religion except through his environment and characters. Despite this, the series becomes more spiritual as it progresses, going from heaven to hell, the afterlife, and beyond, with an ever-increasing focus on personal growth.

Just like in Japan, the main belief systems of the Dragon World are Buddhism and Shintō, with Confucian traits. There are references to Christianity made in the series, but often just for a punchline. There are monks, but in general most people look like average citizens wearing either traditional Chinese clothing or modern Western attire.

Dàoism plays a large role in the series through the martial artists and spiritual cultivators scattered across the land. And even though they often live as hermits, they manage to find one another as they interact with deities and demons amid their travels. This makes sense in a martial arts epic, and each new character is able to introduce new forms of traditional content. For example, the use of *ki* (気, 'kee,' Chinese: *qì*, 氣, 'chee,' "energy," or "spirit"). *Ki* is metaphysical energy of the cosmos that is found in all matter, including our bodies, and the martial artists in *Dragon Ball* use it to augment their strength and develop supernormal abilities.

Because the Dragon World is spiritual without being religious, it contains a lot of symbols. For example, Dàoist immortals are associated with symbols of long life, including turtles, cranes, peaches, pine trees, deer, divine mushrooms, gourds, and long bent walking sticks with a serpentine appearance. Carp, dragons, and other auspicious animals carry unique symbolism as well.

These traditional Eastern symbols are juxtaposed with modern Western designs, such as the contrast between Son

Gohan's hermit hut and Kame-*sennin's* island home.

The end result is that *Dragon Ball* is art, and the way it affects the world is both real and unreal. The Dragon World seems believable yet magical, a surreal realm that portrays more truth than our own reality by inspiring us to look within while being entertained. Akira Toriyama tells his stories with myths, legends, archetypes, symbolism, monsters, and elements from classic stories that have been told for thousands of years around campfires, or while putting children to bed. He then mixes this with religious undertones that do not appear religious, and thus does not cause a dichotomous black and white to offend his readers. His work can be enjoyed by everyone.

Society

The society of Dragon World is avant-garde. The majority of citizens are *ningen* (人間, "human beings"),[4] with every skin tone and race of our own planet, but it is also home to ghosts, demons, and other non-humans. All of the people on Earth are considered *chikyū-jin* (地球人, "Earthlings"), with the subsets of *monsutā-gata* (モンスター型, "monster-type") or *dōbutsu-gata* (動物型, "animal-type").[5]

Talking animals populate the land like in a fairy tale. I

---

4   *Ningen* (人間, "human being," "person," or "man") is a Japanese Buddhist term that refers to all *nin* (人, "people") in the human plane of reincarnation that have entered the *gen* (間, "gate") of man, no matter what planet they are on.

5   *Daizenshū 7* and *Chō-zenshū 4* state that *monsutā-gata* (モンスター型, "monster-type") Earthlings make up approximately 7% of the global population. "Monster" is in *katakana*, suggesting they are considered foreign from normal people. They're not called *yōkai* (妖怪, "specters," or "ghosts"), used for traditional Japanese monsters.

suspect there are two reasons for their presence. The first reason is *Xīyóujì*, with Xuánzàng's animal-like companions, the animal-based demons they fight against, and shape-shifting animals who take on human form with primal characteristics. We see these in the humanoid animal people. The second reason is Disney's influence on Toriyama's young mind. He loves how Disney portrays animals' personalities, so he adds them into his *manga* to enrich the world. We see these in the talking sea turtles and dolphins.

Everyone in the Dragon World speaks the same language, and that happens to be whatever language the series is translated into. *Daizenshū 7* calls it the *uchū kō yōgo* (宇宙公用語, "universal official language"). Toriyama likely does this out of convenience. He wants to do what's easiest, so if he has to create a new language for each species (because it makes logical sense to do so), he won't do it. Of course, since Toriyama loves aliens, you've got to have an alien language in there somewhere. But aside from that one instance, it's a universal language across the cosmos.

Just as with the title of the series being in English, there are instances of English written into the *manga* that appear on clothing, billboards, names of buildings, and places. Toriyama creates his *manga* in the 1980s and '90s, when it's cool to use English in illustrations, so no matter where the series is translated, English will be present.

Despite their differences in appearance, each race lives alongside others without signs of racial or species-based conflict. The humanoid animals are treated the same as humans, regardless of being born a tiger, bear, or rabbit. Everyone wears clothes, drives a car, and goes to work in the morning. In this manner Toriyama presents a world of multiculturalism, with distinct yet integrated races and species, while keeping it light.

Dinosaurs

Humans and dinosaurs walk the Earth together, from tyrannosaurus rex to brontosaurus, pterodactyl, and triceratops. According to the *Dragon Ball* guidebooks, 65 million years ago the dinosaurs on this Earth, "stubbornly refuse to go extinct." So it's common to see a dinosaur on the horizon or a Saber-tooth cat creeping through the jungles.

I believe that Toriyama creates this world of dinosaurs and men living together because of cinematic influences.

The story of why begins with Ray Harryhausen (June 29, 1920 – May 7, 2013), an American visual effects originator, writer, and producer who created several classic films and monsters. When Ray is a child he sees the movie *King Kong* (1933) and is so inspired by its use of stop motion animation that he makes animation and monster design his life's work. Ray becomes obsessed with *King Kong* the same way that Toriyama becomes obsessed with Bruce Lee's *Enter the Dragon*. He goes on to create *Mighty Joe Young* (1949), *The 7th Voyage of Sinbad* (1958), *Mysterious Island* (1961), *Jason and the Argonauts* (1963), *One Million Years B.C.* (1966), *The Valley of Gwangi* (1969), and *Clash of the Titans* (1981), among others. His innovations and accomplishments bring fantasy to life on the silver screen where men fight with giant apes, crab monsters, dinosaurs, Saber-tooth cats, and aliens in flying saucers: all of which appear in *Dragon Ball*.

Many of his films are established on the "Lost World" concept of science fiction or fantasy. This is where human beings stumble into a realm that has been lost to time or is an alternate dimension. The titular example is Sir Arthur Conan Doyle's (May 22, 1859 – July 7, 1930) novel *The Lost World* (1912; turned into a film in 1925), where reporters travel into the Amazon and discover it is filled with dinosaurs and savage ape-men. Another is *The Land That Time Forgot* (1918) by Edgar Rice Burroughs (September 1, 1875 –

March 19, 1950), author of *Tarzan of the Apes* (1914), whom Gokū shares qualities with. These novels and their film adaptations inspire generations of young boys to believe in romance and adventure.

When Tezuka Osamu, Toriyama's young idol, decides to create a new *manga* in 1948, he follows their path and creates *Rosuto wārudo <Zenseiki>* (ロスト・ワールド<前世紀>, "*Lost World <Last Century>*"). It's a 2-volume *manga* adaptation of Doyle's story, where scientists and detectives travel to a planet filled with dinosaurs. Likewise when *King Kong* becomes a hit in Japan, film makers are inspired to create their own giant monster movies and start the *kaijū* genre, beginning with *Gojira* (1954).

So it's these "Lost World" type novels that lead to *King Kong*, that lead to Ray Harryhausen's films, that lead to Tezuka and *kaijū*, that lead to Toriyama reading Tezuka's work and watching these movies.

For *One Million Years B.C.* in particular, Toriyama says in his *Sutārogu* interview that he enjoys the stop motion animation style of the dinosaurs. That's likely why the dinosaurs in this movie are also in *Dragon Ball*.

The cinematic influences on Toriyama's mind not only shape his characters, but the living and breathing world they call home. These additions from a Lost World enrich his own world.

It's also fascinating that this aligns with alternative history theorists who believe that dinosaurs and humans existed at the same time. It's as if the *Dragon Ball* story takes place on an Earth in a period of time when mankind coexists with dinosaurs, or in a prehistoric civilization prior to the dinosaurs' demise. Is Toriyama a believer in such ideas? I don't know, but I can say for certain that it makes for an exciting place. Just imagine if there were a dinosaur outside your window right now!

Timeline

After civilization is formed, a timeline is created to provide a calendar system of chronological progression. In this system the years are referred to as Ēji (エージ, "Age"). Toriyama uses this modern English loanword instead of the traditional *jidai* (時代, "period") used in Japan.

For example, Gokū is born in Ēji 737, and Chapter 1 of *Dragon Ball* occurs in Ēji 749. Most of the events in *Dragon Ball* occur in the Ēji 700s before or during Gokū's lifetime.

The origin of the Ēji system has never been explained. The only time an Ēji is ever mentioned in the *manga* is in *Dragon Ball* Chapter 358,[6] when Torankusu (トランクス, "Trunks") inspects Seru's (セル, "Cell's") time machine and says it comes from "Ēji 788." This is the handle upon which all other events are situated in the official timelines. Prior to this moment the series lacked a specific 'time and place.'

As the series progresses, the canonical *manga* mentions events a few hundred years prior to the start of the story. But the video games, guidebooks, and other media contain content as far back as over 100 million years prior to the establishment of the Ēji system, at Ēji 1. This period is called *kigenzen* (紀元前, "Before Age").[7] So the timeline uses a modern foreign term of Ēji for the current era and a traditional Japanese term of *kigenzen* for the prior era.

---

6   *Dragon Ball* Chapter 358 is titled *Jāku na Yokan* (邪悪な予感, "A Premonition of Evil") and premieres in *Weekly Shōnen Jump* #8 on January 28, 1992.

7   *Kigenzen* is a Japanese word that can also be translated as B.C. or BCE, but the term doesn't inherently refer to Christ, and is used in things besides the Western calendar. In a similar manner, Ēji is sometimes incorrectly Romanized by fans as "A.D.," so they make the mistake of believing that the timeline is divided into B.C. and A.D. But Ēji and *kigenzen* are secular terms.

Government

The world is divided into 43 *chiku* (地区, "districts"), united under a central government led by a king named Koku-ō (国王, "Nation King"). He's a talking dog that lives in Kingu Kyassuru (キング キャッスル, "King Castle") inside the capital Chū-*no-miyako* (中の都, "Central City").

Prior to the unification between Ēji 550 and Ēji 650 the 43 *chiku* are 43 distinct countries. Toriyama's choice of 43 *chiku* is likely inspired by the 43 *ken* (県, "prefectures") of ancient Japan.[8]

We don't know how the world was unified, but Koku-ō is a peaceful ruler who has served 20 consecutive terms by the time of *Dragon Ball* Episode 113. In this episode he says, "As long as I draw breath I pledge to you I will guide our fair domain under the principles of truth, justice, and harmony among all living things."

There is a one world government ruled by a king, but there are also lesser kings and mayors of smaller towns and cities. This means it could be a monarchial democracy,

---

8   In the "Akira Toriyama" chapter I said that Japan has 47 *ken* (県, "prefectures"), which are divisional regions of the country. But here I say there are 43. This is because there are 43 *ken* proper, with an additional 4 regions. These consist of the one *to* (都, "metropolis") of Tōkyō, the one *dō* (道, "circuit") of Hokkaidō (北海道, "Northern Sea Circuit"), and the two *fu* (府, "urban prefectures") of Ōsaka-*fu* (大阪府, "Great Hillside Urban Prefecture") and Kyōto-*fu* (京都府, "Capital City Urban Prefecture"). Altogether they are called the *to-dō-fu-ken* (都道府県), but the difference between them is arbitrary, so they're often referred to as the 47 *ken*. Nonetheless, the 43 *ken* were designated in 1868 at the end of Japan's fuedal era, and the additional 4 were designated in 1871 during the start of its modern era, so I suspect that Toriyama uses the 43 *chiku* (地区, "districts") to give his Dragon World a more traditional feel and connect it to the original 43 *ken*.

unless the king appoints them. The king serves terms, so it is not a dictatorship. And there are a variety of careers and fashions, so it does not appear to be a communist hegemony. Little else is known about the social structure.

Much like a dynastic Chinese feudal system, there are several capitals across the world where power is organized. These include Kita-*no-miyako* (北の都, "North City"), Azuma-*no-miyako* (東の都, "East City"), and Nishi-*no-miyako* (西の都, "West City"), which are similar in concept to China's Běijīng (北京, "Northern Capital"), Nánjīng (南京, "Southern Capital"), and Xī'ān (西安, "Western Peace"). Citizens tend to congregate in these large cities, with outlying plantations and villages.

Outside of the urban centers are large swathes of barren nothingness, which often reflect different wastelands or mountainous regions of our own world. Gokū tends to fight his opponents in these environments in order to ensure that civilians are not harmed. Of course, there is a less profound reason which Toriyama provides in *Daizenshū 4*, saying, "After all, it'd be rough if Gokū and the others fought in the middle of a city. I'd have to draw the residents who lived in the city, and the buildings would get destroyed. That's why whenever they were about to fight, Gokū and the others would want to go to some wilderness where nobody lived. (laughs) They'd just use *bukū-jutsu* to take off, like it had been arranged ahead of time."[9]

The largest and wealthiest technology company in the world is the Kapuseru Kōporēshon (カプセルコーポレーション, "Capsule Corporation"). It has its headquarters in Nishi-*no-miyako*. This "West City" is filled with Western technology and science, while Gokū lives in the Eastern area of the world that reflects Eastern culture. His home is a hermit hut, and he has never seen a piece of technology.

---

9 *Bukū-jutsu* (舞空術, "cloud dancing technique") is the primary technique of self-powered flight used in *Dragon Ball*.

Currency

The centralized government in the Dragon World uses a form of currency called *zenī* (ゼニー, with the symbol of Ƶ).

This sounds like a made up term, but the history of *zenī* begins in Táng Dynasty China. Here the term is *qián* (錢, "money," or "currency"). The character is a combination of "money" (金) with "farm tools" (戔), because in such agrarian days you farmed to earn money. The *qián* coins are often made of copper or iron, and serve as a practical micro unit of silver or gold bars for daily commerce. They're shaped as circles with square holes in the center that allow them to be strung together. Their circular shape earns them the nickname of *yuán* (元, "circles," or "rounds"). Their convenience causes them to become the common currency throughout China for over 1,000 years.

The *qián* is then exported to Japan during the Edo-*jidai* (江戸時代, "Cove Gate Era," 1603 – 1868). Here it's called *zeni* (錢), written with a more modern character for "money" (戋), and takes on the meaning of "spending cash." The *yuán* (元) nickname for the coins carries over along with it, and the Japanese transliterate it as *gen* (元).

In 1871 the Meiji government decides to reform their system in order to modernize it. In the process they establish the *yen* (円, "circle," with the symbol of ¥). It's a modern and simplified form of the ancient *yen* (圓, "circle"). Like the nickname of *gen*, it means circle, but has a greater value and is perceived as modern and therefore better. However, *zeni* are so common that they are still used. They're also now called *seni* or *sen*. Since they're worth so little, the terms carry the meaning of "loose change." They are worth one-hundredth of a *yen* (¥), similar to a United States' cent compared to a dollar. Nevertheless, by the time of World War II the *zeni* (or *seni*) are so devalued that they are taken out of circulation in 1953.

Why does Toriyama name the Dragon World's money after *zeni* instead of *yen*? Because even though *zeni* are taken out of circulation it doesn't mean people stop using the term. It remains a colloquial expression for money among older generations and those in the countryside. I suspect that since Toriyama grows up in the countryside, he hears this term or uses it himself. Then when he has to come up with a currency for his Dragon World, he thinks back to his childhood and remembers *zeni*. By using *zeni* he creates a currency that feels familiar to Japanese readers without being a modern *yen*. This allows him to maintain the comic's fantasy feeling, yet still be relatable.

But when he writes it, instead of using the ancient *kanji* for *zeni* (銭) that his 1980s readers won't understand, he modernizes it in *katakana* as *zenī* (ゼニー) with an elongated 'i.' So *zenī* are different and foreign, yet still Japanese. A perfect source of money for his Dragon World. And how appropriate that Toriyama would use an ancient term for money that originates in the Táng for his adaptation of the Táng Monk's story, whether intentional or not.

How much is a *zenī* worth? In the *Super Exciting Guide: Character Volume* (2009), Toriyama says that to keep it easy to understand, "I envisioned them as the same as *yen*." To give context, the champion of the largest martial arts tournament on Earth, the Tenkaichi Budōkai, earns 500,000 *zenī* (~ $4,200 USD).

Dragon Ball's success causes *zenī* to carry over into other forms of pop culture. Video games created in the late '80s and early '90s tend to use gold as their currency, but some games shift over to *zenī*, including several developed by Kabushiki-gaisha Kapukon (株式会社カプコン, "Capcom," founded 1983) such as *Sutorīto Faitā* (ストリートファイター, "Street Fighter," 1987), *Rokkuman* (ロックマン, "Rockman," aka "*Mega Man*," 1987), and *Buresu obu Faia* (ブレスオブファイア, "Breath of Fire," 1993). The over 100 *Dragon Ball* video games also use *zenī* as the official in-game currency.

Fusion

Toriyama fuses these factors together to create a lush world of extremes and stereotypes of our own world's culture, interwoven and made accessible. Whether it be Western pioneer villages that have a 'cowboy' feel to them, filled with saloons and steam trains inspired by American Wild West films, or a 'quaint Chinese village' surrounded by bamboo, as if taken from a Jackie Chan film, the world comes alive in a magical way that is still believable. Add in super intelligent robots, fairy tale creatures, monsters, alien worlds, and magical wish-granting orbs that are sought after by power-hungry demons, and you have a wonderful setting for our adventure.

This is the Dragon World's charm.

Enter the Dragon World

The Dragon World is a place best experienced firsthand.

So without further ado, let's begin Gokū's adventure and discover the *Dragon Ball* spirit for ourselves.

Conclusion

YOU'VE JUST DISCOVERED the origin of *Dragon Ball* and stepped inside the mind of its creator, Akira Toriyama.

If you're familiar with Gokū's story, then certain elements are clicking together and a bigger picture is unfolding before your eyes. You're starting to see that *Dragon Ball* is a product of its environment, like Akira Toriyama himself. It's a creative fusion of history, language, spirituality, and symbolic illustrations that results in what fans across the world describe as the perfect *shōnen manga*.

Now it's time for you to embark on a journey through ancient times and scientific futures. To enter a realm where witchcraft and technology mix with gods, demons, and martial artists who fight for the chance to summon a wish-granting dragon. You'll enter a world where anything can happen, and a young boy's adventure changes the lives of everyone he meets.

***

A young girl picks up a glowing orange ball and says, "I found this ball in a storeroom in my house. I wondered what it was, so I did some research and found out they're really amazing!"

Gokū asks her, "What's so amazing 'bout 'em?"

She replies, "Want me to tell you?"

Next Steps

Want to find out what happens next?
   Then pick up *Dragon Ball Culture Volume 2: Adventure!*

Thanks for reading my book. I have several more books planned in *The Dao of Dragon Ball* series, but in order to write them I need your help.

Rate this Book

Please rate this book online.
   Your positive review will help me to continue writing.

Share this Book

Please share this book with your friends and let them know you enjoyed it.
   I wrote this book for *Dragon Ball* fans across the world, but as a self-published author I don't have the means to market it on such a wide scale. So tell your friends about it.

Write to the Author

I'm eager to hear from you, so write to me at:
   http://thedaoofdragonball.com

About the Author

Derek Padula is the author of *The Dao of Dragon Ball* website and book series; the first to reveal the deep history, philosophy, and culture of the world's #1 *anime* and *manga*.

Derek first saw the *Dragon Ball anime* in 1997. His love for the series inspired him to start martial arts training in Shàolín *gōngfu, tàijí-quán, qìgōng, karate*, and Fǎlún Dàfǎ meditation. He earned his B.A. in East Asian Studies and a minor in Chinese from Western Michigan University. He studied abroad in Běijīng, China and trained with the Buddhist Shàolín monks and a Dàoist *tàijí* sword master. After returning home, he became an authority on *Dragon Ball*.

Glossary

# #

101 Dalmatians (1961): An animated Disney film about spotted talking dogs and their escape from a cruel lady who wants to turn them into a fur coat. Akira Toriyama says he was inspired by this film.

A

Aichi-ken (愛知県, "Loving Wisdom Prefecture"): Birthplace of Akira Toriyama, creator of *Dragon Ball*, located in central Japan.

Aichi-ken-ritsu okoshi kōgyō kōtō gakkō (愛知県立起工業高等学校, "Aichi Prefectural Okoshi Technical High School"): The art-focused technical high school that Akira Toriyama attends in 1971, graduating from their *dezain-ka*.

Akatsuka Fujio (赤塚 不二夫, September 14, 1935 – August 2, 2008): A *manga-ka* who is considered "the gag *manga* king." His comedy influences Akira Toriyama's work.

Akihito (明仁, "Second Born Brightness"): See "Heisei-tennō Akihito."

Akira (明, "bright," "light," "brilliant," or "clear"): A Japanese *kanji*.

Akira Kurosawa (黒澤 明, March 23, 1910 – September 6, 1998): A Japanese film director famous for his *samurai* films and epic drama's. His *jidai-geki* films influence Akira Toriyama's work.

Akira Toriyama (鳥山明): See "Toriyama Akira."

Alien (1979): A science fiction film about a space alien that hunts and kills human beings. Akira Toriyama says this is one of his favorite films, and the design of the alien influences his character designs.

American International Pictures (AIP, founded 1954): An American film studio dedicated to releasing low-budget independent films that appealed to teenagers. Responsible for the localization of Tezuka Osamu's *Saiyūki* film, retitled as *Alakazam the Great*.

American Shonen Jump: The American magazine that published licensed *manga* from Japan, including *Dragon Ball* and other Akira Toriyama works. Ran from November 26, 2002 to April 2012.

Anime (アニメ, "animation"): The Japanese approximation of the English word of animation, referring to animated cartoons on television and in movies.

Araki Hirohiko (荒木 飛呂彦, born 1960): A *manga-ka*. Author of *Busō pōkā* and *JoJo no Kimyō na Bōken*.

Arare-chan: See "Norimaki Arare."

Arhat (Sanskrit: अर्हत्, Chinese: *luóhàn*, 羅漢, Japanese: *arakan*, 阿羅漢, "worthy one"): A perfect being who has awakened and transcended life and death. The first level of enlightenment.

Asahi Shimbun (朝日新聞, "*Morning Sun Newspaper*," founded January 25, 1879): The second largest national newspaper in Japan.

Ásura (Sanskrit: असुर, Chinese: *āxiūluó*, 阿修羅, Japanese: *ashura*, "power hungry deities"): Deities who fell from heaven and now inhabit a lower realm. Savage brutes who thirst for battle and the satiation of their ego's and vanity. Opposite of the *deva*.

Aurel Stein (1862 – 1943): A Hungarian-British archeologist and explorer focused on Central Asia, including India and China. Discoverer of lost scrolls and cultural relics.

Awawa wārudo (あわわワールド, "*Awawa World*"): The first *manga* that Toriyama submits to Shūeisha in 1977 in an attempt to win the Monthly Young Jump Award. It is never commercially published but does appear in the BIRD LAND PRESS section in Akira Toriyama's fan club newsletter, the *Akira Toriyama Hozon-kai*. It is released in two parts, in issue #5 (March, 1983) and issue #6 (May, 1983). It is also included in the Akira Toriyama Exhibition catalog.

Azuma-no-miyako (東の都, "East City"): An eastern city on the Earth of the Dragon World.

B

Báihuà (白話, "plain speech"): An informal way of writing prose in Chinese. Wú Chéng'ēn writes *Xīyóujì* in *báihuà* rather than in an official imperial style or scholar's style.

Bái Lóngmǎ (白龍馬, Japanese: Shiro-ryūma, "White Dragon Horse"): A dragon prince who committed sins in a previous life by disobeying his father in the story of *Xīyóujì*. He also wishes to return to his original, true self. In order to do so he becomes Xuánzàng's beast of burden and carries him and his luggage to their destination and back. It's my belief that this character inspires Buruma's white motorcycle in the first chapter of *Dragon Ball*.

Báimǎ-sì (白馬寺, "White Horse Temple"): A Buddhist temple near Luòyáng, China, founded in 68 A.D. The location where the Buddhist monk Xuánzàng returns from his trip to India carrying the *sūtra*.

Bali: A tropical island and province of Indonesia, 3.2 kilometers east of Java. The model for Papaiya-*shima*. It is a popular destination for Japanese tourists, so this is likely why Toriyama goes there.

Batoru manga (バトル漫画, "battle *manga*"): A *manga* with battles and fighting as the premise. *Dragon Ball* is the quintessential example.

Biān (編, Japanese: *hen*, "arc," "part of a book," "compilation," "composition," "arrangement," or "volume"): A way of organizing stories into different sub-stories in Chinese and Japanese literature.

Bīru (ビール, "beer"): The Japanese approximation of the English word of beer, referring to an alcoholic beverage.

Běijīng (北京, "Northern Capital"): The current capital of China. Located in the Northeast of the country, west of Korea and Japan.

Bird Land Press: A bi-monthly magazine in Japan created by fans and dedicated to the work of Akira Toriyama.

Bird Studio (バードスタジオ, *Bādo sutajio*): Akira Toriyama's art studio, founded and owned by him. The name is written in English.

Blade Runner (1982): A science fiction film about a detective who hunts down artificial humans called replicants. Stars Harrison Ford.

Bodhidharma (Sanskrit: बोधिधर्म, Chinese: Pútídámó, 菩提达摩, Japanese: Daruma, 達磨, "Enlightened Law," 5th to 6th century A.D.): A sage from Kerala, India who travels to China and spreads the Buddhā Law. Arguably the one who teaches the Shàolín monks the fighting arts of *vajramuṣṭi*.

Bodhisattva (Sanskrit: बोधिसत्त्व, Chinese: *púsà*, 菩薩, "enlightened existence"): An enlightened being who interacts with the world of men to lead people to the Buddhā.

Boku no Son Gokū (ぼくのそんごくう, "*My Son Gokū*," 1953): A *manga* based on *Saiyūki* by Tezuka Osamu. Turned into an animated feature film titled *Saiyūki* in 1960.

Bon (盆, or *obon*, お盆, "the Buddhist festival for dead ancestors"): A traditional and annual *matsuri* in Japan held on the 15th day of the 7th month of the lunar calendar (often in August). A day when ancestors return from the dead and the living pay respects to their family. Influenced by Confucianism.

Bruce Lee (Chinese: Lee Jun-fan, 李振藩, November 27, 1940 – July 20, 1973): Arguably the world's most famous martial artist, despite only filming 4 movies before his unfortunate passing at the age of 32.

Buddhā (Sanskrit: बुद्ध, Chinese: *fó*, 佛, Japanese: *hotoke*, 仏, "enlightened being," or "awakened one"): An enlightened being who awakens to the truth, unlocks their wisdom, and offers salvation to others. Beyond life and death.

Buddhā Law (Sanskrit: *dharma*, धर्म, Chinese: *fófǎ*, 佛法, Japanese: *buppō*). The principles of an enlightened being. Awakened to by Śākyamuni Buddhā and spread throughout India, China, Korea, Japan, and Southeast Asia.

Buddhism ("Beliefs of the Enlightened"): The religion inspired by Buddhā Law. Its teachings profess compassion, and its followers believe it can elicit enlightenment. Originates in India after the enlightenment of Śākyamuni Buddhā. The teachings spread across the world, influencing Chinese and Japanese society and culture.

Bukū-jutsu (舞空術, Chinese: *wùkōng-shù*, "cloud dancing technique," or "dancing sky art") is the technique of self-powered flight that characters in *Dragon Ball* use to fly through the air.

Bunraku (文楽, "puppetry"): Traditional Japanese puppet performances using white-skinned dolls.

Buresu obu Faia (ブレスオブファイア, *"Breath of Fire,"* 1993): One of the world's most famous roleplaying video games. Developed by Kabushiki-gaisha Kapukon.

Burīchi (ブリーチ, *"Bleach,"* 2001): A *shōnen manga* written by Kubo Tite, about a young man who dies and is reborn as a death god.

Buruma (ブルマ): A young woman searching for the dragon balls who encounters Son Gokū and begins the Dragon Ball adventure. Named after *burumā* (ブルマー), the gym shorts worn by Japanese school girls.

Bushidō (武士道, "the way of the warrior"): The Japanese philosophy of self-cultivation through application of martial arts concepts.

Busō pōkā (武装ポーカー, *"Armed Poker,"* 1981): The debut *manga* of Araki Hirohiko.

C

Chan (ちゃん): A Japanese suffix used to refer to young males who are your age or older in an endearing way. It can also be applied to cute girls, such as Arare-*chan*.

Chán (禅, Japanese: Zen, 禅, Sanskrit: *dhyāna*, ध्यान, "oneness," or "contemplation"): The most popular form of Buddhism in China and Japan. Derived from Indian Buddhism.

Cháng'ān (長安, "Perpetual Peace"): The ancient capital of China during the Táng Dynasty. Cháng'ān is the ancient name of Xī'ān.

Chiku (地区, "districts"): The Japanese term for districts or areas of a region. There are 43 *chiku* in the Dragon World, likely inspired by the 43 *ken* in Japan.

Chikyū (地球, "earth ball," or "soil sphere"): The Japanese term for "earth" and the Earth of the Dragon World.

Chikyū-jin (地球人, "Earthlings"): The Japanese term for the citizens of Earth. Not relegated to humans.

Chō-zenshū (超全集, "Super Complete Collections"): The second largest official *Dragon Ball* guidebooks to date, following the *Daizenshū*.

Chū-no-miyako (中の都, "Central City"): The central city and capital of the Earth in the Dragon World.

Christianity ("the anointed one"): An Abrahamic, monotheistic religion, and one of the largest in the world. The principle tenet is salvation through a higher power and compassion for others. It exists in the Dragon World, but does not appear often, and is usually referenced for the sake of humor.

Christopher Sabat (born April 22, 1973): The Voice Director at FUNimation and founder of the recording studio, Okratron 5000, who works with FUNimation to dub the American version of the *Dragon Ball* series. Also a voice actor for several main characters.

Cíbēi (慈悲, "mercy"): A Chinese word for the belief that the gods are good and offer mercy to humanity and other sentient beings.

Confucianism (Chinese: 儒家; *rú-jiā*, "School of Scholars"): A Chinese philosophy and religion founded upon the teachings of Kǒngfūzǐ. Its' teachings profess social order, respect for relationships, and humanistic harmony.

Citta-santāna (Sanskrit: चित्तसंतान, Chinese: *xīn-xiāngxù*, 心相續, Japanese: *shin-sōzoku*, "continual heart"): A Buddhist term for the continual series of moments in the existence of our personality that we call our consciousness.

Clash of the Titans (1981): An action adventure film about the Greek hero Perseus as he battles against mythological monsters.

Clint Eastwood (born May 31, 1930): A Hollywood actor and director, known for his tough guy persona in such films as *Dirty Harry*.

D

Daiei Eiga Kabushiki-gaisha (大映映画株式會社, "Daiei Motion Picture Company," founded in 1942): A Japanese film company that creates *Gamera* to compete with rival Tōhō's *Gojira* series.

Dai Tōzoku (大盗賊, "*The Great Bandit*," 1963): Known internationally as *Samurai Pirate* and in America as *The Lost World of Sinbad*. Akira Toriyama is inspired by this film in his creation of *Dragon Ball*.

Daizenshū (大全集, "*Great Complete Works*"): Guidebooks of the *Dragon Ball* series published from 1995 to 1996.

Dào (道, "the way," or "path"): The universal principles and way of nature, life, and the universe. The "path" followed by a practitioner of the Dào. A "true being" who has awakened to the Dào.

Dàoism ("The Beliefs of the Way"): The native belief system of China. The Patriarch is Lǎozi, and the principle tenet is *zhēn*. The organized religion is called Dào-*jiào*.

Dào-jiā (道家, "School of the Way"): See "Dàoism."

Dào-jiào (道教, "Teachings of the Way"): Religious Dàoism. The native belief system of China, and the principles of those who follow the Dào. Its primary focus is on *zhēn*.

Dàtáng sānzàng qǔjīng shīhuà (大唐三藏取經詩話, "*Tripiṭaka of the Great Táng Seeks the Scriptures, a Tale with Verse*," circa 1280): A fanciful extrapolation of Xuánzàng's real life journey written in China to entertain the masses.

Dàtáng Xīyóujì (大唐西遊記, Japanese: *Ōkara Saiyūki*, 大唐西遊記, "*The Journey to the West in the Great Táng*"): Xuánzàng's biographical journey as transcribed by his disciple in 646 A.D. A cultural and historical record, as well as precursor to the fables that inspire *Xīyóujì*.

Deva (Sanskrit: देव, Chinese: *tiān*, 天, Japanese: *ten*, "gods"): Gods of the Indian belief systems.

Dezain-ka (デザイン科, "design course"): A course in Japanese high school centered around design and illustration. Toriyama graduates from this course.

Dhárma (Sanskrit: धर्म, Chinese: *fǎ*, 法, Japanese: *hō*, "law," or "principles"): Refers to the Buddhā Law as taught by Śākyamuni Buddhā. But not exclusive to only his school of thought.

Dirty Harry (1971): An action film about a cop who takes justice into his own hands, with his iconic magnum revolver. Stars Clint Eastwood, whom Toriyama parodies.

Disney ("The Walt Disney Company," founded October 16, 1923): A multinational animation and film company based in Los Angeles, California. Their films inspired Akira Toriyama during his childhood to continue drawing.

Dìyù (地獄, "Hell"): A lower realm in which beings suffer to repay their *karma* before reincarnating.

Dìyùrén (地獄人, Japanese: *jigokunin*, "hell people"): The people of hell in Buddho-Dàoist cosmology. In contrast to the *tiānrén*.

Dōbutsu-gata (動物型, "animal-type"): A type of Earthling other than a *ningen* on the Dragon World's Earth. Talking animals that may or may not appear humanoid, but are nonetheless sentient.

Dokutā Suranpu (*Dr.* スランプ, "*Dr. Slump*"): See "*Dr. Slump*."

Doraemon (ドラえもん, 1969): A famous *manga* and *anime* about a robotic cat that travels back in time to aid a young boy.

Doragon Bōi (騎竜少年, pronounced in *katakana* as ドラゴンボーイ, "*Dragon Boy*," 1983): A 2-chapter *yomikiri shōnen manga* published in *Fresh Jump* (*Furesshu janpu*, フレッシュジャンプ) magazine in August to October of that year. The precursor to *Dragon Ball*.

Dragon Ball (ドラゴンボール, "*Doragon Bōru*"): A *manga* series written by Akira Toriyama from 1984 to 1995, adapted into a hit *anime*, video game, and merchandise franchise. The quintessential *batoru manga* and the world's most recognized *manga* and *anime*. The anime is 153 episodes long.

Dragon Ball: Bōken Special (ドラゴンボール 冒険SPECIAL, "*Dragon Ball: Adventure Special*," 1987): A guidebook covering the first years of Toriyama's *Dragon Ball manga*, with games, interviews, and data.

Dragon Ball GT (ドラゴンボールGT, "*Doragon Bōru Jī Tī*"): An *anime* inspired by Akira Toriyama's *Dragon Ball manga* and produced by Tōei. It is 64 episodes long and aired in Japan from February 2, 1996 to November 19, 1997.

Dragon Ball Z (ドラゴンボールZ, "*Doragon Bōru Zetto*"): An *anime* based on Volumes 17 to 42 of Akira Toriyama's *Dragon Ball manga*, from Chapter 195 to 519. It is 291 episodes long.

Dragon Ball Z: Kami to Kami (ドラゴンボールZ 神と神, *Doragon Bōru Zetto: Kami to Kami*, "*Dragon Ball Z: God and God*," or "*Battle of Gods*," 2013): The fourteenth *Dragon Ball Z* film, about a *hakai-shin* named Beerusu who comes to Earth in search of a god.

Dragon balls (ドラゴンボール): Seven mystical balls that can be used to summon the wish-granting Shenron.

Dragon World (ドラゴンワールド, "*doragon wārudo*"): The cosmos and mythos of *Dragon Ball's* universe, not just the actual planet that the cast lives on.

Dr. No (1962): First *James Bond* film, based on novels by Ian Fleming.

Dr. Mashirito (博士マシリト): The archenemy of Dr. Slump and a man determined to control everything. He is inspired by Akira Toriyama's editor, Torishima Kazuhiko.

Dr. Suranpu (Dr. スランプ, *Dokutā Suranpu*, "*Dr. Slump*", 1979): Akira Toriyama's breakthrough *manga*. A gag *manga* about a young robot girl with nearsighted vision who is naïve yet super powerful.

Dr. Suranpu Arare-chan (*Dr.*スランプ アラレちゃん, 1981): The *anime* adaptation of the *Dr. Suranpu manga*.

Dr. Suranpu Arare-chan Harō! Wandā Airando (*Dr.*スランプ アラレちゃん ハロー! 不思議島, "*Dr. Slump and Arare-chan: Hello! Wonder Island*," July 7, 1981): The first *Dr. Slump* animated film. Premieres at the Tōei Anime Fea.

Dòu-zhànshèng-fó (鬥戰勝佛, "Buddhā Victorious in Fighting"): The name of Sūn Wùkōng as an enlightened being. Given to him at the completion of his journey west. Also written as *dòu-zhàn-fó* (鬥戰佛, "War Fighting Buddhā"). This name has clear parallels with Son Gokū in *Dragon Ball*, with his love of fighting.

E

Edgar Rice Burroughs (September 1, 1875 – March 19, 1950): Novelist, and author of *Tarzan of the Apes* (1914).

Edo (江戸): The former name of Tōkyō, the capital of Japan, renamed in 1868 at the end of the Edo-*jidai*.

Edo-jidai (江戸時代, "Cove Gate Era," 1603 – 1868 A.D.). An alternate name of the Tokugawa-*jidai*. Edo is the former name of Tōkyō, the capital of Japan, having been renamed in 1868 at the end of the era.

Èguǐ (餓鬼, "hungry ghost"): A state of being in Buddhism where a person is neither dead nor alive, but suffers from hunger, thirst, and discomfort until they reincarnate.

Eitoman (8マン, "*8 Man*," 1963): An *anime* about a human turned android who uses martial arts to defeat villains and maintain world peace. Based on a *manga* written by Hirai Kazumasa and Jirō Kuwata.

Ēji (エージ, "Age"): A "year" in the Dragon World timeline.

Eiji Tsuburaya (円谷 英二, July 10, 1901 – January 25, 1970): Director of special effects at Tōhō kabushiki-gaisha, working on *Gojira* and other *kaijū* films. The creator of *Urutoraman*. Has a great influence on Akira Toriyama's work.

Enter the Dragon (Chinese: *Lóngzhēng Hǔdòu*, 龍爭虎鬥, 1973): Bruce Lee's seminal film that makes him an international star. Akira Toriyama says that this is one of his favorite films and it has a great influence on his work.

F

Fǎlún Dàfǎ (法輪大法, "Law Wheel Great Law"): A Buddho-Dàoist style of *qìgōng* practice founded by Teacher Lǐ Hóngzhì (李洪志, born May 13, 1951) in Gōngzhǔlǐng (公主嶺), China), and made public in 1992. The principles of Fǎlún Dàfǎ are *zhēn, shàn, rěn,* (真, 善, 忍, "Truthfulness, Compassion, Forbearance"). The practice has been persecuted in China by the Chinese Communist Party since July 20, 1999, with at least 60 million people labeled criminals, and thousands tortured and killed for their beliefs.

Fat Man: The fission bomb dropped on Hiroshima-*shi*, Japan, on August 6, 1945.

Fǎxiǎn (法顯, "Manifest Law," 337 – 422 A.D.): A Chinese monk who traveled to India and back to recover *sūtra*. Precursor to Xuánzàng.

Fó-jiā (佛家, "School of the Enlightened"): See "Buddhism." Counterpart to Dào-*jiā*.

Frankie Avalon (born September 18, 1940): An American actor, singer, playwright, and former teen idol. Provided the singing voice of Alakazam (Son Gokū) in the American localization of *Saiyūki* (1960, "*Alakazam the Great*," 1961).

Fresh Jump (*Furesshu janpu*, フレッシュジャンプ): A *manga* anthology publication in Japan.

Fujiko Fujio (藤子不二雄): The name of a *manga* writing duo consisting of Fujimoto Hiroshi (藤本 弘, December 1, 1933 – September 23, 1996) and Abiko Motoo (安孫子 素雄, born March 10, 1934). Creators of *Doraemon*.

Fuji-san (富士山, "Mount Fuji"): The highest mountain in Japan, and a cultural icon.

Fuji Terebi (フジテレビ, "Fuji Television"): See "Kabushiki-gaisha Fuji Terebijon."

FUNimation: The American license holder and English dubbing studio for the *Dragon Ball anime*. Because of their success with *Dragon Ball* they are the largest *anime* dubbing studio in North America.

Furigana (振り仮名, "pronunciation scripts"): A reading aid for pronouncing *kanji*. It consists of writing *hiragana* and *katakana* characters next to the *kanji* to clarify the proper pronunciation.

G

Gairaigo (外来語, "loanwords"): Foreign words transliterated into Japanese.

Gakushū juku (学習塾, "tutoring classes"): A common aspect of modern Japanese society, where students do more studying after their regular school hours are complete.

Gandamu (ガンダム, "Gundam," 1979): The quintessential animated space opera series of *anime* and *manga*.

Ganpura (ガンプラ, "Gunpla"): A portmanteau of "*Gandamu* Plastic Model." This refers to the plastic model kits of *Gandamu meka*.

Gamera (ガメラ, 1965): A film about a giant radioactive turtle *kaijū*. Produced by the Daiei Eiga Kabushiki-gaisha film studio to compete with *Gojira*, produced by Tōhō Kabushiki-gaisha.

Gojira (ゴジラ, "Godzilla," 1954): A film about a giant radioactive lizard monster that attacks Tokyo. The quintessential *kaijū*. Produced by Tōhō kabushiki-gaisha.

Gōngfu (功夫, "great effort," "kung fu"): A catchall term for the martial arts of China.

Gōngfu zhīwáng (功夫之王, *"The Forbidden Kingdom,"* 2008): An American adaptation of the *Xīyóujì* story made for Western audiences, starring Jackie Chan and Jet Li.

Go-Rōshi-sama (ご老師様, "Elder Master"): The master of Tanton in Akira Toriyama's *Doragon Bōi manga*.

Guānyīn Bodhisattva (Sanskrit: Avalokiteśvara, अवलोकितेश्वर, Chinese: Guānyīn-*púsà*, 觀音菩薩, Japanese: Kannon, 観音, "the enlightened being who hears your cries"): An enlightened being who offers salvation to mankind. A main character in *Xīyóujì* who inspires, leads, and protects the pilgrims on their journey.

Guìlín (桂林, "Laurel Trees"): A region of China renowned for its unique karst mountain formations. Toriyama uses this area as inspiration for Paozu-*yama*.

Gyagu manga (ギャグ漫画, "gag comic"): A genre of lighthearted *manga* where the author puts his characters into funny situations and makes jokes along the way.

Gyaru (ギャル, "gal"): A Western expression for a young woman.

Gyaru keiji tomato (ギャル刑事トマト, *"Tomato, Girl Detective,"* August 15, 1979). Toriyama's third published work, a *yomikiri* about a blundering female detective.

H

Hàn Dynasty (漢朝, Hàn-*cháo*, "Dry Riverbed Dynasty," 206 B.C. – 220 A.D.): A golden age of Chinese civilization. The central Chinese people still refer to themselves as the *hànrén* (漢人, "Hàn people") and their written text is called *hànzì* (漢字, "Hàn characters").

Hànrén (漢人, "Hàn people"): The term that mainland Chinese people residing in the central valley use to refer to themselves. Refers to the Hàn Dynasty.

Hànzì (漢字, "Hàn Chinese characters"): The character-based writing system of the Chinese used for thousands of years. Exported to Japan where they are called *kanji*.

Harrison Ford (born July 13, 1942): A Hollywood actor best known for his roles in *Star Wars* and *Indiana Jones*.

Heian-jidai (平安時代, "Era of Peace," 794 – 1185 A.D.): The height of Buddhist, Dàoist, and other Chinese influences in Japan. A period of refined art, architecture, and poetry.

Heisei (平成, "Accomplished Balance"): Refers to a period of television from 1990 to the present, with a more serious tone, shifting from the Shōwa-*jidai's* lightheartedness.

Heisei-jidai (平成時代, "Era of Accomplished Balance"): The reign of *Heisei* Emperor Akihito, from November 12, 1990 to the present.

Heisei-tennō Akihito (平成天皇明仁, "Era of Accomplished Balance Emperor Akihito," born December 23, 1933): Emperor of Japan from December 25, 1926 through January 7, 1989. Succeeded his father, Hirohito, on November 12, 1990.

Hen (編, Chinese: *biān*, "arc," "part of a book," "compilation," "composition," "arrangement," or "volume"): A way of organizing stories into different sub-stories in Chinese and Japanese writing. *Dragon Ball* is organized into *hen*.

Henshin (変身, "body change," or "physical transformation"): The act of transforming the body into another form. Used by *tokusatsu* superheroes and *yōkai* monsters.

Hijiri mefisuto konran-den (聖メフィスト混乱伝, "*The Confusing Legend of St. Mephisto*," 1985): A *manga* written by Akira Toriyama's wife, Mikami Nachi.

Hime-sama (姫様, "princess"): The Japanese word for a princess. The generic name of the princess in *Doragon Bōi*.

Hīnayāna (Sanskrit: हीनयान, Chinese: Xiǎochéng, 小乘, "Small Vehicle"): The original Buddhism as taught by Śākyamuni Buddhā, with an emphasis on self-salvation. In contrast to Mahāyāna.

Hiragana (平仮名, "ordinary scripts"): The syllabic writing system of Japan used for native words, consisting of round letters and shapes. Counterpart to *katakana*.

Hirai Kazumasa (平井 和正, born May 13, 1938): A *manga-ka* and co-creator of *Eitoman*.

Hirohito (裕仁): See "Shōwa-*tennō* Hirohito."

Hiroshima-shi (広島市, "Vast Island City"): A Japanese city, and the victim of the Fat Man fission bomb on August 6, 1945.

Hokkaidō (北海道, "Northern Sea Circuit"): The largest and northernmost prefecture in Japan. One of four main islands of Japan.

Honjitsu no hairai-shima (本口のハイライ島, *"Today's Highlight Island"*): Toriyama's *manga* about a young boy who suffers a toothache.

Hóng Lóu Mèng (紅樓夢, *"Dream of the Red Chamber,"* circa 16th century): One of the world's first novels, and *sìdà míngzhù* Chinese classic. Tells a story of the inner court.

Hugh Hefner (born April 9, 1926): Founder of Playboy Enterprises Inc. and *Playboy* magazine.

I

Ie (家, "family home"): The prototypical Japanese family from the 1930s to '50s. It consists of a father, mother, son, and daughter.

J

Jackie Chan (Chinese: Chan Kong-sang, 陳港生, "Exhibit Harbor Life," acting name Chéng Lóng, 成龍, "Accomplished Dragon," born April 7, 1954): A martial arts actor and fight choreographer with a comedic style. Akira Toriyama loves Jackie Chan's movies and watches them countless times. Chan's film *Zuì-quán* is one of the main sources of inspiration for the creation of *Dragon Ball*.

James Bond (1962): An action adventure film series about a British secret agent named James Bond; an action-oriented man who uses gadgets to fight against megalomaniacs. It has a great influence on Akira Toriyama's work, particularly in Part 2 of the *Dragon Ball* story.

Jason and the Argonauts (1963): An action adventure film based on the ancient tale of Jason, featuring advanced stop-motion special effects and mythical creatures.

Jaws (1975): A horror film about a giant man-eating great white shark that terrorizes a New England beach on the Atlantic Ocean. It is a series of films. The likely source of inspiration for the giant shark in the lake on Shugyō-*no-shima*. Also see "Megalodon."

Jet Li (Chinese: Lǐ Liánjié, 李连杰, born April 26, 1963): A martial artist, actor, producer, and international star. Makes his acting debut in the film *Shàolín-sì* (少林寺, "*Shaolin Temple*," 1982), a landmark movie that inspires Toriyama in his creation of Kuririn.

Jiāhé yúlè jítuán yǒuxiàn gōngsī (Chinese: 嘉禾娛樂集團有限公司, "Golden Harvest Entertainment Group," founded 1970): A Hong Kong film studio that produced and distributed Bruce Lee and Jackie Chan's films. Their iconic logo at the start of each movie inspired the opening of each *Dragon Ball* episode in which there is a Tenkaichi Budōkai.

Jiǎnhuà-zì (簡化字, "simplified characters"): The simplified *hànzì* used in mainland China. They are an altered set of characters, stripped of cultural or historical content.

Jidai-geki (時代劇, "period drama"): A genre of Japanese television set in the feudal era.

Jìn Dynasty (晉朝, Jìn-*cháo*, "Advance Dynasty," 265 – 420 A.D.): An expansion of China's borders into the south and southeast. Refinement of artworks and incorporation of Buddhism.

Jīngāng-lún (金刚轮, Japanese: *kongō-rin*, "thunderbolt ring," "lightning bolt circle," or "*vajra* diadem"): The diadem (or coronet) that binds itself around Sūn Wùkōng's head and tightens whenever Xuánzàng chants *sūtra*, causing such intense and instantaneous pain that it's like being struck by lightning.

Jìngtán-shǐzhě (淨壇使者, "Altar Cleanser Envoy"): The name of Zhū Bājiè's new position given to him at the completion of his journey west.

Jīnpíngméi (金瓶梅, "*Golden Lotus*," 1610): A masterpiece novel alongside *Xīyóujì* and other classics, about the lurid sexual affairs of a nobleman and his many consorts.

Jīnshēn-luóhàn (金身羅漢, "Golden-bodied Arhat"): The title of Shā Wùjìng as an enlightened being. Given to him at the completion of his journey west.

Jirō Kuwata (桑田 二郎, born April 17, 1935): A *manga-ka* and co-creator of *Eitoman*.

JoJo no Kimyō na Bōken (ジョジョの奇妙な冒険, "*JoJo's Bizarre Adventure*," 1987): A famous *manga* written by Araki Hirohiko.

John Bunyan (November 28, 1628 – August 31, 1688 A.D.): Author of landmark Christian novel *The Pilgrims Progress*.

K

Ka (家, "practitioner," or "family"): A practitioner of an art or craft, such as a *manga-ka*. A member of a collective family within that art.

Kabuki (歌舞伎, "song, dance, and skill"): Traditional theater of Japan for displaying folktales and drama.

Kabushiki-gaisha Enu Ti Ti Dokomo (株式会社NTTドコモ, "NTT Docomo," founded 1991): The largest mobile phone operator in Japan.

Kabushiki-gaisha Fuji Terebijon (株式会社フジテレビジョン, "Fuji Television Network, Inc.," or Fuji Terebi (フジテレビ, "Fuji Television") for short, founded 1957): One of the largest television networks in Japan. *Anime* adaptations of Toriyama's work are broadcast here.

Kabushiki-gaisha Kapukon (株式会社カプコン, "Capcom," founded 1983): A Japanese video game company well known for its *Sutorīto Faitā*, *Rokkuman*, and *Buresu obu Faia* series.

Kabushiki-gaisha Shūeisha (株式会社集英社, "Shūeisha Publishing Co., Ltd.," founded 1925): The largest *manga* publisher in Japan, located in Tōkyō. Publisher of Akira Toriyama's *manga*.

Kabushiki-gaisha Tamiya (株式会社タミヤ, "Tamiya Incorporated," founded 1946): A famous modeling and miniature company in Japan. One of Akira Toriyama's favorites.

Kabushiki-gaisha Terebi Asahi (株式会社テレビ朝日, commonly called "asahi tv," founded November 1, 1957): The largest television channel in Japan, owned by the Asahi Shimbun newspaper conglomerate and by Tōei Animation.

Kaijū (怪獣, "strange creature"): The giant monsters in films such as *Gojira* and *Gamera*. Genre of Japanese cinema.

Kaizō ningen (改造人間, "remodeled human," or "cyborg"): A term from the Japanese television series *Kamen Raidā*. Akira Toriyama uses this concept in *Dragon Ball*.

Kakimoji (描き文字, "sound-effects," literally "drawn lettering"): The sound effects used in Japanese *manga*. They are usually written in Japanese *kana*, but Toriyama wrote his in the Roman alphabet, and this is what caught the eye of his future editor, Torishima Kazuhiko.

Kamen Raidā (仮面ライダー, "*Kamen Rider*," 1971): A Japanese TV show about a man who undergoes a cybernetic transformation to become a *kaizō ningen* with the traits of a grasshopper.

Kami (神, Chinese: *shén*, "god," or "spirit"): The spiritual beings or essences of deities in Shintō.

Kamikaze (神風, "divine wind"): The suicide pilots of the Japanese airforce in World War II who flew their planes into naval vessels.

Kanfū (カンフー, "kung fu"): The Japanese pronunciation of *gōngfu*.

Kanji (漢字): The traditional writing system of Japan imported from China. Corollary to the Chinese *hànzì*.

Ka no kuni (華の国, "Flower Country," an epithet for China): A mythical land in Akira Toriyama's *Doragon Bōi manga*. Tanton escorts the princess back to this country.

Kapuseru Kōporēshon (カプセルコーポレーション, "Capsule Corporation"): The largest technological firm in the world, with their headquarters in Nishi-*no-miyako*.

Karma (Sanskrit: कर्म, Chinese: *yèlì*, 業力): An accumulation of metaphysical and spiritual debt, determines the realm into which you are reborn and the type of being you become during reincarnation.

Katakana (片仮名, "fragmentary scripts"): The syllabic writing system of Japan used for foreign words and technical terms, consisting of sharp letters and shapes. Counterpart to *hiragana*.

Kazé: A French licensor of the *Dragon Ball* series.

Keiō Gijuku Daigaku (慶應義塾大学, "Keiō University"): A famous and prestigious university in Tōkyō.

Ken (県, "prefectures"): Refers to large divisions of Japan. There are 43 *ken* in Japan, and these are the likely inspiration for the 43 *chiku* in the Dragon World.

Ki (気, Chinese: *qì*, 氣, "energy"): The energy of the cosmos and metaphysical energy inside the human body.

Kigenzen (紀元前, "Before Age"): The period of time before the Ēji system begins in the *Dragon Ball* timeline.

King Arthur: Legendary British leader of the 5th and early 6th centuries. The source of inspiration for tales and films.

King Kong (1933): The classic film about a giant ape on Skull Island that is captured and displayed in New York City. Inspires the *kaijū* genre and leads to Toriyama's Ōzaru.

Kingu Gidora (キングギドラ, "King Ghidorah"): A threeheaded dragon with wings that fights Gojira and other *kaijū*. Premieres in *San Daikaijū: Chikyū Saidai no Kessen*.

Kingu Kongu (キングコング): The Japanese name of King Kong, the cinematic great ape. Featured in several Japanese made films, including *Kingu Kongu tai Gojira*.

Kingu Kongu tai Gojira (キングコング対ゴジラ, "*King Kong versus Godzilla*," 1962): A blockbuster film in Japan that combines the American *kaijū* of King Kong with the Japanese *kaijū* of Gojira.

Kingu Kyassuru (キング キャッスル, "King Castle"): The capital building of Earth in the Dragon World. Home of Koku-ō.

Kishimoto Masashi (岸本 斉史, born November 8, 1974): Author of the *Naruto shōnen manga*. He idolizes Toriyama.

Kita-no-miyako (北の都, "North City"): A northern city in the Earth of the Dragon World. Likely inspired by Siberia.

Kiyosu-shi (清須市, "Clear Headed City"): Birthplace of Akira Toriyama, creator of *Dragon Ball*. The small rural town on the outskirts of Nagoya-*shi*, within the larger Aichi-*ken* of central Japan.

Koku-ō (国王, "Nation King"): The king of the Earth in the Dragon World. A talking dog that lives in Kingu Kyassuru.

Kǒngfūzǐ (孔夫子, "Confucius," 551 – 479 B.C.): The Chinese sage teacher and philosopher who teaches social harmony and uprightness. His doctrines change all of East Asian society.

Kotatsu (炬燵, "heated table"): A low table with a blanket draped down all four sides with an electric heater attached to the underside.

Kubo Tite (久保 帯人, born June 26, 1977): Author of *Burīchi*.

Kun'yomi (訓読み, "translated reading"): The modern Japanese pronunciation of Chinese *hànzì* and *kanji*. Counterpart to *on'yomi*.

Kuroyanagi Tetsuko (黒柳 徹子, born August 9, 1933): Host of the daytime talk show, *Tetsuko no Heya*.

Kyodai hīrō (巨大ヒーロー, "*giant hero*"): A genre of television where a regular sized man grows to towering proportions to fight a monster.

Kyōgen (狂言, "mad words"): A traditional form of comedic dance and drama on stage.

Kyōto-fu (京都府, "Capital City Urban Prefecture"): A major prefecture of Japan. Home to the ancient capital of Kyōto.

Kyūjitai (旧字体, "old *kanji*"): The traditional *kanji* used in Japan prior to 1947, when *shinjitai* started to be used.

L

Lǎozi (老子, "Old One"): The first patriarch of Dàoism and embodiment of the Dào. Lived circa the Zhōu Dynasty.

Leipziger Buchmesse ("Leipzig Book Fair"): One of the largest book fairs in the world, located in Leipzig, Saxony. Attended by Akira Toriyama and his editor, Torishima Kazuhiko, in 2004.

Liánshuǐ-xiàn (漣水縣, "Rippling Water County"): Birthplace of Wú Chéng'ēn, author of *Xīyóujì*.

Le Comedia ("*Divine Comedy*," ~1321): A novel written in Italian poetic verse by Dante Alighieri. Tells the story of a man who seeks beauty and finds it by traversing through Hell, Purgatory, and Heaven.

Little Boy: Fission bomb dropped on Nagasaki on August 9, 1945.

Liùdào (Chinese: 六道, Japanese: *rokudō*, "six paths"): A Buddhist addition to the cosmological framework that states that all beings are suffering within one of six states of existence. These six states (paths, or roads of life) are those of: beings in hell (Sanskrit: *naraka-gati*, नरक, Chinese: *dìyùdào*, 地獄道, Japanese: *jigokudō*), hungry ghosts (Sanskrit: *preta-gati*, प्रेतगति, Chinese: *èguǐdào*, 餓鬼道, Japanese: *gakidō*), animals (Sanskrit: *tiryagyōni-gati*, तिर्यग्योनिगति, Chinese: *chùshēngdào*, 畜生道, Japanese, *chikushōdō*), *ásura* (Sanskrit: *ásura-gati*, असुरगति, Chinese: *āxiūluódào*, 阿修羅道, Japanese: *ashuradō*, "demons"), humans (Sanskrit: *manusya-gati*, मनुष्यगति, Chinese: *réndào*, 人道, Japanese: *nindō*), and *deva* (Sanskrit: *deva-gati*, Sanskrit: देवगति, Chinese: *tiāndào*, 天道, Japanese: *tendō*, "gods"). Each *gati* (Sanskrit: गति) is a "movement" or "motion" within the wheel of the *liùdào*.

Lúnyǔ (論語, "*Analects*," circa 476 – 221 B.C.): A Confucian classic that enunciates Confucius' ethics. Its contents contain the foundation for much of Chinese, Korean, and Japanese societal customs.

M

Mahāprajñāpāramitā Sūtra (Sanskrit: प्रज्ञापारमिता, Chinese: *Dà bōrě bōluómì duō xīnjīng*, 大般若波羅蜜多心經, "*Great Heart Sūtra*"): A Buddhist *sūtra* that is eighty-four times the length of the *Bible*. Xuánzàng's seminal translation leads to new forms of Buddhism and better understandings of Buddhist principles in China.

Mahāyāna (Sanskrit: महायान, Chinese: Dàchéng, 大乘, "Great Vehicle"): The modified teachings of Buddhism that flourish in China, Korea, and Japan, with an emphasis on salvation of others and the veneration of multiple Buddhā. In contrast to Hīnayāna.

Májiàng (麻將, Japanese: *mājan*, マージャン, "mahjong," or "sparrow"): A Chinese tabletop game with 144 tiles.

Mandarin: A dialect of Chinese from Northeast China. The term comes from the Chinese *Mǎndàrén* (满大人, "*Mǎn* Great Man," or "*Mǎn* Master"), with *Mǎn* (满) referring to the Mǎnzhōurén (满洲人, "Manchurian," or "Full Continent People") rulers of China during the Qīng Dynasty. The Qīng Dynasty was ruled by foreigners from the Northeast, so the term *Mǎndàrén* was used by the Chinese to refer to their foreign rulers, and in turn, their language. The term spread across the world during the 19th century and is now synoymous with the language, but in modern China they call this dialect *pǔtōnghuà* (普通話, "common speech") because it is the standard dialect of Northeast and central China.

Manga (漫画, "whimsical drawing," "comic," or "cartooning"): The Japanese word for comic. A large industry in Japan focused on the production of illustrated entertainment, with many genres.

Manga-ka (漫画家, "comic's family," or "manga author"): A member of the *manga* family or household.

Marco Polo (September 15, 1254 – January 8, 1324): An Italian adventurer who traveled to China and back, helping to establish cultural exchange between the East and West.

Matrëška (Russian: матрёшка, "*matryoshka*"): A series of hollow wooden dolls with a similar appearance and shape, but different size, that you place inside one another.

Matsuri (祭, "festival," or "holiday"): The name for traditional celebratory events in Japanese towns and cities.

Matsuyama Takashi (まつやま たかし, born November 17, 1957): Akira Toriyama's second assistant. They work together for 13 years on *Dr. Slump* and *Dragon Ball*.

Megalodon: An ancient and massive shark that lived 28 to 1.5 million years ago and ruled the oceans. A potential source of inspiration for the giant shark in the lake on Shugyō-*no-shima*.

Měihóu-wáng (美猴王, pronounced 'may-hoh-wahng,' Japanese: Bikō-ō, "Handsome Monkey King"): The name given to the stone monkey after he jumps through the waterfall and into the cave, becoming their king. Another name for Sūn Wùkōng.

Meka (メカ, "mecha"): Japanese shorthand for "mechanical." This is a catch-all term for science fiction stories that feature mechanical or robotic vehicles that can be piloted by a human, or to human beings who undergo a scientific enhancement to become mechanized.

Menzu non-no (メンズノンノ, "Men's Non-No"): A Japanese men's interest magazine. Toriyama is interviewed in this magazine in 2013.

Mighty Joe Young (1949): An American film about a giant ape, and the spiritual successor to *King Kong*.

Mikami Nachi (みかみなち): A *shōjo manga-ka*. Author of *Ue o shita e no rokkunrōru* and *Hijiri mefisuto konran-den*. Akira Toriyama's wife.

Minami-no-miyako (南の都, "South City"): A southern metropolis located on a tropical island on the Earth in the Dragon World. Inspired by Toriyama's trip to Australia.

Míng Dynasty (大明, Dà Míng, "Great Brightness," 1368 – 1644 A.D.): A revival of Hàn controlled China, the Míng is rife with inner rebellion, but its later years marks the beginning of the synthesis of martial arts with spirituality.

Mitsuteru Yokoyama (横山 光輝, June 18, 1934 – April 15, 2004): A *manga-ka* and creator of *Tetsujin Nijūhachi-gō*.

Monsutā-gata (モンスター型, "monster-type"): A type of Earthling other than a *ningen*. *Daizenshū 7* and *Chō-zenshū 4* state that *monsutā-gata* Earthlings make up approximately 7% of the global population on the Dragon World's Earth.

Mosura (モスラ, *"Mothra,"* 1961): A *kaijū* film series about a giant moth. Created by Tōhō to capitalize on the success of *Gojira*.

Mukan no teiō (無冠の帝王, "Uncrowned Emperor"): A moniker that Torishima-*san* refers to Toriyama with. It means that even though his works are popular, he has not received the amount of official awards and recognition that someone of his talent should receive.

Mukashi, mukashi (むかしむかし, "Long, long ago," or "Once upon a time"): A Japanese phrase for beginning a folktale or legend. The Narēshon begins the *Dragon Ball* story with this phrase.

Mysterious Island (1961): A science fiction adventure film based on the work of author Jules Verne, about a group of people who are stranded on an island populated by giant animals and creatures.

N

Nagasaki-shi (長崎市, "Long and Rugged Mountains City"): Victim of the Little Boy fission bomb on August 9, 1945.

Nagoya-shi (名古屋市, "Ancient Name Dwelling City"): Birthplace of Akira Toriyama, creator of *Dragon Ball*. A rural countryside during his birth, but now a burgeoning city. Capital of Aichi-*ken*.

Namekku-sei (ナメック星, "Planet Namek"): A fictitious planet in the *Dragon Ball* series inhabited by a race of aliens.

Nánjīng (南京, "Southern Capital"): An ancient capital of China, located in the south.

Nánjīng Dàxué (南京大學, "Nánjīng University"): One of the most prestigious universities in China and the world. Wú Chéng'ēn is a student here before he writes *Xīyóujì*.

Nara-jidai (奈良時代, "Era of the Flatland," 710 – 794 A.D.): A mostly agricultural period, but modeled after the Táng Dynasty of China. Acceptance of the Chinese writing system, Buddhism, Dàoism, and the martial arts are incorporated into the Shintō-based society and the worship of *kami*, forever changing Japanese society and culture.

Narēshon (ナレーション, "Narration," or "Narrator"): The narrator of the *Dragon Ball* story. Inspired by the narrator in *Xīyóujì*.

Naruto (ナルト, 1997): A best-selling *shōnen manga* written by Kishimoto Masashi about a young *ninja* who follows his *"ninja* way." Kishimoto idolizes Akira Toriyama.

Naui (ナウい, "now-y," or "hip"): A defunct buzzword in Japan during the 1980s for hip or fashionable trends.

Nazi (German: *Nationalsozialistische Deutsche Arbeiterpartei*, "National Socialist German Worker's Party): A political party active in Germany from 1920 to 1945, led by Adolf Hitler (April 20, 1889 – April 30, 1945) that rose in power, spread racism, hatred, nationalism, and death across Europe.

Nazo no rein jakku (謎 の レイン ジャック, "Mysterious Rain Jack"): The second *manga* that Toriyama submits to Shūeisha in 1978 in an attempt to win the Monthly Young Jump Award. It is never commercially published but does appear in the BIRD LAND PRESS section in Akira Toriyama's fan club newsletter, the *Akira Toriyama Hozon-kai*. It is released in two parts, in issue #4 (January, 1983) and issue #6 (May, 1983). It is also included in the Akira Toriyama Exhibition catalog. The original copies of the *manga* were stolen, so these are all that remain.

Ningen (人間, "human being," "person," or "man"): A Japanese Buddhist term that refers to all *nin* (人, "people") in the human plane of reincarnation that have entered the *gen* (間, "gate") of man, no matter what planet they are on.

Nirvāṇa (Sanskrit: निर्वाण, Chinese: *nièpán*, 涅槃, Japanese: *nehan*, "liberation," "extinguishing," or "blown out"): The Buddhist concept of extinguishing all desires and attachments and achieving a state of non-dual bliss, or enlightenment. Liberation from the cycle of *saṃsāra*.

Nishi-no-miyako (西の都, "West City"): A metropolis on the Earth of the Dragon World, with an advanced level of technology. Home of Buruma and the Kapuseru Kōporēshon.

Nō (能, "skillful"): Traditional Japanese dance and drama.

Norimaki Arare (則巻 アラレ): The main character of Akira Toriyama's *Dr. Slump manga*. She is a young and naïve robot girl with nearsighted vision, yet super powered strength. Created by Doctor Norimaki Senbei. She helps Gokū in Part 2 of *Dragon Ball*.

Norimaki Senbei (則巻 千兵衛): An inventor who creates Norimaki Arare, a super powerful robot in the form of a naïve little girl.

O

Oda Eiichirō (尾田 栄一郎, born January 1, 1975): Author of the best-selling *Wan Pīsu shōnen manga*.

Ogyū Sorai (荻生 徂徠, March 21, 1666 – February 28, 1728): An influential Japanese Confucian scholar during the Tokugawa-*jidai*. Responsible in part for the translation of *Xīyóujì* into *Saiyūki* from 1758 – 1831, alongside other classical Chinese literature.

One Million Years B.C. (Japanese: *Kyōryū hyaku man-nen,* 恐竜百万年, *"One Million Years Dinosaurs,"* 1966): A film about a caveman and cavewoman from different tribes who meet and fall in love with one another, but then have to survive in a world full of dinosaurs.

On'yomi (音読み, "sound reading"): The ancient Japanese pronunciation of Chinese *hànzì* and *kanji*. Counterpart to *kun'yomi*, the modern pronunciation.

Orikon Kabushiki-gaisha (オリコン株式会社, Oricon Co., Ltd., founded 1999): A Japanese multimedia and news company focused on the development and social influence of Japanese pop culture.

Ōsaka-fu (大阪府, "Great Hillside Urban Prefecture"): A major prefecture of Japan located on the main island.

Osomatsu-kun (おそ松くん, 1966): A comedic *anime* about the antics of sextuplets with buckteeth. Based on a *manga* by Akatsuka Fujio.

P

Pacific War: The war in East and Southeast Asia from December 7, 1941 – September 2, 1945.

Pangaea ("whole Earth"): The giant land mass that formed 300 million years ago on our own planet, when all the continents were combined together as a supercontinent and dinosaurs ruled the Earth. I suspect it is the model for the Dragon World's Earth.

Papaiya-shima (パパイヤ島, "Papaya Island"): The location where the Tenkaichi Budōkai is held. Akira Toriyama bases its appearance on the island of Bali, located in the South Pacific.

Paozu-yama (パオズ山, "Paozu Mountain"): The mountain where Son Gohan and Son Gokū live. Inspired by the appearance of Guìlín, China. Named after the Japanese pronunciation of the Chinese *bāozi*.

Pengin-mura (ペンギン村, "Penguin Village"): The setting of *Dr. Slump*. A small town on a tropical island filled with a cast of whacky people and talking animals.

Pīnyīn (拼音, "spelled sound"): The written pronunciation of Chinese words in Roman letters.

Playboy: An adult entertainment magazine catering to men's interests. Shūeisha publishes the Japanese version.

Pora ando Roido (ポラアンドロイド, "Pola & Roid," March, 1981): A *yomikiri manga* written by Akira Toriyama. The two main characters are named after the self-processing camera film called *Polaroid*.

Pun-pun (プンプン): The sound used in *manga* for anger.

Puramo (プラモ): A beautiful girl in *Tonpū Daibōken*. I theorize that the name of Puramo (プラモ) is a portmanteau of *purasuchikku* (プラスチック, "plastic") and *moderu* (モデル, "model").

Pútídámó: See "Bodhidharma."

Q

Qián (錢, "money," "currency"): An ancient Chinese term for money.

Qín Dynasty (秦朝, Qín-*Cháo*, "Ash Tree Dynasty," 221 – 206 B.C.): The first imperial dynasty formed through the conquest of six other states. Founded by Qín Shǐhuángdì (秦始皇帝, "Emperor Qín Shǐhuáng," 260 – 210 B.C.).

Qīng Dynasty (清朝, Qīng-*cháo*, "Clarity Dynasty," 1644 – 1912 A.D.): The last dynasty of China. Established by Mongolians. Rife with rebellion, inner turmoil, and external pressure from foreigners. *Dragon Ball* borrows most of its cultural content from this dynasty.

Qítiān-dàshèng (齊天大聖, Japanese: Seiten-*taisei*, "Great Sage Equal to Heaven"): A moniker that Sūn Wùkōng gives to himself after becoming immortal and having disagreements with the gods.

Qítiān-dàshèng zájù (齊天大聖雜劇, *"Variety Drama on The Great Sage Equal to Heaven,"* circa 1450): A fanciful extrapolation of Xuánzàng's real life journey written in China to entertain the masses with a clear emphasis on the Monkey King (the *Qítiān dàshèng*).

R

Ray Harryhausen (June 29, 1920 – May 7, 2013): An American visual effects originator, writer, and producer who created classic films and monsters. His work inspired the dinosaurs in Toriyama's *manga*.

Rén (人, Japanese: *ren*, or *nin*, "people," or "mankind"): Human beings. In contrast to the *tiānrén* and *dìyùrén*.

Rěn (忍, Japanese: *nin*, "forbearance," "endurance," "sacrifice," "fortitude," "discipline," "determination," or "resilience"): An upright characteristic of the universe and all beings within it.

Ribon (りぼん, *"Ribbon"*): A *shōjo manga* magazine in which Toriyama is interviewed in October, 1981.

Robocop (1987): An American film about a police officer in Detroit who undergoes a cybernetic transformation and fights crime.

Rokkuman (ロックマン, *"Rockman,"* aka *"Mega Man,"* 1987): One of the world's most famous side-scrolling adventure video games. Developed by Kabushiki-gaisha Kapukon.

Rōmaji (ローマ字, "Roman letters"): The written pronunciation of Japanese words in Roman letters.

Ronpao (竜宝, "dragon jewel"): A jewel that a dragon comes out of in *Doragon Bōi*. Precursor to the dragon balls in *Dragon Ball*.

Rosuto wārudo <Zenseiki> (ロスト・ワールド<前世紀>, *"Lost World <Last Century>"*): A 2-volume *manga* adaptation of Sir Author Conan Doyle's *The Lost World* where scientists and detectives travel to a far off planet filled with dinosaurs. Written by Tezuka Osamu.

S

Saddharma Puṇḍarīka Sūtra (Chinese: _Miàofǎ liánhuá jīng_, 妙 法蓮華經, _"Lotus Sūtra of the Marvelous Law"_): A _sūtra_ translated by Xuánzàng that leads to a growth of Mahāyāna thought and the establishment of new Buddhist schools in China and Japan.

Saiyūki (西遊記): The Japanese translation of _Xīyóujì_. Akira Toriyama uses it as _Dragon Ball's_ cultural framework.

Saiyūki (西游记, 1960, localized in the United States as _"Alakazam the Great,"_ 1961): An animated feature film adaptation of Tezuka's _Boku no Son Gokū manga_. Produced by Tōei. The film is retitled and localized in the United States by American International Pictures, stripping it of its cultural content by swapping Eastern to Western.

Sakuma Akira (さくま あきら, born July 29, 1952): A freelance writer who collaborates with Akira Toriyama to write the _Toriyama Akira's Hetappi manga kenkyūjo_.

Sakura (桜, "cherry blossom"): An iconic tree of Japan known for its pink petals.

Śākyamuni (Sanskrit: सिद्धार्थबुद्ध, Chinese: Shìjiāmóuní, 釋迦牟尼, Japanese: Shakamuni, 563 – 483 B.C.): An Indian prince who leaves the secular world and enlightens to the Buddhā Law, becoming a Buddhā.

Sammo Hung (Chinese: Hung Gam-bou, 洪金寶, born January 7, 1952): A famous martial arts actor and counterpart to Jackie Chan.

Saṃsāra (Sanskrit: संसार, Chinese: _lúnhuí_, 輪迴, Japanese: _rinne_, "transmigration"): The endless cycle of reincarnation from one body to the next as we die and are reborn.

Samurai (侍, "noble warriors," or "warriors who serve nobility"): A warrior class of nobles in feudal Japan. The subject of many stories.

San (さん, "Mr.," "Mrs.," or "Miss"): A Japanese honorific said after a person's surname to show respect.

San Daikaijū: Chikyū Saidai no Kessen (三大怪獣 地球最大の決戦, _"Three Giant Monsters: The Greatest Battle on Earth,"_ 1964): A major _kaijū_ film produced by Tōhō.

Sānguó Yǎnyì (三國演義, *"Romance of the Three Kingdoms,"* circa 14ᵗʰ century): One of the world's first novels, and *sìdà míngzhù* Chinese classic. Tells the story of the battles and political intrigues of the Three Kingdoms period of ancient China.

Sānjiè (三界, Japanese: *sankai,* "three realms"): The three realms of existence in the Indian and East Asian ideological cosmos, consisting of heaven, earth, and hell. These are abstract places and literal places.

Sararīman (サラリーマン, "salary man"): The stereotypical white collar worker in Japan.

Sen no kuni (仙の国, "Hermit Country"): A fictional land in Akira Toriyama's *Doragon Bōi manga.*

Sengoku-jidai (戦国時代, "Era of Warring States," 1467 – 1573 A.D.): A century of war, intrigue, and unrest. Age of the *samurai.*

Senpai (先輩, "upperclassmen," or "senior"): A Japanese term that denotes a seniority in class and holds a lot of weight in society. A person's *senpai* is established by age.

Seru (セル, "Cell"): An artificial human created by a scientist for the purpose of killing Gokū.

Shàn (善, "compassion," "kindness"): The tenet of Buddhism.

Shàolín (少林, "Young Forest"): Shorthand for the most famous martial artists in the world. Practitioners of the Buddhā Law.

Shàolín gōngfu (少林功夫): A famous style of *gōngfu* practiced by the Shàolín monks. Arguably a product of the *vajramuṣṭi* system taught by the Buddhist sage Bodhidharma.

Shàolín-sì (少林寺, "Young Forest Temple"): The most famous martial arts temple in the world. A Buddhist temple in Dēngfēng (登封, "Mounted Field"), China, located on Sōng-*shān* (嵩山, "Sōng Mountain"), founded in 497 A.D.

Shào shì xiōngdì (邵氏兄弟, "Shaw Brothers," 1958 – 2011): A movie studio in Hong Kong that produced over 1,000 *gōngfu* films. Many of these films inspired Akira Toriyama's creation of *Dragon Ball.*

Shā Wùjìng (沙悟淨, Japanese: Sa-gojō, "Sand Aware of Purity"): A demon who lives in the Liúshā-*hé* and attempts to eat Xuánzàng. He is a former general in heaven who broke a crystal bowl by accident and is condemned to Earth to repay this debt. He becomes the monks' third disciple. Inspires Yamucha in *Dragon Ball.*

Shē (シェー): A physical joke of the main character in *Osomatsu-kun*, where he turns up one foot while standing on the other leg, and then puts one hand above his head in a funny position. It became a popular trend across Japan. Even *Gojira* does it in one of his films.

Shinbutsu shūgō (神仏習合, "amalgamation of *kami* and Buddhā"): The combination of Shintō and Buddhist belief systems in Japan.

Shinjitai (新字体, "simplified *kanji*"): The simplified characters used in Japan starting in 1947. In contrast to *kyūjitai*.

Shinrei (神雷, "soul"): A Japanese word for the spirit, soul, mind, or psyche. Also gods.

Shintō (神道, "the way of the gods"): The native religion of Japan. A development of shamanistic beliefs that mixes with Chinese Dàoism and Buddhism across millennia.

Shōgakukan Manga-shō (小学館漫画賞, "Shōgakukan *Manga* Award"): An annual award for *manga*. Akira Toriyama wins the 27th year for the "best *shōnen* / *shōjo manga* of the year."

Shōjo (少女, "young girls"): *Manga* written for young girls. The counterpart of *shōnen* for young boys.

Shokkā (ショッカー, "Shocker"): A mysterious terrorist organization who kidnaps people, brainwashes them, and uses the *kaizō ningen* process to turn them into animal-based villains.

Shōnen (少年, "few years"): Synonymous with *shōnen manga*.

Shōnen Jump (少年ジャンプ): See "*Weekly Shōnen Jump*."

Shōnen manga (少年漫画, "young boys' comics"). These are *manga* that usually star a young boy that the reader can relate to as they go on adventures or experience funny situations. *Dragon Ball* is the iconic example.

Shōwa (昭和, "Enlightened Peace"): Refers to a period of television in the 1960s to 1980s focused on lighthearted adventures. This is the era of the original *Dragon Ball's manga* and *anime* run. Named as such because of the Shōwa-*jidai*.

Shōwa-jidai (昭和時代, "Era of Enlightened Peace"): The rule of Shōwa-*tennō* Hirohito, from December 25, 1926 to January 7, 1989.

Shōwa-tennō Hirohito (昭和天皇裕仁, "Enlightened Peace Emperor Hirohito," April 21, 1909 – January 7, 1989): The previous Emperor of Japan. Succeeded by Akihito.

Shuǐhǔ Zhuàn (水滸傳, "*Water Margin*," 1589 A.D.): One of the *sìdà míngzhù*, telling the story of 108 bandits in China who unite together.

Shūkan (週刊, "weekly"): A weekly format of *manga* creation and distribution consisting of 14 pages a week, plus a title page. *Dragon Ball* is a *shūkan* in *Weekly Shōnen Jump*.

Shūkan Shōnen Magajin (週刊少年マガジン, "*Juvenile Magazine Weekly*"): A weekly Japanese magazine containing *shōnen manga*. Toriyama attempts to win their prize in the magazine as a young man.

Sìdà míngzhù (四大名著, "four great masterpieces"): The four books that Chinese elites believe a man must read in order to be refined. They include *Xīyóujì*, Shuǐhǔ Zhuàn, *Sānguó Yǎnyì*, and *Hóng Lóu Mèng*.

Sir Arthur Conan Doyle (May 22, 1859 – July 7, 1930): Author of several novels, including *The Lost World*.

Sòng Dynasty (宋朝, Sòng-cháo, "Treetop Dynasty," 960 – 1279 A.D.): A period of rapid growth, economic revolution, invention, and war against the Mongolians to the north.

Son Gokū (孫悟空, Chinese: Sūn Wùkōng, "Monkey Grandchild Aware of Emptiness"): The main character of *Dragon Ball*. A pure-hearted boy with the wish to become stronger. Inspired by Sūn Wùkōng in *Xīyóujì*.

Southern Sòng Period (南宋, Sòng Nán, "Southern Treetop," 1127 – 1279 A.D.): A dynasty of great export and import, as well as complex social infrastructure.

Star Trek (1966): A famous science fiction television and film series about a crew of a 23rd century spaceship who engage with aliens.

Star Wars (1977): The quintessential science fiction space opera film. About a young boy named Luke Skywalker who loses his adoptive parents and becomes a jedi knight to bring balance to the Force.

Stephen Chow (Chinese: Chow Sing-Chi, 周星馳, Mandarin: Zhōu Xīngchí, born June 22, 1962): A Hong Kong actor, writer, and director known for his comedic films.

Sūn Wùkōng (孫悟空, Japanese: Son Gokū, "Monkey Grandchild Aware of Emptiness"): The main character of *Xīyóujì*. An immortal macaque with near boundless strength and supernormal powers who guards Xuánzàng on his journey west. Becomes a Buddhā at the completion of his journey. The inspiration for Son Gokū in *Dragon Ball*.

Sūpā Sentai Shirīzu (スーパー戦隊 シリーズ, "super task force series"): A Japanese superhero team genre of television, with color-coded main characters who fight against monsters.

Super Friends (1973): A Western animated television series about Superman and his super friends.

Superman (1938): The quintessential superhero and a famous series of comics and films. An alien who is sent to Earth by his parents as his home planet explodes. The boy is then adopted and raised as an Earthling, but starts to exhibit super powers, so he upholds the alternate identity of Clark Kent, mild-mannered reporter. Akira Toriyama is a fan of Superman and spoofs his character in *Dr. Slump* and *Dragon Ball*. Toriyama likely uses Superman's alien origin story for Son Gokū's retroactive origin in *"Dragon Ball Z."*

Suppaman (スッパマン, "Sourman"): A man who believes that he is super. Has the alternate identity of Kuraaku Kenta (暗悪健太, i.e. "Clark Kent"). Toriyama's parody of Superman.

Sutārogu (スターログ, "Starlog"): A Japanese magazine about pop culture. Toriyama is interviewed in this magazine in November, 1980.

Sutōrī manga (ストーリー漫画, "story comic"): A *manga* with a more serious tone. The opposite of gag *manga*.

Sutorīto Faitā (ストリートファイター, *"Street Fighter,"* 1987): The world's most famous street fighting series of video games. Developed by Kabushiki-gaisha Kapukon.

Sūtra (Sanskrit: सूत्र, Chinese: *jīng*, 經, "sacred scriptures"): Holy texts in Buddhism that contain the Buddhā Law. The object of Xuánzàng's quest in *Xīyóujì*.

T

Tàijí (太極, "ultimate extremes"): The Dàoist concept of dualism that leads to *yīnyáng*. Opposite polarities in union. For example, North exists because of South, positive exists because of negative, and good exists because of evil.

Tàijí-jiàn (太極劍, "supreme ultimate sword"): The sword-based martial art founded upon the principles of *Tàijí-quán*.

Tàijí-quán (太极拳, "supreme ultimate fist"): The Chinese martial art founded upon Dàoist mind and body principles, incorporating the concepts of *yīn* and *yáng*.

Tanaka Hisashi (田中久志, born April 1959): Akira Toriyama's first assistant at Shūeisha.

Táng Dynasty (唐朝, Táng-*cháo*, "Boastful Pestle Dynasty," 618 – 907 A.D.): The zenith of Chinese culture and a second golden age of civilization. The Táng Dynasty is the period in which the Buddhist monk Xuánzàng travels to India and back in order to retrieve scriptures. His journey inspires the tale of *Xīyóujì* (*"Journey to the West"*) that later inspires *Dragon Ball*. It's also a period of great cultural diversity and the time when China exports Buddhist and Dàoist culture into Japan, alongside their writing system and martial arts.

Tán-gōngdé-fó (檀功德佛, Sanskrit: *Candana-puṇya* Buddhā, चंदनपुण्यबुद्ध, "Sandalwood Buddhā," or "Buddhā of Virtue"): The name of Xuánzàng as an enlightened being. Given to him at the completion of his journey west. Also written as *tán-fó* (檀佛, "Sandalwood Buddhā"). Sandalwood is synonymous with virtue and merit, so it refers to the mighty virtue that Xuánzàng accrues during his journey.

Táng shān dà xiōng (唐山大兄, *"The Big Boss,"* 1971): Bruce Lee's first film, where he fights a corrupt big boss.

Táng Sānzàng (唐三藏, "The Three Baskets Monk of Táng"): A moniker for Xuánzàng, referring to the three baskets (*tripiṭaka*) of *sūtra* that he retrieves from India.

Táng Tàizōng (唐太宗, January 28, 598 – July 10, 649 A.D.): The Emperor of China when Xuánzàng embarks on his journey to India.

Tankōbon (単行本, "standalone volume"): A standard format of publishing volumes of *manga* in Japan. They can be formatted in any size, but the most common are 12.8 × 18.2 cm (5.04 × 7.17"). *Dragon Ball* was published in 42 *tankōbon*.

Tanton (唐童, or たんとん, Chinese: Tángtóng, "Táng Dynasty Boy"): The main character of Akira Toriyama's *Doragon Bōi manga*. Tanton's name is the ancient *on'yomi* Japanese pronunciation of the Chinese *hànzì* of Tángtóng, referring to the Táng Dynasty, the height of Chinese civilization and synonymous with China itself.

Tao Paipai (桃白白, "Peach White White"). A villain in *Dragon Ball* inspired by an actor in a Jackie Chan film.

Tarzan (1912): The story of a young British boy who loses his parents and is raised in the jungle by animals. A series of books and films, premiering in *Tarzan of the Apes* by author Edgar Rice Burroughs.

Tenkaichi Budōkai (天下一武道会, "The Number One Under Heaven Martial Arts Tournament"): The biggest martial arts tournament in the Dragon World. The venue for Gokū's life changing experiences.

Terebaru: A Japanese magazine focused on pop culture, *anime*, and *manga*. Toriyama is interviewed in this magazine in 1986.

Tetsujin Nijūhachi-gō (鉄人28号, "*Iron Man No. 28*," 1963): The first "giant robot" type of *anime*, where a boy controls the robot with a remote control. Based on a manga by Mitsuteru Yokoyama.

Tetsuko no Heya (徹子の部屋, "*Tetsuko's Room*," 1983): Japan's first daytime talk show, hosted by Kuroyanagi Tetsuko. Toriyama was a guest to discuss his success.

Tetsuwan Atomu (鉄腕アトム, "*Mighty Atom*," or "*Astro Boy*," 1952): Masterpiece of Tezuka Osamu, about a robotic boy with human traits.

Tezuka Osamu (手塚 治虫, November 1928 – February, 9, 1989): The father of *manga*, whose work has a great influence on Akira Toriyama.

Tezuka-shō (手塚賞, "*Tezuka Award*"): An award given to up and coming *manga-ka*. Named in honor of Tezuka Osamu.

Tiānrén (天人, Japanese: *tennin*, "heavenly people"): The people of heaven in Buddho-Dàoist cosmology.

The Forbidden Kingdom (2008): See "*Gōngfu zhīwáng*."

The Flintstones (1960): An American cartoon about a family of prehistoric cavemen that live with dinosaurs.

The Land That Time Forgot (1918): Novel by Edgar Rice Burroughs that emulates *The Lost World*, depicting a region filled with dinosaurs.

The Lost World (1912; turned into a film in 1925): A novel by Sir Arthur Conan Doyle about a lost location on Earth filled with dinosaurs and other wild creatures.

The Matrix (1999): A film about a computer programmer who escapes the matrix, a simulation of real life, in order to see the truth of existence and free his fellow humans. A philosophical and psychological film, even though on the surface it's about a programmer fighting against machines.

The Pilgrims Progress (1678): A novel by John Bunyan that tells a story of a man named Christian who experiences a dream and travels from the "City of Destruction" (i.e. Earth) to the "Celestial City" (i.e. heaven) to repent for his sins and attain salvation in Christ.

The 7ᵗʰ Voyage of Sinbad (1958): An action-adventure film about the travels of Sinbad as he fights monsters.

The Statue of Liberty: A neoclassical sculpture on Liberty Island in New York City. An icon of freedom and of the United States. Toriyama parodies it in his early work.

The Terminator (1984): A science fiction film about a robot that looks like a human who is sent back in time to kill the leader of the human resistance. A series of films.

The Tom and Jerry Show (1975): An American cartoon about a cat who tries to eat a mouse, but is outwitted.

The Valley of Gwangi (1969): A film about cowboys and dinosaurs fighting in a world of mixed chronologies.

Tsuzuku (つづく, "it continues"): A standard way to finish a *manga*.

To-dō-fu-ken (都道府県): A Japanese term that refers to the *to* (都, "metropolis") of Tōkyō, the *dō* (道, "circuit") of Hokkaidō, the two *fu* (府, "urban prefectures") of Ōsaka-*fu* and Kyōto-*fu*, and the 43 *ken* (県, "prefectures") of Japan.

Tōei Kabushiki-gaisha (東映株式会社, "Tōei," founded 1950): Japan's largest animation studio and a large film studio. Responsible for the *Dragon Ball* and *Dr. Slump anime*, along with several films that influence Toriyama's work.

Tōhō Kabushiki-gaisha (東宝株式会社, "Tōhō Studios," founded 1932): Japan's largest film studio, creator of *Gojira*, the *kaijū* genre, and *tokusatsu* genre. Their films and television shows influence Akira Toriyama's work.

Tokugawa-jidai (徳川時代, "Era of the Virtuous River," 1603 – 1868 A.D.): A period of social reunification, but also a closed door period where contact with outsiders is forbidden. Also called the Edo-*jidai* (江戸時代, "Cove Gate Era"). Edo (江戸) is the former name of Tōkyō, the capital of Japan, having been renamed in 1868. Most of the traditional Japanese culture in *Dragon Ball* comes from this period.

Tokusatsu (特撮, "special [effects] filming"): A genre of television featuring costumed superheroes who use *henshin* to fight monsters.

Tōkyō (東京, "Eastern Capital"): The capital of Japan. Formerly named Edo.

Tokyopop (founded 1997): An American-based Japanese pop culture company that produced *Tokyopop* magazine, featuring *manga*.

Torankusu (トランクス, "Trunks"): A boy from the future who travels back in time in order to save Gokū's life.

Tori-bot: The robotic likeness of Akira Toriyama, drawn by the author. Named by fans as a portmanteau of "Toriyama" plus "robot."

Torishima Kazuhiko (鳥嶋 和彦, "Bird Island Peaceful Prince," born October 19, 1952): An editor for *Weekly Shōnen Jump* at Shūeisha, in Tōkyō. The man who discovers Akira Toriyama and becomes his editor and lifelong friend.

Toriyama Akira (鳥山 明, "Bright Bird Mountain"): The creator of *Dragon Ball* and *Dr. Slump*. Born on April 5, 1955, in Nagoya-*shi*, Aichi-*ken*, Japan. The most famous and influential *manga-ka* in the world.

Toriyama Akira kōshiki fankurabu (鳥山明公式ファンクラブ, "Toriyama Akira Official Fan Club"): The official fan club of Akira Toriyama, complete with numbered ID cards for over 10,000 members.

Toriyama Akira's Hetappi manga kenkyūjo (鳥山明のヘタッピマンガ研究所, "*Akira Toriyama's Crummy Manga Lab*," October, 1982 – March, 1984): A how-to *manga* written by Akira Toriyama and Sakuma Akira to teach aspiring *manga-ka* how to draw.

Toriyama Akira hozon-kai (鸟山明 保存会, "The Akira Toriyama Preservation Society"): A fan club dedicated to Akira Toriyama's work. Predecessor to the official club.

Toriyama Akira ○ Saku gekijō (鳥山明○作劇場, "*Akira Toriyama's Manga Theater*"): A collection of Akira Toriyama's *manga* short stories, published in 1983, 1988, and 1997 respectively.

Tonpū (トンプー): A cybernetic boy who lands on an unknown planet and meets a girl named Puramo. Main character of *Tonpū Daibōken*.

Tonpū Daibōken (トンプー大冒険, "*Tonpū's Great Adventure*," 1983): Akira Toriyama's *yomikiri manga* about a young space traveling boy named Tonpū who lands on an unknown planet and meets a human girl named Puramo. A precursor to *Dragon Ball*.

Tripiṭaka (Sanskrit: त्रपिटिक, Chinese: *sānzàng,* 三藏, Japanese: *sanzō,* "three baskets"): The *sūtra* Xuánzàng recovers from India. Refers to the *sūtra* lectures, monastic precepts, and systematic philosophy written down by the Indian monks hundreds of years after Śākyamuni Buddhā's death.

U

Uchū kō yōgo (宇宙公用語, "universal official language"): The standard language spoken by every sentient being in the Dragon World cosmos. This language is whatever language the *Dragon Ball* series is translated into.

Ue o shita e no rokkunrōru (下へのロックンロール, *"The Top and Bottom of Rock and Roll,"* 1977): A manga written by Akira Toriyama's wife, Mikami Nachi.

Urutoraman (ウルトラマン, *"Ultraman,"* 1966): The quintessential *tokusatsu* show and series, starring a police force operative who is replaced by an alien that uses *henshin* to fight against giant monsters.

Urutorasebun (ウルトラセブン, *"Ultra Seven,"* 1967): The sequel to *Urutoraman.* Influences Toriyama's *Dragon Ball* and *Dr. Slump.*

V

Viz: The American license holder and English translation company for the *Dragon Ball manga* series. A subsidiary of Shūeisha.

W

Waku-waku (わくわく): The sound used in *manga* for excitement.

Wan (わん, or ワン, "woof," or "bark"): The Japanese onomatopoeia for the sound of a dog's woof.

Wandā Airando (ワンダー・アイランド, "*Wonder Island*"): Akira Toriyama's first published *manga*, premiering in *Weekly Shōnen Jump* #52 in November, 1978.

Wan Pīsu (ワンピース, "*One Piece*," 1997): The world's best-selling *shōnen manga*, written by Oda Eiichirō, about a pirate and his crew.

Warhammer (or Warhammer Fantasy Battle): A popular tabletop wargame created by the British gaming and miniature company Games Workshop (founded 1975).

Weekly Shōnen Jump (週刊少年ジャンプ, *Shūkan Shōnen Janpu*, first issue July 2, 1968): A weekly *shōnen manga* anthology published in Japan. Akira Toriyama's *manga* are published here.

Wèibābù-tiānlóngmǎ (為八部天龍馬, "Heavenly Dragon Horse of the Eight Classes"): The name given to the transformed Bái Lóngmǎ at the completion of his journey west.

World War I: "The Great War"): Taking place from July 28, 1914 to November 11, 1918. Over 16 million fatalities.

World War II: "The Second Great War"): Taking place from September 1, 1939 to 15 August 15, 1945. An estimated 50 to 85 million fatalities. Akira Toriyama is fascinated by this global conflict and incorporates real military weapons and vehicles into *Dragon Ball*.

Wú Chéng'ēn (吳承恩, c. 1505 – 1580 A.D.): Reputed author of *Xīyóujì*. A scholar and poet born in Liánshuǐ-*xiàn* (漣水縣, "Rippling Water County"), Jiāngsū (江苏, "River Province"), in the east of China during the Míng Dynasty.

X

Xī'ān (西安, "Western Peace"): The ancient western capital of China. The place where Xuánzàng departs from and returns to during his journey west.

Xià Dynasty (Xià-*cháo*, 夏朝, "Great Dynasty," c. 2070 – c. 1600 B.C.): Arguably the first dynasty of China in recorded history.

Xīyóujì (西遊記, Japanese: *Saiyūki*, "Journey to the West"): An ancient Chinese legend written in the late 16ᵗʰ century about a Buddhist monk, monkey king, pig man, and sand ogre and their adventures to India and back to recover the holy *sūtra*. It is the inspiration for *Dragon Ball* and provides the cultural framework that makes the series possible.

Xīyóu Jiàngmó-piān (西遊·降魔篇, *"Journey to the West: Conquering the Demons,"* 2013): A cinematic and humorous adaptation of *Xīyóujì* by Hong Kong martial arts actor, writer, and director, Stephen Chow.

Xīyóujì zájù (西遊記雜劇, *"Journey to the West Drama,"* c. the 14ᵗʰ century): A fanciful extrapolation of Xuánzàng's real-life journey written in China to entertain the masses.

Xuánzàng (玄奘, "Great Mystery," 602 – 664 A.D.): A Chinese Buddhist monk who travels to India and back to recover the sacred *sūtra*. He is the inspiration for the character of Xuánzàng in *Xīyóujì*, and in turn Buruma in *Dragon Ball*.

Xuanzang: A Buddhist Pilgrim on the Silk Road (1997): A book on Xuánzàng's life and journey west, written by Salley Hovey Wriggins.

Y

Yamabuki Midori (山吹みどり): Arare-*chan's* school teacher in *Dr. Slump*. Becomes Norimaki Senbei's wife.

Yen (円, with the symbol of ¥, "circle"): A Japanese unit of currency. It's a modern and simplified form of the traditional *yen* (圓, "circle").

Yoga (Sanskrit: योग, Chinese: *yújiā*, 瑜伽, "to yoke"): The practice of unifying the mind and body to attain liberation.

Yogācāra (Sanskrit: योगाचार, "one whose practice is yoga," Chinese: Wéishí-*zōng*, 唯識宗 "Consciousness-Only School," Japanese: Yuishiki, 唯識, "Consciousness-Only"): One of two philosophical schools of Indian Mahāyāna Buddhism. Influences Chinese and Japanese Buddhism.

Yōjinbō (用心棒, *"Yojimbo,"* 1961): A *samurai* film by Akira Kurosawa.

Yōkai (妖怪, "specters," "ghosts," or "phantoms"): A Japanese term for creatures such as ghouls, goblins, and creepy crawlies of the night.

Yomikiri (読み切り, "one-shot"): A single chapter story in a *manga*.

Yuán (元, with the symbol of ¥, "circle"): A Chinese unit of currency,.

Yuán Dynasty (大元, Dà Yuán, "Great Origin," 1271 – 1368 A.D.): A dynasty established by Mongolians. A period of great refinement in the arts and mathematics.

Yújiā shī de lùn (瑜伽師地論, *"Treatise on the Stages of Yoga Practice"*): The Chinese translation of the Yogācāra system of cultivation and Indian logic, as translated by Xuánzàng and his disciples.

Yuen Biao (Cantonese: Jyun Biu, Mandarin: Yuán Biāo, 元彪, born July 26, 1957): A martial arts actor and counterpart to Jackie Chan.

Yùmén-guān (玉門關, "Jade Gate Pass"): The furthermost western border of the Táng Empire that Xuánzàng passes through.

Z

Zájiā xiǎozi (Chinese: 雜家小子, *"Knockabout,"* 1979): A *gōngfu* film starring Sammo Hung and Yuen Biao.

Zeni (銭, or ぜに in *hiragana*, "money"): The ancient Japanese term for money or spending cash. Precursor to Toriyama's *zenī*.

Zenī (Ȥ): The currency in the Dragon World's Earth. One *zenī* (Ȥ) is the equivalent of one Japanese Yen (¥).

Zhēn (真, "truth"): Ethical and spiritual truth. The tenet of Dàoism.

Zhēnrén (真人, Japanese: *shinnin*, "true man"): The living manifestation of the Dào in the body of a man.

Zhèngtǐ-zì (正體字, "traditional characters"): Ancient *hànzì* of China.

Zhōu Dynasty (周朝, Zhōu-cháo, "Circumference Dynasty," 1046 – 256 B.C.): A dynasty in which writing, agriculture, and culture flourish.

Zhū Bājiè (豬八戒, Japanese: Cho-hakkai, "Pig of Eight Restraints"): The man pig in *Xīyóujì* that inspires Ūron's character in *Dragon Ball*. He receives this title from Xuánzàng after joining his pilgrimage west.

Zugaya-san (図画屋さん, "Mr. Drawing Shop"): A local drawing shop for children in Akira Toriyama's home town of Kiyosu. Toriyama spends time here as a child.

Zuì-quán (醉拳, *"Drunken Master,"* 1978): A *gōngfu* film starring Jackie Chan, about a young martial artist who learns drunken style. One of the main sources of inspiration in the creation of *Dragon Ball*.

Index

A

B

Bái Lóngmǎ (*Journey to the West* monk's horse) 104, 107

Battle of Gods Animanga 64

Bird Land Press 54

Bird Studio 54, 62

***Bleach* (Kubo)** 82

***bodhisattva* (enlightened being)** 87

Bruceploitation 77

Buddhā 87, 90, 95, 101–102, 106

Buddhism

    in China 86–90, 95–97

    in India 89, 95

    in Japan 25–26

    self-cultivation 101, 109

    three realms in 98–99

Bunyan, John 109

Burroughs, Edgar Rice 155

Buruma (*Dragon Ball* character)

    inspiration for 102, 132

    white motorcycle, inspiration for 104

C

D

F

G

H

I

J

O

P

R

S

U

V

W

X

Y

Z